D1190824

Despite much recent revisionist analysis of the traditional stereotypes of Victorian women, the downtrodden and helpless 'distressed gentlewoman' has survived or evaded historical scrutiny.

This book examines the distressed gentlewoman stereotype, primarily through a study of the experience of emigration among single middle-class women between 1830 and 1914. Based largely on a study of government and philanthropic emigration projects, it argues that the image of the downtrodden resident governess does inadequate justice to Victorian middle-class women's responses to the experience of economic and social decline and to insufficient female employment opportunities.

Although powerful factors operated to discourage distressed gentlewomen from risking the hardships of emigration, research among emigrants' letters and other records of female emigration societies from Australia, Canada, New Zealand and South Africa, shows that middle-class women without economic resources persistently took advantage of the invariably meagre facilities enabling them to emigrate.

Once out of Britain they proved to be remarkably adaptable emigrants. Instead of the helpless simpering gentility normally associated with the stereotype, women showed a willingness to risk their gentility by undertaking work which would have been unthinkable at home. Their experience raises wider questions about the potential for resourcefulness and adaptability among Victorian women and reveals qualities which are inconsistent with the traditional view of woman as victim.

EMIGRANT GENTLEWOMEN

EMIGRANT GENTLEWOMEN

GENTEEL POVERTY AND FEMALE EMIGRATION, 1830-1914

A. JAMES HAMMERTON

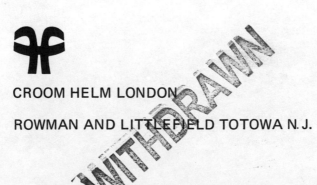

CROOM HELM LONDON

ROWMAN AND LITTLEFIELD TOTOWA N.J.

© 1979 A. James Hammerton
Croom Helm Ltd, 2-10 St John's Road, London SW11

British Library Cataloguing in Publication Data

Hammerton, A James
  Emigrant gentlewomen.
  1. Single women – Great Britain – History
  2. Middle classes – Great Britain – History
  3. Great Britain – Emigration and immigration –
  History
  I. Title
  301.32'5   HQ800

  ISBN 0-85664-608-3

First published in the United States 1979 by
Rowman and Littlefield
81 Adams Drive, Totowa, New Jersey

ISBN 0-8476-6122-9

Printed in Great Britain by offset lithography by
Billing & Sons Ltd, Guildford, London and Worcester

CONTENTS

TABLES

ABBREVIATIONS

BWEA	British Women's Emigration Association
CES	Colonial Emigration Society
CIL	Colonial Intelligence League
CO	Colonial Office Records
FMCES	Female Middle-Class Emigration Society
GBI	Governesses' Benevolent Institution
GFS	Girls' Friendly Society
HRA	Historical Records of Australia
NAPSS	National Association for the Promotion of Social Science
PP	Parliamentary Papers
SACS	South African Colonization Society
SPEW	Society for Promoting the Employment of Women
TNAPSS	Transactions, National Association for the Promotion of Social Science
UBWEA	United British Women's Emigration Association
UEEA	United Englishwomen's Emigration Association
WEA	Women's Emigration Association
WES	Women's Emigration Society

TO MY PARENTS

PREFACE

This book has evolved from a PhD thesis completed for the University of British Columbia in 1969. A revised version of one of the original chapters appeared as 'Without Natural Protectors: Female Immigration to Australia, 1832-36' in *Historical Studies*, XVI, no. 65 (1975) and is not reproduced here. Some of the material in chapter 5 appeared in 'Feminism and Female Emigration 1861-1886', a chapter of *A Widening Sphere: Changing Roles of Victorian Women* (1977) edited by Martha Vicinus, and I am grateful to Indiana University Press for permission to reprint the relevant sections. Most of the research would have been impossible without the assistance of staff at the Fawcett Library; I would particularly like to thank Ms Vera Douie and Ms Mildred Surry for their suggestions and guidance through the records of Victorian and Edwardian emigration societies. Winifred Gerin, Brontë biographer, and Dr Joan Stevens of Wellington, New Zealand, offered helpful comments on the life of Mary Taylor. The Earl of Pembroke kindly allowed me access to the Herbert papers on female emigration at Wilton House, Salisbury. Generous research assistance and study leave from La Trobe University, Melbourne, allowed me time to complete the book. Shirley Gordon's careful typing of most of the final manuscript was an immense help.

My earliest debt has been to my thesis supervisor, Professor James Winter of the University of British Columbia, who a decade ago guided me skilfully through the then uncharted waters of social history. During the process of revision I have benefited from the comments and suggestions of friends and colleagues who read parts of the manuscript. In particular I would like to thank Professor F.B. Smith of the Australian National University, Canberra, David Johansen of La Trobe University, Melbourne, Dr David Philips of the University of Melbourne and Martha Vicinus, editor of *Victorian Studies*. Above all I owe an immeasurable debt to Elizabeth Donoghue, who provided invaluable help at every stage of preparation. Without her patient and incisive questioning, which frequently saved the manuscript, and her emotional support, which frequently saved my morale, this book would never have seen the light of day.

A. James Hammerton
August 1978

INTRODUCTION

Few Victorian stereotypes have endured so thoroughly as that of the distressed gentlewoman. The respectable, unmarried lady, educated for an unlikely and elusive marriage, became an object of morbid curiosity when her father's death or ruin brought her to rely on her own meagre qualifications and seek to earn a precarious living. Forced to barter her gentility for a meagre subsistence as a governess, her life has been depicted by historians and contemporaries as one of humiliation and hardship. A 'standby of Victorian pathos',[1] the working woman of the middle classes had 'little before her but penury, or an occupation so severe as to ruin her health or wear out her mind'.[2] A timid and retiring 'downtrodden governess', her pitiful career became the butt of sarcasm, the object of earnest philanthropists and the focus of feminist energies.

Historians have done more to fill out the details of this picture than to subject it to critical scrutiny. An otherwise quite warranted focus on the serious deficiencies of female education has led to a grotesque caricature of middle-class women as 'Indifferently or frivolously educated, often empty-headed and limited in outlook, idle and dependent upon men for their livelihood and status in society.'[3] More often the single middle-class woman's problems have been approached through the Victorian 'institution' of the governess, usually the resident governess in a well-to-do household.[4] Duncan Crow's stark alternatives for impoverished gentlewomen of casual sewing, governessing or prostitution[5] may suit a sensationalised and impressionistic account, but they bring us no closer to the real lives of such women. Jeanne Peterson's more serious analysis has enhanced our understanding of the 'status incongruence' suffered by the resident governess and the relationship of her position to the fundamental ideals of womanhood upheld by Victorians.[6] But it is doubtful whether we can realistically subsume the lives of distressed gentlewomen under the restricted heading of resident governesses, nor whether the 'downtrodden governess' stereotype will serve as a satisfactory model for the experience of most women who were faced with economic decline.

One purpose of this book is to illustrate the limitations of the distressed gentlewoman stereotype, primarily through a study of the experience of emigration among single middle-class women. The study begins in the 1830s, when official facilities enabling women to emigrate in substantial numbers were first established, and ends in 1914, when sophisticated female emigration societies suspended their operations with the outbreak of war and when conditions which had made the distressed gentlewoman a major social problem began to be more rapidly transformed. There were powerful factors preventing middle-class women from emigrating in the nineteenth century. They must abandon the familiarity of home for the perils of a distant alien land; the voyage was long and hazardous, too often with uncertain protection and disreputable company; employment prospects in the colonies for middle-class women were at best unstable; and the entire venture, at least until past mid-century, could too easily be interpreted as a denial of a woman's respectability − a more certain acknowledgement of loss of caste than becoming a governess at home. Yet, in spite of these inhibiting factors, middle-class Victorian women without economic resources persistently took advantage of the invariably meagre facilities enabling them to emigrate. Moreover, once out of Britain they proved remarkably adaptable as emigrants. The helplessness and simpering gentility normally associated with the stereotype rarely emerged, and instead women showed a willingness to risk their gentility by undertaking work which would have been unthinkable at home. Their behaviour patterns, from the willingness to risk the hazards of emigration to their capacity for exploiting it, reveal perfectly human characteristics of enterprise and courage which are quite inconsistent with the abstract incapacity of the distressed gentlewoman stereotype.

Recent developments in Victorian women's history have already made an encouraging beginning in revising the more general abstract stereotype of passive, ornamental and helpless middle-class women. Patricia Branca has stressed the crucial role of the lower middle-class wife in resolving her family's problems, initiating technological change and showing an active and innovative interest in her own physical and sexual well-being.[7] Equally important, though unfortunately less frequently acknowledged, is Leonore Davidoff's analysis of the energetic role played by upper-class women, even within a severely constricted framework of behaviour, in preserving class solidarity; the power wielded by older women in exacting class conformity, contracting marriage alliances and keeping out threatening intruders is hardly consistent with the dominant image.[8] The title of a recent anthology on Victorian women, *A Widening Sphere*, is an appropriate reminder not only of the social pressure in the nineteenth century to expand women's public roles, but also of the private determination of individuals not to be entirely constrained within the bounds of the prevailing ideal of feminine behaviour.[9] The ideal was of crucial importance, and continues to attract deserved analysis,[10] but it should not be mistaken for the real lives of the women subject to it.

Most of the revisionist work to date, however, has dealt with large, generalised groups of inarticulate women in one or more social classes. Underlying Branca's study of the lower middle class, for example, was the clear rationale that 'we will learn more even about recent women's history by studying the typical situation than by studying the departures therefrom'.[11] This approach raises clear problems for a study of female emigration. Middle-class emigrants were certainly not typical of the majority of their home-bound sisters who never left the country. They were never more than a minority, even among the sub-group known as distressed gentlewomen, and the unconventional dimension of their action suggests that they may have been exceptional women from whom it would be dangerous to generalise about their wider peer group. According to Branca's criteria their representative value must be extremely limited.

Branca's point is an important one, and this study will frequently need to face up to the problem of representative value in the evidence used. But it is far from clear that the 'typical' situation of the inarticulate can be understood only by wide inferences drawn from indirect sources about women in the mass. The less typical usually have the advantage of being better documented, and, except for radical departures from the norm like great political figures, their basic situation rarely differed fundamentally from the lives of more ordinary women. The relatively exceptional and better known may, therefore, illuminate the lives of more typical anonymous women, because, at the very least, they shared the same problems of women in the same society.[12] So far only one study of the exceptional has been used in this way to tease out conclusions of deeper significance about ordinary women. Mary S. Hartman's *Victorian Murderesses*, by any criterion, deals with a 'deviant' group of women, but this does not prevent her from focusing on her subjects as women as well as murderesses, and thus drawing valuable conclusions about 'a group which was especially sensitive to certain problems and tensions which were common to a large number of middle-class households'.[13]

Middle-class female emigrants, although a distinct minority, were certainly less exceptional than Victorian murderesses. But for respectable women, emigration, like murder, was an extreme reaction to deep-rooted social problems experienced by a much larger group. For many it was a response to the fearful experience of downward social mobility, a commonly mentioned but infrequently understood phenomenon, which bore much harder on women than men. Middle-class emigrants might thus illuminate the more general experience of distressed gentlewomen in Britain. More importantly, by glimpsing the reaction of British distressed gentlewomen to relatively new and less urbanised colonial environments, we can gain a novel insight into the real extent of those female characteristics of passiveness, dependence and gentility usually assumed to be second nature to respectable Victorian women. Adaptability and enterprise were not commonly recognised attributes of the ordinary Victorian young lady, whether in prosperity or destitution, and if they appeared so readily in the colonies it is worth asking how durable the passiveness and dependence might have been in the first place, or whether it was there at all.

Exceptional as these emigrant women may have been, they are not the kind of women we usually learn about through first-hand sources. For all the imperfections and inadequacies of the sources used in this study — and there are many — some of them, particularly the emigrants' letters in chapter 5, allow direct contact with individual women undergoing the process of adaptation to new societies. The existence of these sources is of immense value; it is doubtful whether the essay could have been attempted without them. But their use raises some important questions, for a false dichotomy seems to be appearing in women's history — and to an extent social history generally — on the question of appropriate sources. Branca's *Silent Sisterhood* avowedly dealt with 'inarticulate . . . mute inglorious females of whom no biography was ever written, who never did or said or thought a thing that would distinguish them from the mass of women of the day'.[14] In discovering these inarticulate women Branca eschewed direct and autobiographical sources, apparently on the assumption that all female biography and autobiography has dealt exclusively with unrepresentative eminent women or pioneer feminists in the political struggle for emancipation.[15] Her approach, consequently, was an inferential one, interpreting the lives of ordinary women from indirect sources like magazines and household manuals, which, presumably, the women read and found relevant to their daily problems. Her inferential approach is, of course, indispensable to every historian, but the unfortunate result of pursuing it exclusively is that a real woman, coping with the problems Branca describes, never appears throughout the whole book. Direct and autobiographical sources, for all their scarcity, have not been an exclusive preserve of eminent and political women. Vivid, informative memoirs like those of Flora Thompson[16] can bring a vital sense of reality to his-

ιυιγ which is necessarily based largely on indirect sources. They are
also crucial to achieve the 'sense of deeper involvement' and 'immediate
feeling of life', increasingly noticed for being conspicuous by its
absence from much social history.[17] The point is of special importance
when dealing with dominant stereotypes, for their unreal abstraction is
best perceived when confronted with contradictory evidence drawn
directly from life.

At the other end of the spectrum from Branca's approach is one
which is best described as 'experiential'. Relying heavily on direct,
personal sources, and increasingly, for recent times, on oral, interview
material, its primary objective is to convey the immediate flavour of the
personal experience of ordinary people, largely as spoken by themselves.[18] Taken to its logical extreme this has more serious potential
drawbacks than an inferential approach. It is too easy, in the face of
such vivid evidence, to let the facts — that is accounts of personal
experiences — 'speak for themselves'. But the nature of the source in
itself will not necessarily determine the type of questions a historian
asks, and the result can too easily become antiquarian description, with
the historian's interpretation of the meaning of the evidence left out.
The facts have never spoken for themselves, and there is no reason why
the personal sources so crucial to social history should become an
exception.

In this situation the safest course for any social historian must be a
middle ground. It was one adopted successfully in Davidoff's *The Best
Circles*, in which etiquette and household manuals, magazines and even
fiction, were 'balanced' by personal 'memory' taken from diaries,
autobiographies and direct interviews.[19] This book attempts to achieve
a similar balance. Wherever possible full use is made of personal sources
such as emigrants' letters, but more indirect material is used both in
conjunction with and in the absence of correspondence and memoirs.
Periodical literature, emigration propaganda, emigrant societies' records
and official publications therefore figure prominently throughout the
book. It may seem unorthodox to turn to the unlikely records of the
Colonial Office for sources of women's history, but, as chapter 2
should illustrate, the involvement of official bodies with female emigration can yield some surprisingly valuable material.

A logical extension of the historical analysis of personal sources and
memoirs is the case-study method and biography itself. Unfortunately,
though, research has yielded few riches of the Flora Thompson variety
among sources left by distressed gentlewomen emigrants. Most of the
direct sources allow no more than brief snapshots of the lives of women

at one particular stage — usually during or just after the process of emigration — which permit some insight into key attitudes and behaviour patterns, but do little to provide the fuller context of life histories. For this reason the career of Mary Taylor, a Yorkshire friend of Charlotte Brontë who emigrated to New Zealand in 1845, has been chosen for a deeper case study in chapter 3. Taylor was, in many respects, untypical; only in the broadest sense could she be described as a distressed gentlewoman, for she never experienced real genteel poverty and took care to keep herself well-qualified for respectable employment. But her biography is important, for it is one of the main contentions of this book that while the helpless psychological aspect of the distressed gentlewoman stereotype is unrealistic, its socio-economic aspects were only too real for a very wide social range of women. Single women with claims to gentility but a pressing need for employment did not simply come from the fallen families of Burke's Peerage or the great capitalists. As the next chapter will attempt to show, they included women in the most insecure marginal families down to the lower middle class. They also included Mary Taylor, who, while not poverty stricken, was constrained as much as the most distressed gentlewoman by restrictions in Britain on female employment. For her, as for most middle-class women, emigration could provide some genuine solutions to the British dilemma, although conditions in Britain allowed some groups of women to exploit its benefits more easily than others.

Exceptional as these women were, simply by virtue of their emigration, all of them, including Mary Taylor, need to be distinguished carefully from the more exceptional women encountered among a different class of wealthier women explorers. Eminent 'Victorian Lady Travellers' like Mary Kingsley and Isabella Bird[20] were indeed exceptional, and they are not the subject of this book. Ironically, the frequent existence of such women among the Victorian upper and middle-classes has rarely been recognised as a living denial of the more leisured, dependent and unadventurous stereotype. It was an important contradiction, but it sheds little light on the theme of downward social mobility, which is the main concern here. The more ordinary middle-class emigrants who appear in the following chapters contradict an associated but rather different sterotype of helpless female gentility in distress. The inability of middle-class families — usually, but not necessarily, 'ruined' families — to provide for their daughters' livelihood was a recurrent preoccupation of Victorian commentators.[21] The experience of these emigrants may at least cast some light on the daughters' capacity to provide for themselves.

The most traditional historical approach to the distressed gentlewoman has been to concentrate on the work of reformers in Britain
who worked to alleviate her problems. The attempt to improve the
employment opportunities and conditions of governesses, started in the
1840s, led very quickly to a primary focus on the need to improve
education for middle-class women; by the 1860s moderate middle-class
feminist reformers had launched a serious campaign to reform secondary and tertiary education and to open new occupations to middle-
class women. Understandably, historians have concentrated on the
activities and undoubted achievements of these reformers, but the predictable result has been to lose sight of the real fate of the distressed
gentlewoman altogether. The institutional approach to social history
can too easily drift into a facile form of teleology which portrays the
grand culmination of historical development in the ultimate achievement of needed reforms or the attainment of conditions as we know
them today.[22] Women's history seems to be particularly unsuited to
this approach, since there is little that qualifies unreservedly as a clear
success story for women in social development. But it is no effective
reply to this new whiggism to assert simply that it was not a success
story. Rather, social history needs to deal with the ramifications of the
underlying social process. As the first chapter will attempt to show, the
place of distressed gentlewomen in the social process was far from
unequivocal, and certainly not consistent with the success story suggested by institutional history. Too often casualties rather than beneficiaries of social reform, their immediate hope for social and economic
survival lay in their own initiative and adaptability — often in a willingness to leave the country altogether — rather than in the ambiguous
benefits of institutional 'progress'.

Despite the clear advantages of emigration for middle-class women,
which the following chapters try to illustrate, a recurring theme is the
persistence with which a variety of obstacles prevented more women
from emigrating. The disreputable image of emigration in Britain, the
rigid occupational demands of the colonies, the ideological dictates of a
feminist emigration society and competition from other classes of better
prepared women tended to put distressed gentlewomen at a clear disadvantage. Much of the story which follows, therefore, will focus on the
varying impact of these different inhibitions and their relevance for
potential emigrants. The evolution of official and public attitudes and
the contrasting policies of voluntary emigration societies which affected
the opportunities for emigration determine the conceptual framework
of the argument, but in the process this enables an examination of indi-

vidual women who were determined to solve their own problems in their own way, often in the face of heavy discouragement. Their action may not be enough to dispose thoroughly of every aspect of the distressed gentlewoman stereotype, but at the very least it should raise some questions about the extent of its relevance to a body of women who were forced to become pioneers, unexpectedly, in the traumatic process of attaining self-sufficiency.

Notes

1. G.M. Young, *Victorian England: Portrait of an Age*, 2nd edn. (London, 1953), p. 90.
2. John Duguid Milne, *Industrial and Social Position of Women in the Middle and Lower Ranks* (London, 1857), p. 133.
3. Lee Holcombe, *Victorian Ladies at Work: Middle-Class Working Women in England and Wales, 1850-1914* (Newton Abbot, 1973), p. 5.
4. Wanda F. Neff, *Victorian Working Women: An Historical and Literary Study of Women in British Industries and Professions, 1832-1850* (New York, 1929), ch. 5; Patricia Thomson, *The Victorian Heroine, A Changing Ideal, 1837-1873* (London, 1956), ch. 2.
5. D. Crow, *The Victorian Woman* (London, 1971), p. 68.
6. M. Jeanne Peterson, 'The Victorian Governess: Status Incongruence in Family and Society', in M. Vicinus (ed.), *Suffer and Be Still: Women in the Victorian Age* (Bloomington, 1972), pp. 3-19.
7. Patricia Branca, *Silent Sisterhood: Middle-Class Women in the Victorian Home* (London, 1975).
8. Leonore Davidoff, *The Best Circles: Society, Etiquette and the Season* (London, 1973).
9. Martha Vicinus (ed.), *A Widening Sphere: Changing Roles of Victorian Women* (Bloomington, 1977).
10. See, e.g. L. Davidoff, J. L'Espérance and H. Newby, 'Landscape with Figures: Home and Community in English Society', in J. Mitchell and A. Oakley (eds.), *The Rights and Wrongs of Women* (Harmondsworth, 1976), pp. 139-75.
11. Branca, p. 11.
12. A similar objection applies to Branca's claim that single women deserve less attention than wives because they were not in the majority and thus not typical. Branca, pp. 2-4.
13. M.S. Hartman, *Victorian Murderesses: A True History of Thirteen Respectable French and English Women Accused of Unspeakable Crimes* (London, 1977), p. 2.
14. Branca, p. 11.
15. Ibid., pp. 10-11.
16. Flora Thompson, *Lark Rise to Candleford* (London, 1954).
17. M.A. Crowther, 'British Social History', in *Historical Journal*, 20 (4), (1977), p. 999.
18. See, e.g. Mary Chamberlain, *Fenwomen: A Portrait of Women in an English Village* (London, 1975); such collections of oral evidence are certainly valuable, but mainly as compendia of sources still awaiting historical analysis. The case for experiential history was spelt out in Raphael Samuel's general introduction to

Village Life and Labour (London, 1975), where he stressed how rarely history had been written 'from the real life experience of people themselves', p. xiii. But for a caution against the experiential approach in women's history see Mitchell and Oakley, introduction, pp. 10-11. None of this is to deny the importance of much recent analysis based largely on oral evidence, e.g. Paul Thompson, *The Edwardians* (London, 1975) and the women's history issue of *Oral History*, vol. 5, No. 2, Autumn 1977.

    19. Davidoff, p. 18.

    20. Dorothy Middleton, *Victorian Lady Travellers* (London, 1965).

    21. Some of the most vocal commentators were colonial spokesmen like Edward Gibbon Wakefield, but more particularly the philanthropists, educationists and feminists discussed in chs. 1, 5 and 6.

    22. The most obvious examples are Holcombe, Josephine Kamm, *Hope Deferred: Girls' Education in English History* (London, 1965); Ray Strachey, *The Cause: A Short History of the Women's Movement in Great Britain* (London, 1928) and to a lesser extent Neff, chs. 5 and 6.

1 THE PROBLEM OF THE DISTRESSED GENTLEWOMAN

Why has the distressed gentlewoman stereotype been so pervasive? Part of the answer lies in the nature of the sources which gave rise to it in the first place. Decayed gentility resulting from family impoverishment was a powerful literary convention, and it appeared in at least three generations of Victorian novels, from Lady Blessington's *The Governess* (1839) to George Gissing's *The Odd Women* (1893). Thackeray used it to bring the Sedleys down in *Vanity Fair*, depicting the young widowed Amelia as a timid and helpless victim of the system, sheltering behind her gentility, advertising for pupils who never responded and attempting vainly to earn a living from card-painting.[1] More often the product of family decline was a downtrodden governess, exploited by her employers, abused by her pupils and resented by the servants, although fiction, at least, could provide a dramatic rescue from dependent helplessness in the form of a happy marriage, unexpected fortune or both. Clara Mordaunt[2] and Agnes Grey[3] served as prototypes for countless fictional downtrodden governesses in this mould, while Gissing, more realistically perhaps, used the plight of the elder Madden daughters to stress the unrelieved shabbiness and insecurity of the lives of decayed and ultimately unemployable gentlewomen.[4] Whatever the variations, the fictional models have provided a quarry of vivid and persuasive evidence for historians, to the point where we have come to associate fallen gentility in Victorian women with helplessness, timidity, dependence and false dignity.[5] It is not a picture which says much for the resourcefulness and capacity of Victorian women.

A similar picture, paradoxically, was perpetuated by the early feminists who strove to improve education and employment opportunities for unqualified middle-class women. Earnestly committed, and assisted, from the late eighteen-fifties, by the systematic methods of their colleagues in the National Association for the Promotion of Social Science, these moderate reformers portrayed a gruesome situation in need of urgent change. Most of their analysis of the plight of middle-class women was not exaggerated, but much of their rhetoric provided further support for the distressed gentlewoman stereotype. The well-known phenomena of family impoverishment and genteel poverty served as useful devices to dramatise the folly of female dependence,

husband-hunting, and the inadequacy of female education. The middle
class, Bessie Parkes argued, was at the mercy of countless accidents of
commercial or professional life forcing thousands of destitute and
superficially educated women to earn their living. She estimated that
every reader had 'a female relative or intimate friend whom trade-
failures, the exigencies of a numerous household, or the early death of
a husband or father, has compelled in this course'. The sons of such a
family were equipped, through a more useful education to survive
and succeed, but for untrained women the future was grim:

> the mother and daughters are helped on by friends, exhaust their
> little store of well-wishers, take in sewing, drift lower and lower out
> into that vast ocean of destitution, of which the shores are so steep
> that a bold swimmer and a hard climber may hardly ascend the brink
> thereof.[6]

In a similar tone Jessie Boucherett attacked the prejudices which left
such women unprovided for and unqualified, so that when they
attempted to earn 'they find themselves unable to do it, their hay is
spoilt, and their life, which began so cheerfully, ends in sadness and
sorrow, and in vain regrets for the lost opportunity'.[7] More ominously,
John D. Milne suggested that for untrained gentlewomen the hardships
of a governess's life were so severe that to many they were 'more than
they can bear; either health fails, or, which is of as great importance,
the geniality of the mind gives way'.[8] The image of such downtrodden
casualties of the system was undoubtedly an inspiration to overdue
reforms, but the accuracy of the image has never been called into question. Certainly there was no denying the reality of economic distress;
distressed gentlewomen in this sense were a genuine problem, but the
nature of this problem will be misunderstood if we accept too uncriti-
cally the helpless image developed by novelists and feminists.

The persuasiveness of this image owes a good deal to the more
general and widespread stereotype of Victorian gentlewomen, who,
economically at least, were in no way viewed as distressed. The attack
on middle-class female idleness and aimlessness constituted a key element in the feminist campaign for education and employment, and
while most of the analysis was accurate, in the process it projected a
dehumanised image of helpless, frivolous women which is barely credible as a generalisation for an entire class. Emily Davies deplored the
mental and physical weakness of middle-class women at a NAPSS congress in these terms:

It is a rare thing to meet with a lady, of any age, who does not suffer from headaches, languor, hysteria, or some ailment showing a want of stamina . . . Dulness (*sic*) is not healthy, and the lives of ladies, are, it must be admitted, exceedingly dull.[9]

Charlotte Brontë, in *Shirley* (1849), lamented the declining health and 'wondrous narrowness' of minds and views resulting from feminine aimlessness.[10] More didactic writers blamed uncultivated leisure for a condition of 'ennui' which only useful activity could cure.[11] The condition was far more serious than mere loneliness or mental stagnation. J.D. Milne's socio-psychological diagnosis, with its hints of alienated anomie, has a familiar, modern ring.

As it is — prevented from mingling her regard in much that is of vital importance to the well-being of mankind, and from undertaking many duties to which she feels naturally called — there is entailed upon her a constant sense of alienation from society, and the still more oppressive sense of a purposeless existence.[12]

Speaking, no doubt, from direct observation, Mary Taylor, a close friend of Charlotte Brontë, who had once escaped to New Zealand from relative idleness in England, described the fearful but logical conclusion of an aimless existence.

To receive few impressions, then — to lead the uneventful and almost solitary life which is often thought fit for women — is to approach the borders of insanity; of the state in which the mind cannot distinguish the real from the ideal, and is more under the dominion of the latter than the former.[13]

It was easy to believe that women whose aimless drift left them so helpless in prosperity would be incapable of helping themselves after family misfortune.

It is not the intention of this book to analyse the stereotype of the idle middle-class woman. Some efforts have already been made in this direction, one stressing the active ingenuity of the lower middle-class wife,[14] another focusing on the central, willing and engaging role of the upper and middle-class woman in a system of etiquette designed to guarantee class cohesion among polite Society.[15] But much research is still needed to unravel the extent and meaning of idleness among the middle class. Certainly the passion of Florence Nightingale's denunciation of aimless triviality among middle-class women in *Cassandra*[16] suggests that for some women, at least, idleness and isolation constituted a real problem, although the most voluble protests invariably came from women who solved the problem for themselves. Clearly, though, the preoccupation with idleness did much to colour the attitude towards the equally powerful stereotype of the helpless distressed gentlewoman.

It is a formidable task to question a stereotype which is supported so widely and consistent with such a wide range of credible evidence. Much of the argument which follows will, in fact, draw on and support many of the same sources which sustained the pathetic distressed gentlewoman stereotype. At issue here are the behaviour characteristics of a very wide social range of women, and it would be fanciful to anticipate anything but an infinite variety of personal reactions to the experience of downward social mobility and genteel poverty, including the full measure of the helpless distressed gentlewoman model just described. But the psychological stereotype of the helpless submissive victim and downtrodden governess needs serious qualification. On the other hand contemporary descriptions of socio-economic conditions which gave birth to the stereotype, that is, inadequate female education, middle-class insecurity, family impoverishment and employment difficulties for women, form a much more accurate and reliable picture. A concept of ambivalence is therefore crucial, for the objective conditions making for the stereotype were by and large accurately perceived by Victorians, but their descriptions of the consequences for women's behaviour, though not always false, did a gross injustice to too many of them.

The image of ladylike helplessness in the face of the rough masculine employment marketplace certainly suited the role which had been recommended for respectable women by nineteenth-century writers. Women, quite simply, were expected to refine and civilise their husbands, and any exposure to the harshness of the world of business and politics would disqualify them for that home-based duty. There is no need to repeat the already well-rehearsed details of the image of the 'perfect lady',[17] but the pervasive doctrine of the feminine civilising mission had a long pedigree, which could be put to various uses. The most important nineteenth century manifesto for the doctrine came from Hannah More in 1799, when, in condemning the same frivolity in female education which had stirred feminists like Mary Wollstonecraft and Catherine Macaulay in a different direction, she insisted that women should make a Christian use of more serious studies through a gentle religious influence, or 'moral power', on man. 'Have men no need.' she asked, 'to have their rough angles filed off, and their harshnesses and asperities smoothed and polished by assimilating with beings of more softness and refinement?'[18] More's Victorian successors agreed, and the middle-class drive for respectability was wholly consistent with the image of Coventry Patmore's much cited poem, *The Angel in the House*.[19] More significantly, the same doctrine could be used consistently to urge women to undertake their civilising duty outside the home, in occupations which were simply an extension of their mothering and supportive role. Ruskin's 1864 tribute to woman's 'queenly power' included a plea for her to 'assist in the ordering, in the comforting, and in the beautiful adornment of the state', a thinly disguised reference to nursing, teaching and associated 'feminine' work.[20] As we shall see, the civilising mission could also be used to urge women to leave their homes and undertake a perilous emigrant's journey overseas to civilise pioneer male colonists, which for all its internal consistency with the basic doctrine, hardly left women unexposed to the rigours of the harsh outside world.

The ladylike ideal may well have been realised, on the surface at least, among leisured women of the prosperous middle class. The diaries of Ellen and Emily Hall, daughters of a well-to-do provincial family, record a day to day existence preoccupied largely with the private dramas of courtship, entertaining, visiting, rides, picnics, Sunday School teaching and minor household chores.[21] But lack of contact with the world of work or men's affairs did not necessarily produce a 'Victorian Miss all simpers and swooning'[22] who would be unable to cope with family crises. Nor did it prevent essentially idle and cultivated women from adapting to strange and initially alien circumstances. Emily Hall, who in 1839 was ashamed 'to get into such a thing' as an omnibus, nevertheless was quick to adapt to the freer atmosphere when she visited a household far more high-spirited and less reserved than her own. Initially disgusted by the rowdy manners of the Shore family, she soon noted 'how very quickly one is apt to forget one's proprieties when they are perpetually forgotten by others . . . I could not have fancied I should so quickly have come to like staying here'.[23] The Hall girls were spared from the family impoverishment which would have forced them to find employment, but Emily's readiness to adapt to new conditions was a quality which less fortunate women might turn to their economic advantage.

More pertinently, it is ironic how frequently the same feminists and reformers who made so much of the pathetic distressed gentlewoman stereotype had themselves experienced, fought and survived, through their own efforts, the trauma of family impoverishment. Elizabeth M. Sewell, who wrote at length of distressed gentlewomen who 'begin life penniless, and in all probability . . . will end it penniless',[24] had been driven to keep a small school after her father's death left her, together with her mother and sisters, with an inadequate income.[25] A more prominent example was Harriet Martineau, who resorted to writing, successfully, only after the economic crisis of 1825-6 had virtually ruined her family.[26] The careers of eminent writers are, admittedly, an unreliable guide to the lives of the inarticulate majority, but their experience is a useful reminder of ways in which women might resist the dramatic fate of the downtrodden governess.

The presumed high proportion of governesses in insane asylums formed one of the most common arguments used to illustrate the incapacity of distressed gentlewomen. The observation was not confined to feminist reformers. The Colonial Reformer, Edward Gibbon Wakefield, asserted in 1833 that governesses formed the largest occupational class in insane asylums.[27] Harriet Martineau agreed in 1859[28] and Elizabeth Sewell lamented that 'Our lunatic asylums, our workhouses, and — alas for England that it should be so! — even our penitentiaries, are too often homes for decayed, distressed, destitute governesses.'[29]

Most of these observations were impressionistic, and certainly vague about the precise nature of the mental illness suffered by governesses. The ultimate significance of any such evidence would, anyway, need to be qualified by consideration of the nature of Victorian definitions of insanity. But on the surface there was hard evidence to support the observations. The reports of the Governesses' Benevolent Institution, a society formed in the 1840s to assist unemployed, ill and aged governesses, frequently commented that the illnesses of governesses were usually nervous or mental, 'the effects of early labour, anxiety and fatigue, acting on a delicate frame and weakened nerves', and often cited specific cases of women, young and old, who suffered from such ailments as 'a nervous and brain fever' or periodic insanity with 'lucid intervals'.[30] Florence Nightingale encountered similar cases during her tenure at the Institution for Care of Sick Gentlewomen in Distressed Circumstances in 1853. 'I had more than one lunatic,' she wrote of her governess patients to Dr Pincoffs, adding 'I think the deep feeling I have of the miserable position of educated women in England was gained while there.'[31] European medical opinion confirmed the susceptibility of governesses generally. The psychiatrist, Krafft-Ebing, attributed it to such occupational hazards as

Homesickness; unpleasant family and social relations that often drive these poor creatures away from home; insulting, harsh treatment; in general, depressing social position; disappointed love; over-exertion in work, usually appear as causes.[32]

The national census count of asylum inmates by occupation is not wholly reliable, since nearly a third of the total women had no occupation recorded. But with this qualification the 1861 figures shown in Table 1 bear out the pessimistic estimates. The proportion of governess inmates to total governesses, at 0.55 per cent was higher than any other occupational group, including schoolteachers, and much higher than that among the highest numerical group of women, domestic servants; it was also higher than the proportion of corresponding male occupation groups in asylums.

Table 1: Selected Former Occupations of Lunatics Compared to Total of Each Occupation in Population, England and Wales, 1861

Occupation	Female			Male		
	Total in occupation	Lunatics	Percentage of total	Total in occupation	Lunatics	Percentage of total
Musician	1,618	5	0.31	10,300	27	0.26
Schoolmistress, master, and other teachers	58,350	121	0.21	31,811	80	0.25
Governess	24,770	136	0.55	–	–	
Domestic servant	962,786	2,695	0.28	109,990	119	0.11
Charwoman	65,273	240	0.37	–	–	
Gentlewoman, gentleman, independent	27,420	631	2.30	12,407	121	0.98
No stated occupation		4,026			1,594	
Total listed	10,289,965	13,096	0.127	9,776,259	11,249	0.115

Source: Extracted from Summary Tables, Census Report, England and Wales, 1861, *PP* 1863, LIII, Pt. I (3221), pp. viii, xlii-lxvv, ciii-cix.

It would be too easy though, to exaggerate the significance of the governess statistics. The phenomenon is striking, but it can be explained partly by the more general increase of professional, educated and 'independent' persons in lunatic asylums from about mid-century, which William Farr noticed in his census report for 1861.[33] Governesses might form the highest occupational group in asylums, but they were greatly outnumbered by unoccupied women from the ranks of the leisured, presumably idle or 'independent gentlewomen' at 2.30 per cent. The proportion for 'independent gentlemen' was also higher, at 0.98 per cent. The meaning of these figures may need to be qualified by the probability that the wealthy would be more able to afford to put their mentally ill relatives out of the way, although this would not explain the preponderance of women over men. But feminists were conscious of this problem, too, and their concern for it probably exceeded that for governess inmates. 'Ask medical men the effects of idleness in women', fulminated Barbara Leigh-Smith. 'Look into lunatic asylums, then you will be convinced something must be done for women'.[34] Emily Shirreff argued that the fashionable pursuit of charitable work by wealthy women stemmed not from pious altruism, but from the need for some escape, however inappropriate, from 'morbid feeling and mental suffering bordering more nearly on derangement than we like to allow'.[35] If idle women were actually more subject to mental illness than working governesses, it might suggest that such an occupation, for all its hazards, might provide a welcome relief to many women from the frustrations of leisured gentility. The real distressed gentlewomen, psychologically at least, might have been the wealthy.

It is also worth recalling that even in literature the downtrodden victimised woman was not the only type to appear as a governess, a fact rarely acknowledged by historians. For every Emily Morton or Agnes Grey there was an upstart, ambitious and scheming Becky Sharp, upwardly mobile, or, as Lady Eastlake put it, 'underbred' and interfering 'with the rights of those whose birth and misfortunes leave them no other refuge'.[36] More genteel literary governesses, too, departed from the downtrodden image, as Charlotte Yonge noted in her criticism of the 'pathetic governess style'.[37] For all her trials, Charlotte Brontë's Jane Eyre displayed far too much independence and self-respect to fit the stereotype, earning Lady Eastlake's contempt in the process.[38] Similar women of competence and dignity appeared in Wilkie Collins's novels of the 1860s, and countless others.[39] Less subject to sensationalising than the distressed variety, and hence lost in relative obscurity they nevertheless testified to a recognition that ladylike governesses might fend for themselves with some success.

Before we encounter more direct, personal evidence, then, there are sufficient grounds to question the classic psychological stereotype seriously, even from the scattered evidence produced above. Much of the history of female emigration, in subsequent chapters, should reinforce this impression. But this is not to say that a wide cross-section of middle-class women did not experience the economic distress described so often by feminists and others. Employment for impecunious ladies was no easy matter throughout the nineteenth century, and philan-thropic and feminist societies like the GBI and the Society for Pro-moting the Employment of Women knew from their records that the large numbers seeking work for which they were poorly qualified con-stituted a basic social problem. What, then, was the precise nature of this problem, which class of women were most affected and what remedies could Victorians offer?

By the middle of the century most commentators seemed convinced that the problem was a simple demographic one. There were more women than men in Britain, and the assumption that if the numbers were equal all women would marry and be cared for tended to domin-ate the discussion. The same controversial notion bedevilled the launching of a serious feminist attempt in the early sixties to help middle-class women to emigrate, the Female Middle-Class Emigration Society. The 'redundancy' of women in Britain could easily be put down to the greater emigration of males, and wholesale shipments of prospective wives to the colonies seemed a natural solution.[40] Others, and not simply the feminists, saw emigration as a possible employment outlet for 'excess' women. The Registrar-General accepted this view in his comments on a female surplus of 718,566 in the 1871 UK census, which was balanced by a complementary surplus of males in the New World. 'Those who seek to extend the sphere of labour for women,' he concluded, 'will find therefore in Australia and America a most fruitful field for such of the sex as are willing to play a part in the foundation of the great states of the future'.[41] Certainly the sex disparity was sub-stantial, and from mid-century it increased steadily, as Table 2 illus-trates. Actually the male birth-rate was higher than that for females, but male infant mortality was also higher, as was male mortality generally, so that by the age of 15 there were more females living. The effects of male emigration were substantial, but as can be seen in Table 3, the disparity was aggravated by the permanent absence abroad of men in the armed forces and merchant navy.[42]

An alarming aspect of the sex disproportion, though, was the 'bulge' of 209,663 excess women in the most marriageable ages between 20 and 30 (see Table 3), which seemed to explain the apparent surfeit of young unmarriageable gentlewomen. In fact the bulk of the excess, 312,749, occurred among women over 30. Moreover, analysts of the census were convinced that the figures were distorted. Successive census

Table 2: Females per 1,000 Males, England and Wales

Year	England and Wales Females per 1,000 males
1851	1,042
1861	1,053
1871	1,054
1881	1,055
1891	1,063
1901	1,068
1911	1,068

Source: B.R. Mitchell, *Abstract of British Historical Statistics* (Cambridge, 1962), p. 6, Table 2.

Table 3: Excess of Males and Females, England and Wales, 1861

Ages	Male excess	Female excess	Army, navy and merchant seamen abroad
0- 4	9,032	–	–
5- 9	1,854	–	–
10-14	14,602	–	1,604
15-19	–	16,782	27,121
20-24	–	109,073	55,292
25-29	–	100,590	35,328
30-34	–	63,398	19,110
35-39	–	43,982	11,574
40-44	–	32,011	6,367
45-49	–	24,220	3,021
50-54	–	22,171	1,595
55-59	–	16,004	780
60-64	–	25,168	365
65-69	–	25,496	125
70-74	–	24,489	–
75-79	–	17,080	–
80-84	–	11,147	–
85-89	–	5,249	–
90-94	–	1,803	–
95-99	–	440	–
100+	–	91	–

Source: General Report, Census, England and Wales, 1861, *PP* 1863, vol. LIII, Pt. I (3221), Appendix, p. 115, Table 70.

reports complained that many women had an irritating inclination to mis-state their ages. Girls under 20, they argued, frequently over-stated their age in the hope of qualifying more readily for domestic service, while women over 30 under-stated their age for reasons of personal vanity or presumed eligibility for marriage. After 1841 each census revealed disproportionately more women in the 20-24 age group than had appeared in the 10-14 age group ten years earlier. A similar anomaly appeared in the disproportionately low numbers progressing each decade from the 20-29 age group to 30-39.[43] This in no way denied the existence of an excess of women, but it did suggest that the numbers were more evenly distributed between the ages of 10 to 40 than the census indicated.

None of these figures, however, can prove that the sex disproportion occurred primarily among middle-class women. The meagre national statistics that exist do suggest that middle-class men emigrated in larger numbers than their female counterparts, but the system of recording middle-class women emigrants was extremely unreliable, including only self-described 'gentlewomen' and 'governesses'. Certainly one might expect more middle-class men than women to emigrate under nineteenth-century conditions, but the difference in the available figures would not have been sufficient to leave a major excess of middle-class spinsters, and the accuracy of the figures must be severely qualified by the failure of most women to state any occupation.[44]

The available evidence makes it impossible to be precise about the class composition of the large numbers of unmarried women. A simple comparison of population figures in predominantly middle and upper-class districts with those in predominantly working-class districts, attempted by one historian,[45] can be grossly misleading, since a very large proportion of the female population in the wealthier districts was made up of domestic servants. In Kensington, for example, the 1861 census revealed 69,810 females (41,345 unmarried) and 45,422 males (18,216 unmarried), but the striking implications of the disparity are modified substantially when the female domestic servant total of 19,288 is considered.[46] In 1890 Clara Collet, who worked with Charles Booth on his survey of London, used the 1861 and 1881 censuses to compare the numbers of unmarried women between 35 and 45 (i.e. those considered to be permanently single) in Kensington with those in Hackney. She found that among the 'servant-keeping classes,' or those with an income of £150 and over, there were, in Kensington, 36 unmarried women to 30 married women, while in Hackney the ratio was 12 to 24 for the same class and 9 to 76 for the working class. Collet's figures applied to an age group of women (35 to 45) where single domestic servants were not in the majority, and in any case excluded one-third of single women who were presumed to be servants at that age, so they begin to give a clearer picture of the peculiarly middle-class dimensions of the problem.[47] Collet guessed, without supporting evidence, 'that the unmarried women are, to a large extent, the daughters of clerks and professional men'.[48] but it did not follow that the problem of 'redundant' unmarried women was simply a demographic one. Jessie Boucherett, at the height of the controversy, insisted that experience in other countries where there were more men than women

> showed clearly that the excess of women above the number of men was not the sole or even chief cause of the existing distress, and that if we could equalise the number of men and women in Great Britain we should still not be out of our difficulty.[49]

Most writers linked the demographic argument to a popular belief that the middle class, and especially middle-class men, were delaying marriage until later ages, creating a growing force of reluctant spinsters.[50] There is at least some substantive evidence, though it is far from conclusive, to suggest that the middle-class tendency to postpone marriage was increasing. In 1871 C. Ansell Jr. conducted a private survey of marriage and mortality among 8,000 families from the clergy, legal and medical professions and a large number 'of other gentlemen and Noblemen' in England and Wales. The results, shown in Table 4, indicated a significant increase in the male age at marriage over the period 1840-1870 to 29.95 years from a prior figure of 28.64, and a widening gap between the male and female ages.[51]

Table 4: Middle-Class Age at Marriage, 1840-70

| Period of marriage | Mean age at marriage | | Mean difference in ages of |
	Bachelor years	Spinster years	husband and wife years
Before 1840	28.64	24.75	3.89
During and since 1840	29.95	25.53	4.42
Both periods	29.32	25.16	4.16

Source: Ansell, p. 45.

By contrast the mean age at marriage for the population as a whole between 1861 and 1870 was 27.8 years for men and 25.6 for women, and other research has suggested a trend towards earlier marriage among the general population from 1851 to 1881.[52] Here, then, was the essence of the problem that fascinated novelists and provoked feminists; middle-class women, raised exclusively for marriage, had progressively fewer opportunities of realising it, and without the support of a husband there was no certain guarantee that their fathers or other relatives would be able to support them indefinitely. Since the majority were wholly unqualified for the narrow range of respectable, well paid work which was open to women, the picture of economic distress seems to be irrefutable for a substantial minority.

The GBI, founded in the 1840s, and feminist reformers from the 1850s were clearly convinced that the distress was substantial.[53] But the problem was even more complex, because it was far from clear to what extent the 'distressed' were actually 'gentlewomen'. The preoccupation of the feminists with the plight of 'ladies' who had suffered family impoverishment marked out their own main priorities, and testified to the reality of downward social mobility among women from the professional classes and higher. The complaint that the 'great difficulty ladies usually find in securing congenial and sufficiently well-paid employment arises from the pressing necessity they are generally under of earning money at once',[54] formed one of the most frequent arguments for better female education. But the feminists were conscious of another dimension to the problem; lower middle-class women, and daughters of the upper levels of the working class, were competing for the same limited range of respectable occupations. Jessie Boucherett complained that the teaching profession was so overcrowded and difficult for unqualified gentlewomen because of the increasing entry of young women 'who are not gentlewomen by birth' with an entirely different motive, 'for the sake of social advancement, just as men sometimes go into the church or the army in order to become gentlemen by profession'.[55] A phenomenon frowned upon by many feminists, it made teaching a platform where two classes of women met, in Bessie Parkes' words, 'the one struggling up, the other drifting down'.[56] Downward mobility, in short, clashed with the more ambitious upward mobility.

Such complex social mobility may have caused reformers to exaggerate the real extent of genteel poverty, but it also provoked a continuing discussion of the meaning of gentility which helps to clarify the problem. By the second half of the century there was growing confusion over what, precisely, constituted a gentlewoman, how far down the social structure she might exist and how wide a range of employment she might safely adopt. All women, an etiquette guide noted, now called themselves 'ladies', but true gentility was marked less by breeding, wealth or social rank than by behaviour, that is, restraint, self-control and conduct towards others, especially towards poorer people. True refinement was never a product of dress or speech, but rather of a refined mind, ideas and education.[57] Gentility, then, was democratically accessible to all women, at least in theory. The practical work of reformers soon brought them to similar conclusions. Much as they deplored the lower middle-class 'mania for gentility' they were soon forced to come to terms with it.[58] On the one hand, anxious to open new occupations to the impoverished daughters of once-prosperous families, they sought to persuade them that true gentility could never be compromised by the nature of a woman's work; in Louisa M. Hubbard's words, 'no such external accident as her profession can either make or unmake a lady'.[59] On the other hand, their increasing contact with unemployed daughters of the lower middle class convinced them that the problem, for both groups, was similar. Their families could no longer support them, they insisted on work which would be deemed respectable and their education and training was invariably inadequate for the narrow range of available employment. All of them, up to a point, could be described as distressed gentlewomen.

The feminists' discussion of social class, however, continued to produce ambivalence and confusion. The confusion is understandable, since historians today still find it difficult to explain the place of women within an analysis of class structure based essentially on male categories. One historian of the lower middle class recently acknowledged that 'historical stratification theory' has great difficulty in coping with female occupations.[60] The problem was no less elusive for contemporaries, particularly when new white-collar occupations were slowly becoming accessible to women. Clara Collet's location of the middle-class female employment problem among the daughters of clerks and professionals earning upwards of £150 was probably accurate,[61] but it covered a huge social range, and still ignored the upwardly aspiring daughters of the working class. There was a clear distinction, for example, between mid-Victorian schoolmistresses in local elementary schools, recruited from the working class, and those not far removed socially, but 'who have been brought up as ladies' and would find the position 'extremely repulsive'.[62] Yet by the 1870s feminists were urging the well born 'lady' to undertake the very same work, assuring her that while she might have to tolerate some 'unpleasant slights and discomforts', 'the more real are her pretensions to the true title of lady, the less she will feel the sting of such petty grievances, and the more easily will she be able even to smile at prejudices to which she is running counter'.[63] Feminist reformers accustomed to making such proposals soon accepted a wider definition of gentility. In 1878 the *Women's Gazette* identified the daughters of the 'professional and clerical classes . . . women who frequently begin life as nursery governesses at eighteen or so', with those of 'gentle-birth'.[64] The admission is consistent with literary evidence. Elizabeth Gaskell described Molly Gibson's governess, Miss Eyre, in *Wives and Daughters*, as

> a respectable woman, the daughter of a shopkeeper in the town, . . . a 'lady' . . . in the best sense of the word, though in Hollingford she only took rank as a shopkeeper's daughter . . . She was sensitive and conscientious, and knew the evils of an ungovernable temper.[65]

It may seem incongruous to include destitute shopkeepers' daughters among the ranks of distressed gentlewomen, but the state of social mobility in the later nineteenth century requires a broadening of the concept at least in that direction.

This is not to suggest the absurd notion that there were no distinctions of substance between the lower middle class and the more comfortable multiple-servant-keeping middle and upper middle classes. But the differences between these classes carried different meanings for women than they did for men. Since, as the feminists noticed, gentility was becoming an acquired characteristic of the lower middle classes, and since many daughters of both groups continued to be raised for a leisured future, each class continued to produce its quota of distressed gentlewomen with basically similar problems of employability and declining status. Undoubtedly, by the late nineteenth century, the daughters of all these classes were taking advantage of educational reforms and filling the new skilled and semi-professional occupations created by an expanding economy. But each class continued to produce casualties with appropriate qualifications for the title of distressed gentlewoman.

Despite their liberal interpretation of gentility the feminists did not abandon the concept altogether, and on some issues an obsession with gentility could determine their basic attitude. From the beginning they deplored the 'insane notion' that a woman should be unable to turn to conventionally male or working-class occupations without retaining the status of a gentlewoman.[66] But there was a limit to the distance a woman might move in this direction. In the early 1870s there were a number of proposals to open domestic service to gentlewomen.[67] Initially the reaction was mixed and prompted familiar sermons stressing the 'dignity of labour'.[68] But after some serious experiment and long discussion feminist opinion turned decisively against the proposals, on the grounds of class incompatibility. The journal *Women and Work* compared the notion with the unthinkable possibility of clergymen's and physicians' sons becoming valets, footmen and butlers, and drew the logical conclusion: 'Classes and sexes must sink or swim together; that which is impossible for the man cannot be made available — speaking from the class point of view — for the woman.'[69] The language of class evident here was never far removed from feminist analysis of the problems they encountered. A widened interpretation of gentility did not prevent most feminists from maintaining a clear dividing line between respectable and unrespectable work, between gentlewomen and at least ambitious daughters of the working class. The very existence of distressed gentlewomen was attributable in part to class-based prejudices of Victorians which identified respectability with idleness and dependence; it is hardly surprising that moderate Victorian feminists should have addressed themselves to the problem in terms of class.

From the 1840s the efforts of feminists and other reformers to assist the distressed gentlewoman became increasingly ambitious, and in many ways effective. Initially, through the GBI, the focus was on the plight of the governess; from the late fifties feminists attempted to open a huge range of occupations to women which had previously been inaccessible. Yet, despite the massive incursion of women into the occupations feminists promoted,[70] despite basic changes in the standard of female education, by the 1890s the problem of the distressed gentlewoman seemed as intractable as ever. In 1894 H.C. Davidson, after a long description of occupations available to women, regretted having to tell unqualified young ladies of the 'melancholy' fact 'that the only openings nowadays are those involving special training and much hard work'.[71] Louisa Hubbard, summarising eighteen years' work of her women's magazine, *Work and Leisure*, in 1893, lamented the fact that feminist reformers still had to cater to the most 'forlorn members of society'; she blamed the 'enormous increase of population' for the apparently disappointing results.[72] The continued complaints of well-informed feminists like Clara Collet[73] and the indignation of novelists like George Gissing in *The Odd Women*[74] confirmed that in the midst of progress for women there was stagnation, possibly deterioration. Why, then, did the feminists' determined efforts do so little to solve the central problem which had stirred them in the first place?

The earliest feminist analyses were quick to diagnose the fundamental social causes of genteel poverty. Women raised for a state of dependence in marriage but not provided for in the event of spinsterhood were bound inevitably for 'educated destitution'.[75] It was a simple, logical step to blame this situation on parents for neglecting their daughters' future. In fact the early criticisms tended to accept the assumption of natural female dependence on male relatives by stressing the duty of fathers to make financial provision for their daughters and wives, if necesssary by sacrificing the extravagant habit of 'keeping up appearances'. At the very least, Bessie Parkes argued in 1865, this required fathers to take out sufficient life insurance to make financial provision for their daughters and wives. But such forethought was rare.

It is lamentable to think how small a proportion of our population insures, when it is so cheap, easy and safe for the *young* married men to do so, and creates help for the women of a family just when, by the death of the breadwinner, they would otherwise be left without resource. To insure, or to save up a portion for every female child, this is a father's sacred duty. Style, position, the keeping of many servants, all should be stinted to effect this end.

As she went on to explain, the passion for material acquisitions and a large establishment of servants to maintain mother and daughters in fashionable idleness precluded any outlay on insurance premiums.[76] Even the anti-feminist writer, Elizabeth Eastlake, stressed that 'we need the imprudencies, extravagancies, mistakes or crimes of a certain number of fathers to sow the seed from which we reap the harvest of governesses'.[77] If blame had to be apportioned anywhere this was surely the place for it. As late as 1893 Gissing underlined the irony of the situation in *The Odd Women.* Dr Madden, the father of six daughters, to whom the thought 'of his girls having to work for money was so utterly repulsive that he could never seriously dwell upon it', is accidentally killed in the first chapter, leaving his daughters penniless, immediately after announcing to the eldest that on the next day he would insure his life for a thousand pounds.[78]

In view of the failure of families to guarantee financial support for young women, the point about insurance was a valid one, but it remained a virtually inaccessible luxury for most marginal middle-class families. There is certainly clear evidence that most middle-class Victorians were chronically under-insured. In 1846 a committee of civil servants asked William Farr, for many years Superintendent of the Registrar-General's Statistical Department, to investigate the existing civil service superannuation scheme and to examine their proposal for an alternative widows' and orphans' pension scheme. Farr found the old scheme extremely ineffectual. The yearly salaries of 16,353 civil service officers averaged £141, among which 8,704 under £100 averaged only

£86. The premiums of the superannuation scheme, established in 1829, fell most heavily on those with the lowest incomes, requiring a 2½ per cent deduction from salaries under £100 and 5 per cent from those over £100. The 7,964 employees who returned Farr's completed questionnaire drew an average of £106. Of this group 5,367 were married, of whom 4,290 had 16,331 children, an average of 3.81 children for each productive family. Farr's sample was not fully representative of the entire civil service, but his point was well taken that the superannuation deductions left the majority of those with the greatest need quite unable to insure their lives or provide for their widows and children. Farr noticed that this deficiency had already caused considerable distress among the families of deceased civil servants, and recommended a combined superannuation-pension scheme along the lines of that of the East India Company, which, among other things, provided a £50 yearly pension to orphan daughters until marriage. But more important, in view of his intimate acquaintance with British population problems, was Farr's conviction that the same conditions obtained among most of the middle classes, not least those more prosperous than the civil servants he surveyed. Life insurance in these circumstances became a moral duty.

Life insurance meets the risk of mortality; but it unfortunately happens in all professions — and in the civil service among others — that life insurance, to an adequate extent, is not effected by the great majority of husbands — and more particularly by those whose lives are liable to be cut short, and whose large families are likely to prove the severest pressure of want — the heaviest burden on the community. Society has, therefore, a right, and whenever an opportunity offers, perhaps a duty to see, that such a deduction is made from the adequate income in active life as will lighten the sufferings of the fatherless children and widows of its members. If the Government set the example in the public service, it may be copied by other classes; and would ultimately prove a great boon and economy to the nation.[79]

Insurance alone, though, was no fundamental solution to the problems of middle-class female employment. Before long some feminists began to argue that the proceeds of insurance were inadequate anyway, and that there was no substitute for sound education, training, or instruction of wives and daughters in a business, even in that of the father.[80] Again the responsibility rested upon the father for neglecting to give his daughters a useful education. After gathering substantial

evidence and opinion on the state of female secondary education, the
Taunton Commission concluded that the fault lay in 'the apathy and
want of cooperation, often the active opposition, of too many of the
parents . . . they will not pay for good teaching when they might have
it; and . . . oppose what is not showy and attractive'.[81] Shortly afterwards Barbara Bodichon told the Commissioners of Popular Education
that parents were responsible for the most basic weakness in the education system, the shortage of good teachers.

> Fathers will not expend capital in training girls as teachers, or in any
> other profession; it is not a good investment of capital they think, as
> the girl may marry and leave her profession, after exercising it a
> short time, or before exercising it at all.[82]

This, no doubt, was the crux of the problem. So long as fathers found it
too expensive, unfashionable or wasteful to educate their daughters for
specific work, as they educated their sons, and so long as fathers continued to die, become incapacitated or insolvent, there would be an
army of unqualified middle-class women seeking work. Until educational reforms could compel all fathers to give their daughters a useful
education the problem would remain.

The feminist diagnosis of the problem led logically to the many-
faceted campaign to reform female education. The earliest, halting
impulses followed the formation of the Governesses' Benevolent Institution, which in 1843 began to give financial aid to unemployed governesses; it also established a savings scheme and awarded a few annuities
to aged and infirm governesses. Subsequently it began a 'Home for dis-
engaged governesses', a free employment register, an asylum for the
aged and a savings bank. But its experience in all these ventures demonstrated that inadequate education was the root cause of governess hardship, and in 1847 it assisted in the founding of Queen's College, Harley
Street, where it encouraged potential and actual governesses to obtain a
thorough secondary education.[83] The GBI committee was slow, however, to admit that only thorough educational reform would eliminate
the distress it sought to cure, and even while establishing Queen's
College it proclaimed a remarkably backward-looking philosophy of
education.

> The Committee disclaim any idea of training Governesses as a separ-
> ate profession. They believe and hope, that the ranks of that profes-
> sion will be still supplied from those, whose minds and tempers have

been disciplined in the school of adversity, and who are thus best able to guide the minds and tempers of their pupils.[84]

The process by which educational reform left casualties in its wake was a simple one. In 1895 the Royal Commission on Secondary Education (Bryce Commission) enthused that of all the recent improvements in secondary education, the most conspicuous and beneficial was the welcome fact that 'School-keeping is less frequently than it used to be the mere resort of ladies possessing no other means of support.'[85] The difficulty was that educational reform had not developed to a point where 'ladies possessing no other means of support' ceased to be a problem. The more fortunate women, whose parents had wisely enabled them to take advantage of the new secondary schools, now fully qualified and certificated, were able to turn to the publicly recognised profession of teaching. But the higher salaries and status were reserved for the well-trained, while those without the training found their opportunities steadily narrowing, the casualties of professionalisation. Mercy Grogan, in 1880, acknowledged that although teaching was still the most suitable and remunerative employment open to women,

> an ordinary education no longer qualifies a woman for the position of governess in any educational establishment; if she wishes to be tolerably certain of securing an engagement it is necessary that she should be certificated, or, still better, have completed her education at Girton, Newnham or one of the new halls opened at Oxford, and it is most desirable that she should pass the new examination of teachers instituted by the Teacher's Training Syndicate of Cambridge.[86]

Teaching, an Associate of Newnham College concurred, was 'ceasing to be a refuge for the destitute'.[87] The situation applied equally to the schoolteacher and private governess. As early as 1876 Charlotte Yonge told parents that no 'professional teacher' under 25 '*ought* to be engaged for girls over fourteen, who cannot produce a certificate from a University'. Such a governess would require a good salary but, if necessary, parents should share her with two or three other families rather than engage the poorly qualified at a pittance.[88]

The fate of those without 'certificates' left to earn a mere pittance was a major problem facing feminist reformers.[89] One reaction in the early years was, like that of the GBI, to urge that ladies who had turned to teaching through 'reverse of fortune' had, nevertheless, 'seen much of life', and had worthwhile experience to offer, not, perhaps as efficient instructors, but for their 'moral influence, which is most important in giving a refined and cultivated tone to the whole course of education'.[90] But it was too inconsistent with the central feminist stress on the value of professional education and training to argue for long that the untrained should be given a special educational role. Other alternatives had to be found, but in the meantime, as their gentility became less marketable, many 'incapables', as Louisa Hubbard called them,[91] continued to turn to teaching. Many of the advertisements placed in a late-nineteenth century governess register demanded salaries as low as £20, and continued to appear in successive issues without any successful response.[92] Institutions like the GBI continued to offer assistance to women tenacious enough to remain governesses in the face of more professional competition, but feminists soon realised that the only solutions lay in other occupations, training if possible or escape if necessary.

Feminist reformers set themselves the daunting task of bringing a new air of respectability to less genteel occupations in order to induce middle-class women to turn away from governessing. Their efforts were aided by late-nineteenth century socio-economic tendencies which stimulated the expansion of white-collar occupations.[93] Elementary school-teaching was one of the early targets chosen to secure middle-class entry. Since 1846 this had been the almost exclusive province of working-class 'pupil-teachers', trained first through the system and later at training colleges. The rough, crowded conditions of working-class schools had been sufficient to deter most middle-class women from attempting to gain entry. But with the expansion of the system and improvement of conditions feminists soon began to urge ladies without higher certificates to turn to elementary teaching.[94] The problem was that time and money still needed to be expended on specific training. A special Church of England training college, Bishop Otter Memorial College, began in 1873 to train 'ladies' as elementary teachers, and there is no question that middle-class women able to obtain the training took advantage of the new opportunities in increasing numbers.[95] But the annual fee of £50[96] put such an option far beyond reach of the genuine distressed gentlewoman in need of an immediate income. Fortunately for the most determined, women able to find co-operative headmasters or headmistresses could become assistant-teachers in their schools with a salary of £20 or £30, continue to study while 'on probation', and eventually take examinations to become fully certificated elementary teachers.[97] It is impossible to know how often the middle class resorted to this outlet; certainly for the more enterprising it offered a real solution. But the relentless drive in the direction of more thorough college training prevented it from becoming a more widely canvassed outlet.[98]

With the establishment of the Society for Promoting the Employment of Women in 1859 feminist reformers (familiarly known as the 'Ladies of Langham Place') issued a constant flood of suggestions for alternative employment which might suit distressed gentlewomen.[99] At the same time they were attempting to open new occupations to women generally, so it was unlikely that all the opportunities would be appropriate to women without the relevant education and specialised training. The most obvious areas for concentration were those undergoing the most rapid expansion in the later nineteenth century: office work, shop work and nursing. In addition feminists offered a seemingly infinite range of suggestions, many of them bordering on the bizarre, but all seriously put forward as possible relief from the distressed gentlewoman's economic dilemma. The following list is a mere representative sample: bee-keepers, cashiers, cooks, detectives, domestic pet-rearers, embroiderers, engravers, hairdressers, gardeners, illuminators, journalists, lithographers, masseuses, photographers, prison-warders, wood-carvers.[100] From the 1870s 'dictionaries' and 'handbooks' of female employment proliferated, and the authors insisted that employment had already been obtained for ladies in the most unlikely positions which they recommended.[101] The overall scope of expansion in female employment was indeed vast,[102] and despite obvious and frequent drawbacks like long hours, low pay (invariably lower than the prevailing male wage) and insecurity, the new openings meant real opportunities for middle-class women over what had been available before. But difficulties remained which tended to place the genteel and untrained at the end of the queue.

The more serious and skilled occupations, such as nursing, remained virtually inaccessible to distressed gentlewomen, for reasons similar to those which excluded them from elementary schools. In nursing a minimum of one year's training at £30, and in office work, shop work and various trades and crafts a period of lesser training or apprenticeship all raised formidable obstacles to women lacking the necessary fees and living expenses.[103] Acutely conscious of the dilemma, feminist workers assiduously sought out employers willing to offer special conditions for the truly 'deserving'. At Saint Thomas's Hospital, in London, through the Nightingale Fund, occasional vacancies occur for the admission of gentlewomen free of expense, together with, in some cases, a small salary during the year of training. These advantages will be strictly limited to those whose circumstances require such aid.[104]

Similarly, the Prudential Life Assurance Company in 1880 employed 160 ladies, stressing that only daughters of 'professional men' with an ordinary English education' were eligible, and that conditions were provided, such as a library, piano and separate amenities, catering to the special comfort of 'lady-clerks'.[105] Mercy Grogan also found that a large proportion of shop assistants with the larger linen drapers were daughters of professionals.[106] Most of these positions were in 'living-in' accommodation provided by the employers, and were notorious for their harsh exploitative conditions;[107] their suitability for the genteel thus stretches credulity, but after questioning the women themselves Grogan was convinced, insisting that

> Their universal opinion is that they are much better off than they would be if they were governesses; in fact many of them have been governesses, and have given it up from the difficulty of obtaining comfortable engagements.[108]

Special favours, though, could only benefit the fortunate few when the dominant trend increasingly favoured young women who sought education and training with the deliberate intention of finding work. The feminists soon found that the less genteel were better situated to exploit the new opportunities than women who had anticipated a more leisurely future or more respectable work. The secretary of the SPEW told the Taunton Commission that the well trained from all classes could always get work, but 'sometimes the daughter of a small tradesman is rather better educated than those who have been in a higher position'.[109] Once again crucial reforms had worsened the competitive position of women most in need of help.

Competition was not the only obstacle facing the untrained middle class. The feminists' task of bringing new respectability to occupations traditionally considered unsuitable was hard fought, and too often resisted most strongly by the women themselves. Law-copying, for example, was consistently one of the employment societies' favourite occupations for young ladies.[110] But after fifteen years of propaganda and hard work, and despite potential salaries of £100, a feminist journal complained in 1874 that nine out of ten women 'have an idea that law-copying is "vulgar", "wretchedly paid for"', and refused to entertain the prospect.[111] In nursing, where the most dramatic revolution in public image took place, and where there was no doubt of growing middle-class participation, there were continued complaints about the 'tinge of shame' associated with the work, which prevented some women from adopting it and caused others to leave it.[112] Women were slowly overcoming the long Victorian obsession with gentility, but by the 1890s it was still pervasive enough to limit the range of occupations they would accept. The matter was crucial for the distressed gentlewoman, since her major hope lay increasingly in a willingness to sacrifice her carefully nurtured sense of gentility.

There was little in the way of a comprehensive solution for the severe economic dilemma facing distressed gentlewomen. The relentless competition and progressive narrowing of opportunity created a situation which, admittedly, lends some credibility to the familiar pathetic stereotype of the distressed gentlewoman. But we need to look beyond the convenient conclusions suggested by this assumption. The decayed gentlewoman forced into needlework to eke out a livelihood, for example, conjures up a picture which is curiously inconsistent with scattered first-hand evidence. The once destitute middle-class milliner, Louisa Baker, interviewed by A.J. Munby in 1859, was sufficiently independent and prosperous to bear no comparison with the stereotype.[113] Millinery and dressmaking, for all their hardships and severe working conditions, may have provided a regular and viable living for the daughters of professionals, clergy and half-pay officers.[114] Moreover, feminists liked to cite cases of gentlewomen succeeding in business as examples to others. 'Miss Sinclair of Hull', a doctor's daughter, did so well as a confectioner in her own business after her father's death that by 1881 she had

> already purchased many a cosy bit of property, and looks forward to settling in a suburban residence now being built for her. She remarks humorously that she has never had the expense of a husband, and 'no man-person' is employed in her establishment.[115]

Such random examples constitute little more than hints of the range of possibilities for the more enterprising. But there is no reason why the enterprising should be seen as mere isolated exceptions from the norm of the pathetic decayed gentlewoman. Some of the most promising solutions available to women required precisely the sort of determination shown by Miss Sinclair of Hull. Emigration was one of those solutions, and it had potentially vital attractions for distressed gentlewomen.

By the later nineteenth century many reformers had seen the advantages of emigration for middle-class women, and worked unremittingly to encourage distressed gentlewomen to emigrate.[116] But the connection between emigration and the dilemma of single middle-class women was perceived much earlier, in the 1830s.

Significantly, one of the earliest and most astute analyses of the socio-economic origins of the distressed gentlewoman was combined with an elaborate theory of colonisation and lofty claims for the unique role of women in emigration and the founding of new societies. The author was Edward Gibbon Wakefield, a Colonial Reformer and a promoter of emigration whose first book, published anonymously in 1829 while he was serving a sentence for abduction in Newgate, criticised convict transportation to Australia and pleaded for a system of self-supporting respectable emigration.[117] In his second book, *England and America*, in 1833, he insisted that the vulnerability of most of the middle class, or, as he called them, the 'uneasy class', to economic misfortune was a powerful argument in favour of a system of patrician emigration. He was the first to locate and describe the 'uneasy class' systematically with such prime emphasis on one of its major victims, the portionless daughter. He also offered a ready solution: emigration, or more properly, a central role in colonisation. One of Wakefield's chief interests was to encourage the middle class to emigrate, especially to Australia, in order to establish an extension of the British social hierarchy there;[118] consequently he was prone to exaggerate the case for middle-class emigration, but his analysis of the 'uneasy' or 'anxious vexed or harassed class', was highly pertinent, and anticipated much of the feminist analysis a generation later. The uneasy class in the thirties, he argued, consisted of all classes above labourers who suffered from various forms of economic distress; to be more precise, as many as nine-tenths 'of all who are engaged in trades and professions, as well as all who not being very rich, intend that their children should follow some industrious pursuit'.[119]

Wakefield's basic thesis was that there was an insufficient field for investment and an overcrowding of talent in Britain; consequently, with excessive competition and inadequate markets, the profits and incomes of all small investors, entrepreneurs and professionals were perilously unremunerative, leaving them highly vulnerable to economic fluctuations and crises. Their plight was aggravated by the constant increase in expenditure necessary to maintain social rank, especially the daunting task of educating and providing for a large family. Those on fixed incomes, particularly, were desperate to prevent their daughters' descent to a lower social class through imprudent marriage, but it was exceptional for women of small resources to marry men of the wealthier 'spending class'.

The general rule with the daughters of men of small income, whether fixed or not, is a choice between celibacy and marriage with one of the uneasy class. Now, a great proportion of young men in the uneasy class dread marriage, unless there be fortune in the case, as the surest means of increasing their embarrassment. This is one of the most important features in the social state of England.

The result was 'exuberant prostitution' and middle-class women left to 'pine in celibacy'. Their only employment outlet lay in education. Governesses faced greater competition for work than labourers, and hence were the most common occupants of lunatic asylums.[120] Wakefield's solution was to employ both the capital and labour of the uneasy class abroad, and in that process women had a central role, which he expanded upon further in 1849. It had been New England matrons rather than fathers who had 'made New England for a long while, the finest piece of colonisation the world has exhibited'. Similarly, in the new colonies of the nineteenth century, successful colonisation depended on the participation of the best and most virtuous women.

The influence of women in this matter is even greater . . . than that of the men. You may make a colony agreeable to men, but not to women; you cannot make it agreeable to women without being agreeable to men . . . A colony that is not attractive to women, is an unattractive colony: in order to make it attractive to both sexes, you do enough if you take care to make it attractive to women.[121]

Women were to emigrate, then, in order to bring 'honour, virtue and refinement' to new societies,[122] and to escape the unnatural state of celibacy to which they were condemned in an overcrowded Britain. Their importance in the process of colonisation rested on the familiar assumptions of the feminine civilising mission. As wives and mothers of respectable colonists they would refine and cultivate the New World.
　　The doctrine of feminine civilising influence had obvious implications for female emigration. The promoters of all the various emigration schemes regularly paid lip-service to the probable reform that the feminine touch would effect on a crude, male-dominated, pioneering colony.[123] Moreover, there seems to have been a widespread belief in

the innate superiority and refinement of Englishwomen over other
nationalities, which gave them a unique capacity to influence male
society. A women's magazine, at about the same time as Wakefield,
attributed the superiority to the distinctive form of Christianity prac-
tised in England.[124] William Farr, in his introduction to the 1851 census,
noticed the large number of women — wives, mothers and daughters —
without official employment, and added, with significant italics, 'but it
requires no argument to prove that the *wife*, the *mother*, the *mistress*
of an *English Family* — fills offices and discharges duties of no ordinary
importance'.[125] Mary Maurice, sister of F.D. Maurice, made a similar
point through invidious comparison with foreigners. She deplored the
exposure to a lower moral tone faced by English governesses teaching in
France; the damage was permanent, but not complete. 'When she
returns home, her salary may be higher, but her tone is lower, though
she is still a safer teacher than a French woman, who never had any
right principle, to counterbalance her natural frivolity.'[126] It was a
simple step from here to argue, as Wakefield did, that Englishwomen
should civilise abroad as well as at home.

The appearance of Wakefield's arguments in the late twenties and
thirties was timely, for as early as the 1830s some distressed gentlewomen, against enormous obstacles, began, in effect, to follow his
advice by obtaining passages to the colonies.[127] Their object, though,
was invariably work rather than a pioneering husband in need of
feminine cultivation. Emigration had some obvious advantages for
middle-class women. Those fearing the loss of caste and humiliation
which would accompany a wage earning career at home might more
safely pursue the same career anonymously in the colonies, where most
women of all social classes were accustomed to harder work generally
and a wider range of menial chores normally performed by servants.
Feminists themselves began to promote emigration for gentlewomen in
the 1860s.[128] But there were formidable hurdles to be overcome. Emigration, until at least the second half of the century, was a hazardous
undertaking, most especially for middle-class women, who were unused
to travelling alone in Britain.[129] Courage and enterprise were therefore
essential qualifications for potential emigrants. Furthermore, until mid-
century at least, critical public attitudes and lack of facilities discouraged many middle-class women from emigrating. Most emigration
promoters looked to Australia, where there was a severe shortage of
women, as the best haven for British gentlewomen. But before the
1850s the public associated Australia, and to a lesser extent emigration
generally, with convict transportation, distress, depravity and prostitu-

tion, and these assumptions were bound to work as a deterrent against any system of middle-class emigration in the early-Victorian period. The history of early-Victorian female emigration is thus partly an account of its gradual emergence from this hostile stereotype; it is also an uncharacteristic story of women who were sufficiently courageous to defy the conventions which bound them.

Notes

1. W. Thackeray, *Vanity Fair* (London, 1848), chs. 17, 18, 50.
2. Lady Blessington (Marguerite Gardiner), *The Governess* (London, 1839).
3. Ann Brontë, *Agnes Grey* (London, 1847).
4. George Gissing, *The Odd Women* (London, 1893).
5. Cf. Katherine West, *Chapter of Governesses: A Study of the Governess in English Fiction, 1800-1949* (London, 1949), chs. 2, 3, 4; Bea Howe, *A Galaxy of Governesses* (London, 1954), chs. 5, 6; Thomson, ch. 2.
6. Bessie R. Parkes, 'Educated Destitution', in *Essays on Women's Work* (London, 1865), pp. 76-83.
7. Jessie Boucherett, *Hints on Self-Help: A Book for Young Women* (London, 1863), pp. 1-3.
8. John Duguid Milne, *Industrial and Social Position of Women in the Middle and Lower Ranks* (London, 1857), p. 131.
9. Emily Davies, 'On Secondary Instruction as Relating to Girls', *Transactions*, National Association for Promotion of Social Science (hereafter TNAPSS), 1864, p. 396.
10. C. Brontë, *Shirley* (London, 1849), ch. 22.
11. Emily A.E. Shirreff, *Intellectual Education and its Influence on the Character and Happiness of Women* (London, 1858), p. 23.
12. Milne, pp. 19-20.
13. Mary Taylor, 'Feminine Idleness', in *The First Duty of Women* (London, 1870), p. 118. See the detailed discussion of Taylor in ch. 3, below.
14. Branca.
15. Davidoff; see also J.A. and Olive Banks, *Feminism and Family Planning in Victorian England* (Liverpool, 1964).
16. Fragment from unpublished manuscript, *Suggestions for Thought to Searchers after Religious Truth*, printed in Strachey, Appendix I, pp. 395-418.
17. For the fullest discussions see Vicinus, *Suffer and Be Still*, introduction; Banks, chs. 5, 6; Walter E. Houghton, *The Victorian Frame of Mind* (New Haven, 1957), pp. 348-53.
18. Hannah More, *Strictures on the Modern System of Female Education* (London, 1799, 2 vols.), Vol. I, pp. 67-9, 178-81, vol. II, pp. 1-4, 22-3, 31-3. See also More's model woman in *Coelebs in Search of a Wife* (London, 1808).
19. Cf. Houghton, pp. 341-5, 392. Most of the nineteenth century moralising literature of feminine obligation simply echoed More's sentiments; see, e.g. Sarah Lewis, *Woman's Mission* (London, 1839); Mrs S. Ellis, *'The Women of England* (London, 1839) and *The Daughters of England* (London, 1842); A.B. Muzzey *The English Maiden: Her Moral and Domestic Duties* (London, 1841).
20. J. Ruskin, 'Of Queen's Gardens', in *Sesame and Lilies* (London, 1865), pp. 122-3, 160-1, 177-9. Cf. David Sonstroem, 'Millet Versus Ruskin: A Defense of Ruskin's "Of Queen's Gardens" ', *Victorian Studies*, XX(3), Spring 1977,

pp. 283-97.
21. O.A. Sherrard, *Two Victorian Girls* (London, 1966).
22. Ibid., p. 2.
23. Ibid., pp. 31, 71.
24. Elizabeth Missing Sewell, *Principles of Education* (London, 1865), Vol. II, p. 229.
25. E.M. Sewell, *Autobiography* (London, 1907), pp. 70, 74, 80, 116-17; her later writing was largely prompted by 'the pressure of pecuniary anxiety'. (p. 80). She established the school in 1852, ten years after her father's death,after finally overcoming her mother's resistance to the idea.
26. The small amount salvaged by her father was lost in a further failure of 1829. H. Martineau, *Harriet Martineau's Autobiography* (London, 1877, 3 vols), vol. I, pp. 128-30, 141-7; see also Martineau, *History of England During the Thirty Years' Peace* (London, 1849-50, 2 vols), vol. I, p. 365; also her comments in her article 'Female Industry', *Edinburgh Review*, vol. CIX (April, 1859), p. 331, and her novel, *Deerbrook* (London, 1839), in which Maria Young, the governess, is an uncharacteristically independent departure from the downtrodden stereotype.
27. Edward Gibbon Wakefield, *England and America* (London, 1833, 2 vols), vol. I, pp. 96-8.
28. Martineau, 'Female Industry', p. 307; see also her *Society in America* (London, 1837, 3 vols), vol. III, p. 149.
29. Sewell, *Principles of Education*, vol. II, p. 245. The anti-feminist, Elizabeth Eastlake, claimed that the governess problem was based on 'wounded vanity . . . the rock on which most minds go to pieces'. '*Vanity Fair* and *Jane Eyre*', *Quarterly Review*, Vol. LXXXIV, Dec. 1848, p. 177.
30. GBI, *Reports*, 1843, p. 11; 1844, p. 11; 1848; pp. 24-35, case no. 80; 1850, p. 14; see also Mary A Maurice, *Mothers and Governesses* (London, 1847), pp. 158-9.
31. Quoted, Howe, p. 116.
32. Dr R. von Krafft-Ebing, *Text-Book of Insanity, Based on Clinical Observations* (Engl. transl.,Philadelphia, 1904), p. 154.
33. Census Report, England and Wales, 1861, *Parliamentary Papers* (hereafter *PP*), 1863, LIII, Pt. I (3221), p. 69.
34. Barbara Leigh-Smith (afterwards Bodichon), *Women and Work* (London, 1857), p. 13.
35. Shirreff, p. 410; see also the stress on insanity in a plea for the reform of female education in *English Woman's Journal*, vol. I, June, 1858, pp. 219-20.
36. Eastlake, p. 180.
37. Charlotte Yonge, *Womankind* (London, 1876), p. 37.
38. Eastlake, pp. 162-76.
39. Miss Gwilt in *Armadale* (London, 1866), and Miss Garth in *No Name* (London, 1862); see also Martineau, *Deerbrook* and Thomson, pp. 49-56.
40. See the discussion of W.R. Greg's article, 'Why Are Women Redundant?' in ch. 5, below.
41. Preliminary Census Report, 1871, *PP* 1871, LIX (381), p. xxiv.
42. General Report, Census, England and wales, 1861, *PP* 1863, LIII, Pt. 1 (3221), pp. 6-7.
43. Results and Observations, Census, Great Britain, 1851, *PP* 1852-53, LXXXVIII (1691-1), Pt. I, pp. xxiv-xxv; General Report, Census, England and Wales, 1881, *PP* 1883, LXXX (3797), pp. 15-19; T.A. Welton, *On the Inaccuracies Which Probably Exist in the Census Returns of Ages* (Liverpool, 1876), pp. 1-13.
44. The figures include all 'passengers from the United Kingdom' and not just emigrants, and thus are of even more limited value. For 1854-60 2.53 per cent of all male passengers were recorded as 'Gentlemen, Professional men, Merchants etc.', while 0.70 per cent of all female passengers were recorded as 'Gentlewomen

and Governesses'. For 1861-70 the figures were 6.68% and 5.75% respectively, 1871-76: 13.00% and 10.93%, 1877-80: 16.14% and 1.39%, 1881-90: 11.57% and 0.61%, 1891-1900: 16.21% and 0.84%, 1900-02: 11.89% and 2.84%. But notice the discrepancy, e.g. in the figures to Canada, in 1861-70: 9.26% male and 22.43% female, 1871-76: 14.70% male and 36.82% female. Only 20% of the recorded women stated a gainful occupation in 1871-76; 65% stated 'married woman' or 'spinster' and 15% made no statement. N.M. Carrier and J.R. Jefferey, *External Migration: A Study of the Available Statistics, 1815-1950* (London, HMSO,*Studies on Medical and Population Subjects* No. 6, 1953), Tables 11 and 12, pp. 57-9. Cf. Banks, p. 29.

45. Holcombe, p. 11, simply reproduced the argument of M.A. in *The Economic Foundations of the Women's Movement* (London, Fabian Society Women's Group, 1914), but neglected to mention that M.A. only counted women and men between 35 and 55. The districts counted, from the 1911 census, were Hampstead, Kensington and Chelsea (5,758 men, 19738 women), and Woolwich, Shoreditch and Bethnal Green (5,185 men, 3,850 women).

46. Calculated from Census, 1861, England and Wales, Summary Tables, *PP* 1863, LIII (3221) Pt. I, Div. III, pp. 21-33.

47. Clara Collet, 'The Economic Position of Working Women,' (Feb. 1890), reprinted in *Educated Working Women* (London, 1902), pp. 33-7.

48. Ibid., p. 37.

49. J. Boucherett, 'On the Cause of Distress Prevalent Among Single Women', *TNAPSS*, 1863, pp. 767-9.

50. W.R. Greg, 'Why Are Women Redundant?' *National Review*, XXVIII, April 1862, pp. 447-50; Anna Jameson, *Memoirs and Essays* (London, 1846, rev. ed. 1860), pp. 231-2. Cf. J.A. Banks, *Prosperity and Parenthood* (London, 1954), ch. 3.

51. C. Ansell, Jr., *On the Rate of Mortality at Early Periods of Life, the Number of Children to a Marriage, the Length of a Generation, and other Statistics of Families in the Upper and Professional Classes* (London, 1874), p. 45. Ansell conducted his survey for the National Life Assurance Society; the clergy experienced the highest age at marriage at 30.44; p. 48.

52. General Report, Census, England and Wales, 1871, *PP* 1873, LXXI (872–I), Pt. II, p. xvii; D.V. Glass, 'Marriage Frequency and Economic Fluctuations in England and Wales, 1851 to 1934,' in L. Hogben (ed.), *Political Arithmetic: A Symposium of Population Studies* (London, 1938), p. 252, Table 1; cf. Banks, *Feminism and Family Planning*, pp. 29-30.

53. See, e.g. GBI, *Annual Reports*, 1844, pp. 17-24; 1847, pp. 22-33; SPEW, *Report,* June 1879, pp. 3-10.

54. Mercy Grogan, *How Women May Earn a Living* (London, 1880), p. 10. See also *Women and Work*, 22 Aug. 1874, p. 2; Emily A.E. Shirreff, *The Work of the National Union* (London, 1872), p. 24; Sewell, *Principles of Education*, vol. II, pp. 228-35, 254-9.

55. Boucherett, *Hints on Self-Help*, p. 25.

56. Parkes, "The Profession of Teacher', in *Essays on Woman's Work*, p. 1.

57. *What is a Lady?* (London, 1885), pp. 9-24, 42-7.

58. Shirreff, *The Work of the National Union*, p. 8; *Woman's Gazette*, vol. II, March 1877, p. 90.

59. Louisa M. Hubbard, *Work for Ladies in Elementary Schools* (London, 1872), p. 5.

60. Geoffrey Crossick (ed.), *The Lower Middle-Class in Britain, 1870-1914* (London, 1977), Introduction, p. 18.

61. Collet, p. 37.

62. A.F. Foster's report, Reports of Assistant Commissioners Appointed to Inquire into the State of Popular Education in England, 1861, *PP* 1861, XXI, Pt.

II (2794 — II), p. 365. One commissioner drew attention to the social isolation suffered by most trained working-class schoolteachers, since 'It is difficult to point to the class with whom they can associate at all', p. 95.

63. Hubbard, p. 20.

64. 'Ladies as Dressmakers', *Woman's Gazette*, vol. III, Aug. 1878, pp. 115-17.

65. Elizabeth C. Gaskell, *Wives and Daughters* (London, 1866), ch. 3, quoted, West, p. 116.

66. B.R. Parkes, 'The Profession of Teacher', *Englishwoman's Journal*, vol. I, no. 1, 1 March 1858, p. 11; (reprinted in *Essays on Woman's Work*, pp. 87-109).

67. For a fuller discussion of these proposals see chs. 5 and 6 below.

68. *Women and Work*, no. 9, 1 Aug. 1874, pp. 4-5.

69. *Women and Work*, no. 32, 9 Jan. 1875, p. 4; see also no. 11, 15 Aug. 1874, p. 5; no. 68, 18 Sept. 1875, p. 6; Mrs H.C. Davidson, *What Our Daughters Can Do For Themselves* (London, 1894) pp. 151-6.

70. See Holcombe, pp. 18-20 and *passim* for a detailed discussion of the extent of the incursion and its relationship to the expanding industrial economy.

71. Davidson, p. 259.

72. *Work and Leisure*, vol. XVIII, Dec. 1893, p. 312.

73. Collet, 'Prospects of Marriage for Women', (first published, 1892), in *Educated Working Women*, pp. 61-5.

74. Significantly, Gissing was a close friend of Clara Collet and drew on much of her research for his portrayal of the position of women in his novels; J. Korg, *George Gissing, A Critical Biography* (Seattle, 1963), pp. 12, 22, 189-92.

75. Parkes, *Essays on Women's Work*, pp. 73-84.

76. Ibid., pp. 77-82, 217-18.

77. Eastlake, pp. 176-7; see also Sewell, *Principles of Education*, vol. II, pp. 228-30; A.T. Vanderbilt, *What to do with Our Girls* (London, 1884), p. 1.

78. Gissing, ch. 1.

79. W. Farr, *Remarks on a Proposed Scheme . . . for the Support of Widows and Orphans of Civil Servants of the Crown* (London, 1849), pp. 3-5, 7-13, 16, 29-31.

80. 'Women and Work', *Victoria Magazine,* Oct. 1876, pp. 570-1.

81. Report from Schools Inquiry Commissioners, 1868, *PP* 1867-8, XXVIII, Pt. I (3966), General Report, p. 570.

82. Answers to the Circular of Questions to the Commissioners of Popular Education, 1861, *PP* 1861, XXI, Pt. V (2794 — V), 7th vol., pp. 103-5 (dated Aug. 1859); see also Grogan, p. 12; *Women and Work*, no. 2, 13 June, 1874, p. 4.

83. GBI *Annual Reports*, 1843, pp. 12-15; 1846, pp. 11-13; 1847, pp. 14-15; 1849, pp. 16-18.

84. Ibid., 1848, p. 17.

85. Royal Commission on Secondary Education, General Report, 1895, *PP* 1895, XLIII (c. 7862), p. 15.

86. Grogan, pp. 15-16.

87. Miss E.P. Hughes in Christabel Osborn and F.B. Low, *Manuals of Employment for Educated Women* (London, 1900), vol. I, *Secondary Teaching*, introduction, pp. xvi-xvii.

88. Yonge, pp. 33-4.

89. See, e.g., Sarah Harland, 'Educated Women as Technical Workers', *TNAPSS*, 1884, pp. 417-18.

90. Letter from Anne J. Clough to Schools Inquiry Commissioners, Miscellaneous Papers, *PP* 1867-8, Vol. XXVIII, Pt. II, (3966 — I), pp. 84-7.

91. Letter from L.M. Hubbard, to Editor of *Labour News*, April, 1874, quoted in *Work and Leisure*, vol. XVIII, Dec. 1893, pp. 311-12.

92. *Madame Aubert's Governess List* (1883-1914); see, e.g. no. 364, which first appeared in 1883 and was still appearing in 1890, listing the same age, 26; by

August, 1914, 50,041 advertisements had appeared in the register.
93. Cf. Holcombe, pp. 18-20; O.R. McGregor, *Divorce in England* (London, 1957), pp. 86-7.
94. Hubbard, *Work for Ladies in Elementary Schools*, Kay-Shuttleworth introduction, pp. iv-viii, pp. 1-23; *Woman's Gazette*, vol. I, Oct. 1875, pp. 5-6; Holcombe, p. 35.
95. Howarth Barnes, *Training Colleges for Schoolmistresses* (London, 1891), pp. 64-70; F. Harrison, 'Elementary School Teaching', in *Ladies at Work* (London, 1893), pp. 122-5.
96. Barnes, pp. 64-70.
97. Hubbard, *Work for Ladies in Elementary Schools*, pp. 15-16.
98. Grogan, pp. 18, 40-45; Christabel Osborn, *Manuals of Employment for Educated Women* (London, 1900), vol. II, *Elementary Teaching*, pp. 6-8; Holcombe, 36-46.
99. SPEW, *Report*, June, 1879, pp. 3-4; J. Crowe, 'Report of the Society for Promoting the Employment of Women,' *TNAPSS*, 1861, p. 85.
100. *Women and Work*, no. 9, 1 Aug. 1874, p. 6; Davidson, contents.
101. Davidson; Selina Hadland, *Occupations of Women Other than Teaching* (London, 1886); Elizabeth Kingsbury, *Work for Women* (London, 1884); L. Phillips, *A Dictionary of Employments Open to Women* (London, 1898); Phillis Browne, *What Girls Can do* (London, 1880); Vanderbilt; Osborn, *Manuals*, vols. I – III; *Ladies at Work*.
102. Holcombe, pp. 18-20.
103. Grogan, pp. 72-95; some training, like the SPEW's book-keeping course, at sixpence weekly for four to five months, was relatively accessible, but still involved a long period without an income; pp. 82-4.
104. Ibid., p. 73.
105. Ibid., pp. 87-8.
106. Ibid., p. 91.
107. Cf. Holcombe, pp. 108-17.
108. Grogan, pp. 91-2.
109. Report of Schools Inquiry Commissioners, vol. V, *PP* 1867-8, XXVIII (3966 – IV), p. 718, QQ. 16006-9, evidence of Gertrude King, 19 April 1866.
110. See below. ch. 5, for details of Maria Rye's law-copying venture, associated with the SPEW, in Lincoln's Inn Fields.
111. *Women and Work*, no. 11, 15 Aug. 1874, p. 2.
112. *Ladies at Work*, p. 97; see also Grogan, p. 82.
113. Derek Hudson, *Munby, Man of Two Worlds: The Life and Diaries of Arthur J. Munby, 1828-1910* (London, 1972), pp. 19-20.
114. Sally Alexander, 'Women's Work in Nineteenth-Century London; A Study of the Years 1820-50' in Mitchell and Oakley, pp. 84-6, stresses the severe working conditions in millinery and dressmaking, but see 'Ladies as Dressmakers', *Woman's Gazette*, vol. III, Aug. 1878, pp. 115-17 for details of special conditions made available for ladies through the Ladies' Dressmaking Association
115. The writer commented on the increasing quantity of 'sons and daughters of professional men, well educated and highly intelligent [who] are now pursuing mercantile avocations'. Hadland, pp. 12-13.
116. See below, ch. 5, 6.
117. Edward Gibbon Wakefield, *A Letter from Sydney* (London, 1929, first published 1829). The Colonial Reformers were a political pressure group closely connected with the Philosophic Radicals, and best known for arguments for colonial self-government, their campaign against convict transportation to Australia and the founding of new Wakefield-style colonies in South Australia and Canterbury, New Zealand. On Wakefield's abduction of the heiress, Ellen Turner

in 1826, and his subsequently annulled marriage, see Paul Bloomfield, *Edward Gibbon Wakefield: Builder of the British Commonwealth* (London, 1961), pp. 1-14.

118. Wakefield, *Letter from Sydney*, pp. 82-6.

119. Wakefield, *England and America*, vol. I, p. 84.

120. Ibid., vol. I, pp. 82-106, vol. II, pp. 106-7.

121. E.G. Wakefield, *A View of the Art of Colonization* (London, 1849), p. 156.

122. Ibid., p. 157.

123. Maria S. Rye, during the formation of her Female Middle-Class Emigration Society in 1861 spoke of the need to uproot colonial 'vice and immorality' by means of importations of high class women, 'an elevation of morals being the inevitable result' of their mere presence. *Emigration of Educated Women* (London, 1861), pp. 9, 12.

124. *The Christian Lady's Friend and Family Repository*, vol. I, Sept. 1831, pp. 2-3.

125. Census Report, 'Results and Observations', 1851, *PP* 1852-3, LXXVIII (1691 – I), p. 1 xxxviii. Farr traced the Englishwoman's special character from the Roman *materfamilias* and the Anglo-Saxons.

126. Maurice, p. 40.

127. See below, ch. 2.

128. See below, ch. 5.

129. *The Perils of Girls and Young Women Away from Home* (London, 1884). For a less restrictive view see L.C. Davidson, *Hints to Lady Travellers at Home and Abroad* (London, 1889), although a note of caution persisted, p. 63.

2   PIONEER EMIGRANTS, 1832-1836

At first glance the problems of distressed gentlewomen seem to bear little relationship to the world of British emigration in the 1830s. Emigration was, unmistakably, an activity attracting increasing attention and participation by the early 'thirties. But it was related most directly to the problems of the poor, of destitution and the poor-rate, and, in the Wakefieldians' stinging phrase, 'shovelling out paupers'.[1] Whatever might be the destinations of emigrants, the great majority came from the poor, the dispossessed, the unskilled — rural and urban — and predominantly from the male sex.[2] The connection between emigration and destitution was further reinforced in the 'forties by the Irish famine, and it receded only slowly and fitfully in the second half of the century. The emigrants' voyage, too, whether of two weeks' duration to North America or up to four months to the Antipodes, was not one to attract the distressed gentlewoman as we have come to know her. But people rarely behave as predictably as our fixed stereotypes might require, and behind thousands of working-class emigrants seeking an escape from bleak prospects in Britain there are enough hints of the unexpected to provoke some rethinking of our traditional notions of impecunious middle-class spinsters.

There was, though, little reason in the 'thirties to expect that Australia, of all possible destinations, might attract single middle-class women from Britain. In public comment the Australian colonies were associated invariably with convicts, disorder and moral depravity, even by Colonial Reformers who wished to reform Australian settlements through 'systematic colonisation'.[3] Most writers and public figures linked the presumed moral depravity with the social evils flowing from the serious disproportion of the sexes.[4] By 1836 the New South Wales population included 2.6 males for every female, a clear consequence of the uneven effects of convict transportation.[5] Australian colonists, British politicians and Colonial Reformers were united in seeing female emigration, in various forms, as a solution to all the evils. In sufficient numbers, and with the right qualifications, women, they argued, would civilise Australia, as they civilised all societies.[6] But the right qualifications were anything but those of a refined young lady. The women sought for Australia were domestic and farm servants who would first relieve overworked colonial wives and eventually make wives themselves

53

for the rough convict and settler population. It was not a world made for Britain's distressed gentlewomen, which makes their eventual intrusion into that world all the more remarkable.

The first serious attempt to correct the sexual imbalance in Australia came in 1831, when the Colonial Office accepted the principle of government assistance for free emigrants financed out of the sale of colonial lands.[7] This simple principle was to provide the basis for innumerable colonial immigration schemes, later run by the colonists themselves, up to the First World War. But the immediate result was to make the Colonial Office itself responsible for organising a system of mass assisted emigration, mostly of unmarried working-class women, to New South Wales and Van Diemen's Land (Tasmania). The task was a daunting one, but from 1832 to 1836 the system accounted for the movement to Australia of more than 3,000 women, most of them in sixteen separate ships (5 from Ireland, 11 from England).[8] The large numbers involved meant that each ship, on average, carried close to 200 single women — in 1835 the *James Pattison* took 288 women from Cork to Sydney — with all the attendant problems relating to selection of the women in Britain, provisioning and order during the voyage and reception and integration in Australia. Clearly the Colonial Office was in no way equipped to manage such a task, and it rapidly accepted offers from volunteers to select the emigrants and handle shipboard arrangements. Emigrants for the first two ships were thus selected by a number of charitable institutions, and the later ones by a group of men known as the London Emigration Committee in collaboration with a shipowner-contractor, John Marshall.[9]

Criticisms of the scheme were quick to appear in England soon after the first ships reached Australia, and the critics invariably blamed the incompetence of the voluntary committee and the corruption of John Marshall. Prostitutes and paupers, opponents claimed, had been swept off the streets of London to make up Marshall's full quota of passengers on each ship. Management on board had been lax, leading to riotous scenes of drunkenness, debauchery and seduction among ships' crews and the women, and, worst of all, the women were badly behaved, creating disgusting scenes on arrival, augmenting the population of prostitutes in the colony and doing more to corrupt than to civilise Australia. I have argued elsewhere that these charges were often unfounded and always exaggerated.[10] The excitement of arrival in a new country after more than 100 days at sea undoubtedly produced boisterous behaviour among the women, which must have done little to encourage their potential colonial employers. But the vast majority of the women rapidly assumed a correct and docile demeanour more in keeping with their prescribed colonial role, were promptly employed as servants and not heard from again. The colonial authorities themselves, always the first to complain of improper conduct, usually acknowledged later 'that the mischief has been by no means as great as might have been anticipated'[11] and that the women had integrated into colonial society without difficulty.

Such was the reality, but to most people in Britain it was an unseen reality, and the reputation of the scheme there had a more far reaching influence on the future of female emigration. *The Times*, after a persistent campaign against the venture, wrote it off as 'a wicked knavish trick'.[12] Politicians like William Molesworth had their own reasons for insisting that the scheme had caused Australian free emigrants to 'outstrip in vice and obscenity' the convict population.[13] But powerful civil servants at the Colonial Office, once convinced of the failure of such projects, were unlikely to acquiesce in a repetition of the exercise. James Stephen pointed the way to future policy in his insistence that, despite the London Emigration Committee's precautions,

> no care and vigilance can guard against the recurrence of evils, which appear naturally to flow from the separation of females at an early age from their natural guardians and protectors, and their exposure, notwithstanding the asylum provided for them by the Government on their arrival, to more than ordinary temptations.[14]

Apart from inhibiting potential emigration outlets for women, Government policy in itself was not of central importance in determining attitudes to emigration. But it provides a valuable indicator of public attitudes to female emigration, especially to Australia. The prevailing social code concurred with Molesworth in insisting that 'respectable women will not consent to go alone to dwell among convicts'.[15] Respectable women, indeed, would not consent to travel anywhere alone, in theory, but nineteenth-century realities forced continuous violation of rigid middle-class social rules.[16] The rules were wholly irrelevant to the vast majority of working-class women who embarked under the scheme, although there is evidence that after the worst outbreaks of hostile publicity it became difficult for several months to recruit the usual number of willing emigrants for the next ships.[17] It was too easy to confuse wholesale shipments of women with the evils of convict transportation. Warnings of the physical rigours of emigration were traditional, and not necessarily daunting to the middle class.[18]

But moral warnings were conclusive, especially for women — or at least they should have been.

In this setting middle-class spinsters could expect little official encouragement to emigrate to Australia. Colonists were anxious to receive domestic servants;[19] politicians and public officials, keen to provide Australia with a 'hardy peasantry',[20] also tried to prevent harmful criticism about unsuitable emigrants. But, as suggested in the previous chapter, by the 1830s there were new influences working in the opposite direction. Wakefield's vision of a reproduction of British class structure in the colonies underlined the need for encouragement to his 'uneasy class' to emigrate. His views were reflected rapidly in Wakefieldian propaganda from the early thirties, which pointed to the unrelenting pressure for some form of middle-class emigration of both sexes. The Wakefieldian model colonies in South Australia and New Zealand were, according to theory, intended as exact replicas of the British social structure, a precise transplantation of every class from the humblest to the highest. But the Colonial Reformers directed their greatest persuasion to the class most traditionally reluctant to leave. R.S. Rintoul's *Spectator*, the Wakefieldian mouthpiece, argued that the new South Australian colony in 1834 offered most advantage to

> men of small or moderate fortunes, *having large families to provide for* — a career for all the sons, be they ever so many, husbands for all the daughters, however large the brood; and for the contented father, a field of profitable exertion and honourable ambition.[21]

The Wakefieldian stress was confined largely to the emigration of families and young couples, but all the arguments inducing middle-class families to emigrate applied with equal force to single women of the same class. Wakefield's reliance on the concept of the feminine civilising mission made the connection unavoidable. The evidence from the 1830s suggests that the connection was soon perceived.

Despite the clearly expressed working-class character of the scheme inaugurated in 1832, various pressures emerged rapidly for some kind of assistance to middle-class women. An extraordinary proposal from R.F. Breed, a Liverpool shipowner, suggests that commercial interests soon calculated that potential lucrative profits might flow from such a scheme. Breed solicited the Government's support for a project initially to send to Hobart Town fourteen to sixteen 'respectable young females' under twenty-three. He would not charge for the passage but expected, rather naively, to be paid 150 guineas when each woman married. At that time, also, he hoped that the Government would allow each of the emigrants a small grant of land as a 'marriage portion'.[22]

Not surprisingly the Colonial Office declined Breed's proposal,[23] but he remained persistent. In a subsequent letter he requested simply that the Government guarantee protection of the women in the colony until their marriage. He claimed to have contacted three families 'overburthened with Females of excellent standing and character'. One of the fathers was an artillery captain with twelve children, 'all well educated but in straitened circumstances. These families expressed delight at the idea of being able to embrace an opening to better the fortunes of some of their Daughters with comfort and protection'. But comfort and protection was the key term, and assuming that his own scheme was to lapse, Breed asked

> whether some revisal of the Circulars may not hereafter be made so as to hold out inducement to the Emigration of Females of a higher order than seems to be contemplated. The scale of passage money in these circulars would admit of beggarly accommodation fit only for paupers, or the lowest order of society, and in vessels that must I take it be crowded with passengers in which a respectable Female would not embark under any consideration.

Goderich, the Colonial Secretary, dismissed this as 'absurd', and in his scribbled note displayed a marked ignorance of the situation of middle-class women:

> He says the aid should be such as to tempt respectable (meaning *wealthy*) females to emigrate. It does not appear to have occurred to Mr Breed that wealthy females would be able to pay for themselves. The sooner the letter is put out of sight the better.

It does not appear to have occurred to Goderich that, as the artillery captain's daughters knew only too well, middle-class respectability was no guarantee of middle-class wealth. Similar women in 'straitened circumstances' consequently were quick to seek the same solution from their genteel poverty.[24]

At a time when a 'respectable' cabin passage to Australia cost from £40 to £80,[25] which was the usual annual salary range of a well qualified governess, it is not surprising that some middle-class women attempted to take advantage of Government assistance, which by 1835 consisted of a wholly free passage. Free emigration could present a rare opportunity to escape from an apparently hopeless situation, but some women, at least, had first to be convinced that all other alternatives at home were exhausted. Mary Scheidweiler, for example, only petititoned the Crown from Buttevant, Ireland, after passing through all the familiar experiences of distressed gentlewomen. The educated daughter of an officer who had retired in Ireland, she had maintained her accustomed rank so long as he drew half-pay, but on his death was left at the age of 20 to support a younger sister and brother. Excessive competition had prevented her from obtaining 'a situation in the capacity of Governess or in some other respectable line'. She had recently equipped her sister to emigrate to New South Wales, but was herself unable to make a living 'in consequence of which disappointments she would be inclined to avail herself of the opportunity afforded by Your Majesty's benevolence to young unmarried females of emigrating to the colony of New South Wales'. With a fourteen-year-old brother also in need of assistance, it is unlikely that Scheidweiler's petition was successful, but her case is typical of those who turned to emigration as a last resort. For women resolved on such a course, public warnings about the moral depravity of New South Wales seemed irrelevant.[26]

The Colonial Office was usually quick to discourage casual middle-class applicants like Scheidweiler. The passage money, they insisted, was provided out of colonial funds to populate Australia with badly needed domestic and farm servants from the working-class; consequently educated women were not eligible for any form of grant. Elliot advised a Miss Fitzpatrick that the Government's arrangements

> have reference principally to females of the working-classes, and that they are scarcely calculated to furnish the inducement which you observe would be requisite to lead Ladies in your circumstances to the Colonies.[27]

At times the Colonial Office showed more diligence in this respect than the colonists themselves. In 1833 it emerged that two assisted emigrants were daughters of Mr Yeoland, the Van Diemen's Land Auditor-General. 'It is quite clear', wrote Hay, 'that they are not the class of females whom the Government intended to assist in emigrating to the colony', and he requested that Lt Governor Arthur demand immediate repayment from Yeoland.[28] In most cases, at least, the Colonial Office was intransigent on the point that assistance must be confined to those qualified for the roughest domestic service.[29]

Despite these official discouragements, however, it is quite clear that substantial numbers of middle-class women did in fact receive the Government grant, and others were able to emigrate under the scheme's protection at a lower cost than would otherwise have been possible. The frequent colonial protests at receiving governesses and nursery governesses suggest that one of the chief Australian resentments against the scheme was that so many women had social backgrounds which did not suit them for rough colonial work.[30] On the other hand one complaint in 1836 from Van Diemen's Land could imply that it was not so much soundly educated middle-class women the colonists resented as those with humble backgrounds and middle-class aspirations. The Ladies' Reception Committee noted that

> that class which usually style themselves 'nursery governesses' are little required . . . A few good governesses, who are thoroughly competent to undertake the education of children in respectable families would find situations.[31]

The problem, of course, was that the best qualified governesses in most cases had neither the need nor desire to emigrate. But whatever the women's qualifications the surviving passenger lists indicate that at the point of departure Marshall and the Emigration Committee were less reluctant than the Colonial Office to admit middle-class women. Consequently the alleged working-class scheme soon came to include a regular minority of middle-class women.

Once the scheme was well established even the Colonial Office attitude to middle-class emigrants apparently softened. In 1833 Under-Secretary Hay sent Governor Bourke a list of women on the *Layton* who 'are of superior habits and education, whom misfortunes in life have compelled to seek a maintenance in another Hemisphere', and requested special treatment for them in the colony to ensure that they found suitable employment.[32] It is not clear exactly what prompted this attitude but in some cases undoubtedly it was due to the intervention of persons with some influence. Sophia Eyre, a governess recommended by the Earl and Countess of Denbigh and Viscountess Fielding, received exceptional attention from the Colonial Office, who requested Bourke's personal assistance for her in the colony.[33] In 1835 Arthur took special pains to place two sisters, one as a schoolteacher, and one as a governess, after a request from Stanley, then Colonial Secretary.[34] Elliot's deferential tone in his communications with a Miss Igglesden contrasts sharply with his abrupt rejection of Miss Fitzpatrick's request noted earlier. He had been approached by friends sufficiently influential to prompt him to go to considerable lengths to obtain an assisted passage for her: She had, he told a shipowner. 'been in very respectable circumstances, but the limited extent of her means would preclude her from engaging any accommodation but the cheapest'.[35] With the right friends, it seemed, the Government was quite prepared to help women to escape from genteel poverty.

Patronage, though, was not the only means to an assisted passage. By 1834 the pressure from middle-class applicants was so great that Marshall and the committee made special arrangements to segregate their shipboard accommodation from the steerage emigrants. For an extra charge of £5 women 'of great respectability' could be accommodated in the poop deck cabin. The *Charles Kerr*, in 1835, carried fourteen of these 'poop governesses'. as they came to be known.[36] Marshall described these arrangements in a pamphlet written to defend the scheme in 1834, stressing that apart from accommodation all other conditions, including provisions, were identical to those for women in the steerage compartment, 'and they are allowed the conveniences alluded to more to preserve their own peculiar associations than for any other personage'.[37] This constituted a significant departure from Goderich's original policy to provide the Australian colonies with a 'hardy peasantry' by means of the scheme,[38] and had the scheme itself not proved abortive, it may have provided a growing outlet for middle-class women. Certainly the shift in selection criteria illustrated how quickly social pressures in Britain, at the point of origin, came to overshadow the labour demands of the colonists.

Despite the willingness to admit the middle class there seems to have been a general understanding between Marshall and the committee that emigration was suitable only for genuine gentlewomen who were genuinely distressed. Marshall was quick to point out to potential emigrant teachers that the least well-educated fared little better in Australia than in England, rarely earning more than £20 in the most junior teaching positions. Furthermore, women in search of adventure whose conditions were less than desperate met with a firm rebuff. When Mrs Caulfield enquired on behalf of a young woman who 'can readily obtain employment here at a high salary,' Marshall immediately questioned the prudence in leaving contentment and prosperity for such a 'distant contingency.' Although, he admitted, she would probably do well in Australia, where solid ability and accomplishment were needed, she was unable to reach it without

passing through considerable annoyance, trials, and even, to a certain
extent, privations, and I am no advocate for young women of
refined mind and acquirements encountering all this when they are
happy in this country.[39]

Quite clearly Marshall's notion of the distressed gentlewoman was an
economic and not a psychological one. His experience had shown that
only the most economically desperate middle-class women resorted to
emigration. Since these women were invariably those with the least
attractive occupational qualifications his approach may have reinforced
the tendency of economic and social forces to drive those middle-class
women to emigrate who were least equipped by family and educational
background to adjust to such a fundamental change. Certainly, as far as
the surviving passenger lists permit reliable generalisation, they suggest
that the women who did emigrate came either from the most severely
depressed of their class or from upwardly mobile lower middle-class
women.

Some passenger lists have survived from eleven out of the fourteen
ships managed by the London Emigration Committee,[40] and a basis for
comparison between British and Australian occupations exists for seven
ships.[41] To be useful here, however, it is necessary to make the unprov-
able assumption that all those listed with middle-class ocupations necessarily had middle-class backgrounds. In a few instances, at least, this
was almost certainly not the case. In Australia it is evident that middle-
class gentility was not a universal pre-requisite for governesses; some
cases occurred on the *Strathfieldsay*, for example, of previous servants
or milliners being hired as governesses on arrival. Conversely, the
instances in which ex-governesses took positions as housemaids,
nurserymaids and dressmakers almost immediately after arrival could
imply falsification of previous occupations, drastically lowered job expectations or the more significant possibilities that the Australian
supply of governesses exceeded demand and that domestic servitude in
Australia carried with it less of a social stigma. But the evidence already
cited confirms that several middle-class women experienced as governesses did receive assistance, and there are other casual references in
correspondence to qualified middle-class governesses.[42] Absolute certainty is impossible but it is reasonable to assume that most of the
women listed as governesses and teachers before departure actually had
middle-class backgrounds.

Appendix I shows the known Australian occupations taken up by
emigrants with putative middle-class origins. To the 86 listed with

middle-class occupations in Britain should be added 6 from the *Amelia Thompson*, for which no British list exists, who obtained teaching positions in Australia. Thus there were 92 middle-class women out of 2170 female emigrants on the 11 ships with passenger lists, or 4.24 per cent of the total. This excludes 49 women listed as teachers and nursery governesses, among whom there may have been some emigrants with middle-class backgrounds. Furthermore, there is little reason to suppose that this percentage would be reduced if figures were available for the remaining ships. Even the first ship managed by William Fry in 1832, the *Princess Royal*, included eleven women (out of a total of 193) whom Fry described as 'Teachers and Upper Servants' selected from casual applicants,[43] suggesting at least the possibility that some middle-class women may have been admitted when the rules against them were most strict. The obstacles to genteel female emigration were still strong enough to prevent a larger number of middle-class women from using the scheme, but at a time when working-class emigrant ships were generally regarded with horror, it is significant that any 'young ladies' at all were hard pressed enough yet sufficiently enterprising to resort to such a drastic solution.

As if the act of emigration itself was not enough, it is clear from the passenger lists that some middle-class women entered distinctly non-middle-class occupations in Australia.[44] Leading colonists repeatedly stressed their need for domestic and country servants, not 'governesses, nursery governesses and ladies' maids'.[45] But the rapidity with which these women accepted domestic service or needlework — usually within two weeks of arrival and before many genuine servants had been hired — suggests that the social opprobium of ungenteel menial work in Australia was not nearly so great as in Britain. The fear of class decline might be substantially allayed after a congenial meeting with a potential employer of high social standing and respectability. Most of these women, indeed, obtained servants' positions with families of high social position and gained recognition of their gentility in above average salaries. Mary Anderson, an ex-teacher aged 29 from the *William Metcalfe*, became a general servant in Major Newman's family at Hobart Town with a salary of sixteen pounds, 'to be raised', while most servants from the same ship received only eight to twelve pounds.[46] Elizabeth Chippett, a Somerset teacher off the *Sarah*, became a nursery-maid at sixteen pounds for a Mrs Hewett at Hobart Town.[47] Ann Rowe, an Irish governess aged 25 off the *Canton*, took work as a lady's maid at fourteen pounds in the home of Mr Plunkett, the Solicitor-General at Sydney.[48] Although, like those of many governesses who took up their usual employment in Australia, these women's salaries were low, it is safe to assume that they accepted work they would never consider in Britain simply because it was judged to be less demeaning in the new country and because they no longer had to reckon with the embarrassing disapproval of their peers in Britain.[49] Once out of Britain their main concern was not so much money as a sense of solidarity with the social class closest to their own — in this case a colonial elite — and in Australia such solidarity was not inconsistent with most forms of domestic work.

These findings are supported by the testimony of a later emigrant in the forties. Susannah House, a lady's maid in England who became a nursemaid at a salary of twenty-five pounds in Van Diemen's Land in 1841, told a Committee on Immigration that there were many women in England who would emigrate if they could get employment. She thought that women would do much better than men in Van Diemen's Land, but added 'we are obliged to lend a helping hand to so many things here that we do not do in England', and later elaborated her complaint, 'I have no servants here to wait upon me; I had always two or three servants under me.'[50] But she gave no hint that she found this extra work and less exalted position in any way humiliating or that her employers thought less of her for it. Clearly the complex British rules which established social identity required revision in a pioneering colonial society like Australia; if the keeping of servants was sufficient to define 'middle-classness' in Britain,[51] it certainly was not the case in early Colonial Australia, where most people, regardless of background, frequently had to dirty their hands. Women especially, therefore, were forced to fall back on cultural notions of gentility as the mainstay of middle-class status. Certainly in Britain any middle-class woman forced to share in as much rough domestic work as her colonial counterpart would be considered, and would consider herself, to have lost caste irrevocably, whereas in Australia a common class origin with her equally industrious employers was often sufficient to preserve her dignity. In a more primitive and egalitarian, albeit still socially stratified, society, it soon became clear that her problem lay less in hostility towards manual work than in easily removable social implications involved in that work. The point assumes particular importance in view of developments towards the end of the century when the prospect of domestic work became the surest means of attracting larger numbers of middle-class women to the colonies.

A picture begins to emerge, then, of a small group of women whose behaviour was substantially at variance from that of our traditional model of the distressed gentlewoman. Undoubtedly most of these women were 'distressed' in an economic sense but no amount of 'status incongruence' or conditioned dependence prevented them from defying social convention as they knew it, risking their own reputations and turning to menial employment which would have been unthinkable in Britain. If these women were in any way representative of distressed gentlewomen then the stereotype requires some revision to allow for a degree of psychological resilience not previously thought to be realistic.

On the other hand it must be admitted that even the evidence produced so far provides some small support for the traditional 'dependent-helplessness' image of the distressed gentlewoman. For a tiny minority the emotional effects of emigration made it impossible to exploit its advantages. While statistically insignificant, it is still noteworthy that out of 3,098 women sent to Australia between 1832 and 1836 the only four reported cases of insanity should have occurred in two described as governesses and two as nursery governesses.[52] One of the governesses, Frances Haydon on the *Strathfieldsay*, was sponsored by the Corporation of Sons of the Clergy. The destitute daughter of a deceased clergyman, she only consented to emigrate to Van Diemen's Land 'after many trials and disappointments' in England. As the Registrar of the Corporation, Oliver Hargreave, put it:

> She has considerable repugnance to the transplantation to so distant a possession of the British Crown, but I hope she may find reason to repent her resolution, as situations here are not to be obtained always by persons of the best character.

Soon after departure the surgeon and superintendent noticed that 'she was labouring under an aberration of mind, which continued more or less the whole voyage', and when admitted to hospital at Hobart Town showed such 'considerable imbecility of mind' that Lt Governor Arthur determined to send her back to England. Hargreave denied the colonial suspicion that Haydon had been persuaded to emigrate against her will, asserting that her case

> was one of pure compassion, calculated, as far as we could see, to extricate her from inevitable misery and destitution in this country, and enable her to earn an honest livelihood and independence in a new colony.[53]

One is reminded of the frequent contemporary references to the fact that governesses constituted the largest percentage of any occupational group in insane asylums,[54] but in this case, at least, it seems that the act of emigration was itself responsible for producing serious psychological disturbance. Obviously some women who were likely to be driven to emigration were the least capable, from family upbringing and qualifications, of turning its potential to their profit. For most impoverished middle-class women − indeed, for many working-class women − the life-long implications of emigration were certain to prove a traumatic emotional wrench, and in extreme cases could produce a personal tragedy like that of Frances Haydon. Nevertheless, the most remarkable fact remains not that a few succumbed to the obstacles, but that so many overcame them.

After 1836 more than two decades elapsed before a facility as cheap, secure and accessible as the female emigration scheme became available to enable determined middle-class women to emigrate. With the scheme's termination it became increasingly difficult for middle-class women to emigrate with the kind of financial assistance they had obtained between 1832 and 1836. Under the new emigration procedures from 1837 the colonists exercised the greater amount of control, and were entitled to refuse to grant the Government bounty for any emigrants they considered ineligible. A few governesses continued to appear in the returns of assisted immigrants from Australia,[55] but on the whole the colonists attempted strictly to exclude middle-class women from the Government scheme. In 1842 the New South Wales authorities refused the bounty on Mary O'Connor, whose dress and appearance 'showed her to be very much above the class of persons eligible for a free passage under the regulations now in force'.[56] Even nursery governesses were excluded from government assistance,[57] and Earl Grey, who, as Colonial Secretary, vigorously prosecuted the assisted emigration of working-class women in large numbers and mass shipments − predominantly Irish orphans − from 1848 to 1851, remained steadfastly opposed to assisted middle-class emigration.[58]

Despite the elaborate colonial and British efforts to exclude middle-class women from subsidised emigration, there is evidence that some impoverished gentlewomen were ingenious enough to obtain the assisted passage, and their final resort to the assumed degradation of an emigrant ship − without the earlier segregated accommodation for 'poop governesses' − must be seen as a measure of their courage as well as their desperation. In these circumstances their genteel origins could easily provoke the enmity of ship's officers or working-class emigrants on the voyage. In 1842 Roger Therry, a judge of the New South Wales

Supreme Court, prosecuted the Captain and Surgeon of the *Carthaginian* for encouraging the persecution of Mary Ann Bolton throughout the voyage. Whenever 'any disturbance arose, or impropriety was committed by some of the vile women who filled the vessel, they attributed the blame to her', and she was frequently brought on deck in her nightclothes to be doused with buckets of cold water. She died from consumption soon after the trial in Sydney, but not before she had become a personal friend of Therry, who claimed that he soon detected her social background:

> I learned little of her history beyond the fact that she had been a governess. She was certainly a highly educated person, and her language and sentiments were those of a lady who had seen happier days.[59]

For Mary Ann Bolton some of the well publicised horrors of middle-class emigration proved, unhappily, to be well-founded, but they were insufficient to deter other women who recognised that the British social system had no place for them.

The small numbers involved in this study and its limited scope are clearly inadequate to permit any conclusive statements about the psychology and behaviour of distressed gentlewomen generally. But the evidence suggests a picture well beyond the level of mere plausibility. Indeed, the evidence itself points again to the need for ambivalence rather than one-sided firmness in interpreting the meaning of economic decline for middle-class women. It may well be that the women who turned to emigration were an exceptional minority rather than the tip of a social iceberg, but the rapidity with which they took advantage of such a hazardous and ill-promoted prospect suggests something beyond adventurous eccentricity. While confirming the severity of their economic desperation, it hardly accords with the helpless defeatism associated with the usual image. Most middle-class emigrants seem to have been able and eager to adapt to a new social situation which could require them to work at a range of occupations previously deemed beyond the pale. On the other hand, the degree of mental disturbance which emigration could provoke in women like Frances Haydon, the clergyman's daughter, indicates that psychological resilience was not always a necessary product of the middle-class woman's economic decline. Significantly, though, the Haydon stereotype, in full accordance with the conventional image, appears here more as a departure from the norm. The problem is certainly not clear cut, for there are frequent reminders that emigration might attract the very women who were least equipped to exploit its advantages. Far more striking, though, is the regularity with which women took all the risks involved in emigration and were able to turn it to their profit. An apparently unlikely alternative could quite suddenly be transformed into a promising solution.

Notes

1. The term was first coined by Charles Buller. Wakefield, *A View of the Art of Colonization*, p. 39.
2. I. Ferenczi and W.F. Willcox, *International Migrations*, Vol. I (New York, 1929), Table IX, pp. 401-410.
3. See, e.g. Wakefield, *A Letter from Sydney*, pp. 47-54.
4. Ibid., pp. 51-2.
5. R.B. Madgwick, *Immigration into Eastern Australia, 1788-1851* (Sydney, 1937, 1969), pp. 230-1.
6. P.M. Cunningham, *Two Years in New South Wales*, Vol. I (London, 1827), pp. 262-281. Wakefield, *A Letter from Sydney*, pp. 51-3. 'New South Wales', *Edinburgh Review*, Vol. XLVII, Jan. 1828, p. 92.
7. Viscount Goderich to Governor Bourke (NSW), 28 Sept. 1831, *Parliamentary Papers* (hereafter PP), 1831, vol XIX (328), pp. 126-31.
8. Initially the system of mass shipments was operated alongside a 'bounty' system which required women to emigrate with their families in order to receive assistance. This form of aid was provided to 430 women by 1835, after which the system was discontinued following the discovery of numerous abuses by shipowners and contractors. Madgwick, pp. 97-8.
9. A.J. Hammerton, " 'Without Natural Protectors': Female Immigration to Australia, 1832-36," *Historical Studies*, XVI, no. 65 (1975), 539-66.
10. Ibid.
11. Lt. Governor Arthur (Van Diemen's Land) to R.W. Hay (Permanent Undersecretary, Colonial Office), 5 Oct. 1833, Colonial Office Papers (hereafter CO), 280/43.
12. *The Times*, 16 Oct. 1837.
13. W. Molesworth, 'Life in the Penal Colonies', *Westminster Review*, XXVII, July 1837, p. 85. Molesworth's intention was to demonstrate that all systems of Australian immigration would be futile so long as convict transportation continued.
14. Stephen (Permanent Under-Secretary from 1836) to A.Y. Spearman (Treasury), 19 Aug. 1836, *PP*, 1837, vol. XLIII (358), p. 60.
15. Hansard, *Parliamentary Debates*, 3, LIII, cols. 1257-8 (5 May 1840).
16. The bias against unaccompanied travel inhibited female mobility in England as well as female emigration, and it was not confined to the middle class. In 1834 a Liverpool emigration agent advised the Colonial Office that he had selected many respectable women for emigration if a ship could be despatched from Liverpool rather than London, but 'there seems an unwillingness on the parents' parts, of the lower better order of society, to trust their children so far from their sight previous to embarkation'. Lt. R. Low to Hay, 21 June 1834, CO 384/35.
17. Hammerton, pp. 554-5.

18. See, e.g., Susanna Moodie, *Roughing it in the Bush*, (Toronto, 1962), pp. xv, 166, 236-7. Moodie's account of her hardships in the Canadian backwoods stressed that for the impoverished middle-class emigration was 'an act of severe duty,' because, to remain independent, 'they cannot labour in a menial capacity where they were born and educated to command'. First published in 1852, her book went into many subsequent editions.

19. See, for example, the evidence of Alexander McLeay, New South Wales Colonial Secretary, to the Committee of the NSW Legislative Council on Immigration, Minutes of Evidence, 18 Sept. 1835, *PP* 1837, XLIII (358), p. 16.

20. Goderich to Bourke, 28 Sept. 1831, *PP* 1831, XIX (328), pp. 126-31.

21. *Spectator*, 4 Jan. 1834, pp. 7-8.

22. R.F. Breed to Colonial Secretary, 15 Dec. 1832, CO 384/30.

23. Hay to Breed, 22 Dec. 1832, CO 202/29.

24. Breed to 'Commissioners for Emigration,' 5 Jan. 1833, and Goderich's note dated 7 Jan. 1833, CO 384/33.

25. See T.F. Elliot's replies to enquiries. e.g. to T. Borrows, 13 Oct. 1831, CO 385/12, and to J.B. Monck, 5 April 1832, CO 385/14.

26. Petitition of M. Scheidweiler, Buttevant, Cork, Ireland, 24 July, 1835; forwarded from Home Office to Hay, 29 July, 1835, CO 384/39. Scheidweiler was the daughter of a Hanover immigrant who had served as Quartermaster in the First Regiment of Lifeguards for 28 years; her petition included a testimonial from the Vicar of Buttevant, James Law, who concluded that 'she would be a very valuable acquisition to the colony of New South Wales'. There is no surviving record of a Colonial Office reply. The usual response to eligible enquiries was to send application forms to be completed and returned to the Emigration Commitee.

27. Elliot to Miss Fitzpatrick, care of Rev. John Robinson, Mexford, 20 Jan. 1832, CO 385/13.

28. Hay to Arthur, 20 April, 1833, CO 408/9.

29. See, for example, Elliot to Miss Chambers, Kennington Cross, 23 June, 1832, CO 385/14.

30. See Arthur to Hay, 9 Oct. 1832, CO 280/36; Evidence of Alexander McLeay to the Committee of the NSW Legislative Council on Immigration, op. cit. p. 16. The same opinion reached England. In an otherwise favourable description of the *Amelia Thompson*, a reporter in *The Times* suggested that the demand for governesses in Van Diemen's Land must be less than the supply on this one ship. 29 April 1836, p. 5.

31. Ladies Committee Report, *Boadicea*, 11 April 1836, in Arthur to Glenelg, 29 April 1836. CO 280/65.

32. Hay to Bourke, 10 August 1833, *Historical Records of Australia* (HRA), I. Vol. XVII, p. 186.

33. J. Lefevre to Bourke, 4 July 1834, CO 202/32; S.A. Eyre to Hay, 9 July 1834, CO 384/36.

34. Arthur to Stanley, 1 Feb. 1835, CO 280/55.

35. Elliot to Miss Igglesden, 4, 5, 21, 28 June, 23 July 1832; Elliot to John Masson, 20, 23 June, 23 July 1832, CO 385/14.

36. Passenger list, *Charles Kerr*, Launceston, 18 Nov. 1835, CO 280/60.

37. J. Marshall, *A Reply to the Misrepresentations which have been put forth respecting Female Emigration to Australia* (London, 1834), p. 13.

38. Goderich to Arthur, 27 Jan, 1832, CO 408/7.

39. Marshall to the Hon. Mrs Caulfield (Hackley, Armagh, Ireland), 13 and 19 Feb. 1835, in Appendix 55, Report from the Select Committee on Transportation (II), *PP* 1838, XXII (669), p. 304.

40. See Appendix I. The same kind of information does not exist for the first

two ships, the *Red Rover* and *Princess Royal* in 1832, whose emigrants were selected by charitable institutions in Ireland and London under the direction of the philanthropist, William Fry. Hammerton, pp. 543-6.

41. For five ships there are two lists, one compiled by the Committee before departure showing the previous occupations of each emigrant, and one compiled in the colony showing the type of work obtained, the employer and the salary received. Two other colonial lists indicate previous as well as colonial occupations. The figures in Appendix I are based on the following passenger lists: *Sarah*: CO 384/35, 280/55; *Strathfieldsay*: CO 384/35, 280/49; *Canton*: CO 384/38, 201/252; *Charles Kerr*: CO 384/38, 280/60; *James Pattison*: CO 384/39, 201/255; *Boadicea*: CO 280/65; *William Metcalfe*: CO 280/78; *Duchess of Northumberland* (I): CO 201/245; *Layton*: CO 384/32; *David Scott*: CO 384/35; *Amelia Thompson*: CO 280/67. The following lists from Australia were copied in the *Parliamentary Papers*: *Sarah*: PP 1836, XL (76), pp. 39-40; *Strathfieldsay*: PP 1835, XXXIX (87), pp. 33-7; *Duchess of Northumberland* (I): PP 1836, XL (76), pp. 30-3.

42. Van Diemen's Land Colonial Secretary's Memo., 1 Dec. 1835, in Arthur to Glenelg, 26 Dec. 1835, CO 280/60; Bourke to Stanley, 26 Dec. 1833, PP 1834, XLIV (616), pp. 32-5.

43. Fry to Van Diemen's Land Ladies Committee, 15 April 1832, CO 384/30.

44. See Appendix I.

45. Evidence of A. McLeay, NSW Colonial Secretary, to the Committee of the NSW Legislative Council on Immigration, op. cit., p. 16.

46. Passenger List, *William Metcalfe*, CO 280/78.

47. Passenger Lists, *Sarah*, CO 384/35; CO 280/55.

48. Passenger Lists, *Canton*, CO 384/38, CO 201/252.

49. Most governesses and teachers obtained salaries from about £15 to £30, not high by English or Australian standards; a few only obtained as much as £60. Marshall made this quite clear to applicants; he told Mrs Caulfield that 'I believe the scale of remuneration is not generally high; some of the least educated have not obtained more than £20 a year, as assistants in schools etc.' Marshall to the Hon. Mrs Caulfield, op. cit. p. 304.

50. Evidence to Committee of the VDL Legislative Council on Immigration, 30 Sept. 1841, PP 1842, XXXI (301), p. 165, QQ 177-90.

51. J.F.C. Harrison proposes this definition in *The Early Victorians, 1832-51* (London, Panther, 1973), pp. 136-7.

52. See Appendix I.

53. Arthur to Spring-Rice, 4 Feb. 1835, with Hargreave's recommendation, 28 April 1834, Ladies Committee Report, 22. Oct. 1834, Colonial Surgeon's Report, 26 Sept. 1834, Ship's Surgeon's Report, 24 Sept. 1834, and Superintendent's Report, CO 280/55; Hay to Hargreave, 7 July 1835, CO 385/16; Hargreave to Hay, 13 July, 1835, CO 384/39; Glenelg to Arthur, 15 Dec. 1835, CO 408/12.

54. See above, ch. 1.

55. See the Report of J.D. Pinnock, the NSW Agent for Immigration, for 1838, 28 Feb. 1839; under the 'bounty system,' by which shipowners selected the emigrants and received payment, upon approval, in the colony, there were 9 governesses out of 162 single women in 1838; in ships chartered by the Government in Britain there were 6 governesses out of 1,096 married and single women. PP 1840, XXXIII (113), p.25; see also the report of F. Merewether, the NSW Immigration Agent, for 1841, 14 May, 1842, PP 1843, XXXIV (109), p. 48; and the return of unmarried adult immigrants to NSW for 1848, PP 1850, XL [1163], p. 68. For a full discussion of the various systems of assisted emigration to Australia to 1851 see Madgwick.

56. Merewether and Brown to NSW Colonial Secretary, 8 Feb. 1842, in

Governor G. Gipps to Stanley, 24 Feb. 1842, *PP* 1843, XXXIV (323), pp. 100-2.
    57. Return of trades of bounty emigrants, 1 July 1841 to 30 June 1842, 22
Aug. 1842, *PP* 1843, XXXIV (109), p. 70.
    58. Grey to Fitzroy, 16 June 1849, *PP* 1849, XXXVIII (593), pp. 116-23,
Madgwick, pp. 189-216.
    59. R. Therry, *Reminiscences of Thirty Years Residence in New South Wales
and Victoria* (second edition, London, 1863), pp. 221-2. This episode is also
described in M. Kiddle, *Caroline Chisholm* (Melbourne, 1950), p. 52, but under
the name of Margaret Ann Bolton.

3 MARY TAYLOR IN NEW ZEALAND: A CASE STUDY

The previous chapter's generalisations from a minority of successful early Victorian emigrants about the meaning of emigration for distressed gentlewomen, while illuminating, must remain partial in the absence of greater statistical precision. But statistical precision is not the only road to historical truth, especially in the realm of social attitudes, outlook and behaviour, and the congruence between social ideals and reality. No less essential is the often neglected biographical dimension which can bring a more reliable sense of close personal context to the elusive and uncertain lives of the inarticulate. The descriptive evidence already presented does, to a limited extent, hint at the implications of the experience of emigration for disadvantaged middle-class women. Most descriptive evidence seldom allows social historians to do more than this; certainly it can rarely provide the close texture of direct personal experience and the sense of proximity to which social history aspires. The incorporation of social biography can do much to add vital context to history which otherwise would deal with little more than elusive shadows.

The near-universal and unavoidable problem, of course, is that historical sources which permit reliable descriptive accounts of the inarticulate by definition preclude reinforcement with detailed social biographies. This is nowhere more evident than with the institutional records of emigration. While the occasional correspondence from and references to individual women point to clear trends, they can only offer the most limited and frustrating glimpse into the place of emigration in the totality of their lives. The middle-class women who braved social opprobium by turning to working-class emigration schemes were unlikely to record their experience in memoirs, diaries or regular and well-preserved correspondence, and if they did there was little chance of their story surviving or coming to light. The reinforcement of social biography must, of necessity, then, be found elsewhere, whenever the relative abundance of sources allows. While this might initially seem to involve some sacrifice of immediate relevance, it should be seen quite readily that the parallels between the women already examined and a case study of one woman from a rather different background who emigrated to a different colony are far more striking than the differences.

The choice of Mary Taylor for a sample biography must at first seem incongruous in a study dealing mainly with the emigration of distressed gentlewomen.[1] According to the contemporary sense of the term Mary Taylor could not qualify as 'distressed' either in an economic or psychological sense. Her family was never left destitute or unable to support her and she was able to obtain financial support from her brothers when she most needed it, even in New Zealand. She came from an established Yorkshire family and had close connections with the Brontës, and hence quickly aspired to, and eventually was part of a regional literary elite. Accordingly her emigration was less an act of economic necessity than one of determined independence and a resolve to make her own way in the world. There was little in common here with the 'poop governesses' of the 1830s, and her choice of Wellington, New Zealand, only established for six years when she left in 1845 and much too young to attract the attention of official or voluntary female emigration schemes, underlined the unusually independent quality of her action.

On the other hand Mary Taylor's experience goes far to illustrate the dilemma facing all single women tarred with the confining brush of middle-class gentility. Except for the financial details, her emigration was the product of circumstances strikingly similar to those faced by women who left under the protection of institutions, and the results of her emigration brought the same change in her outlook and behaviour. The activity and independence she sought could only be found outside England, just as escape offered the only apparent resolution of the distressed gentlewoman's social impasse. The relative wealth of surviving Taylor correspondence certainly testifies to this woman's eccentric individuality for her time, but it also serves as a detailed exposition of a process already witnessed in outline among less well documented emigrants.

The Taylor family of Gomersal in the West Riding of Yorkshire was well established by the nineteenth century, and according to Charlotte Brontë's description in *Shirley*, 'the first and oldest in the district'.[2] The 'Red House', (the 'Briarmains' of *Shirley*), an imposing two-storey building of red brick, sharply distinguished from the ubiquitous grey Yorkshire stone, had formed the Taylor residence since 1660 when William Taylor built it after prospering in the woollen cloth trade. His descendants rose to greater prominence as cloth manufacturers during the eighteenth century. Mary Taylor's grandfather, John Taylor, built a large textile mill nearby at Hunsworth in 1785, and his specialisation in army cloth manufacture brought further prosperity during the Revolutionary wars. Commercial middle-men during the Industrial Revolution, the Taylors also took in the productions of most small manufacturers in the Spen Valley. John Taylor was sufficiently wealthy in 1803 to survive easily the destruction of his mill by fire. He built a new one promptly in 1804 and bequeathed a prosperous enterprise to his eldest son, Joshua, Mary's father and the Hiram Yorke of *Shirley*.[3]

Joshua Taylor was a keen entrepreneur and expanded his inheritance enthusiastically. To supplement his role of cloth manufacturer and merchant he became a banker after building the 'Gomersal Bank' behind the 'Red House', and issued his own notes under 'Joshua Taylor and Sons'. The turning point came during the financial crisis of 1825-26, the same depression which reduced Harriet Martineau's family, when Taylor's bank failed in the general crash. The crash did not ruin Taylor entirely for he continued with the manufacture and trade in woollen cloth. But, significantly, he conducted his business, until his death in 1841, with the sole aim of repaying his creditors, and an interval of nearly thirty years elapsed before his eldest son, Joshua, finally cleared the debt of several thousand pounds.[4]

Although financial crises like those of 1825-6 were the making of countless distressed gentlewomen, both in fact and fiction, this was hardly the case with Mary Taylor. She was only eight years old at the time, and her family were far from penniless. Nevertheless, for the Taylor household, which included Mrs Taylor, four sons and two daughters, the long term debt brought constant parsimony and a grave reduction in their standard of living, which had permanent effects on Mary. Ellen Nussey, the third member of the group of friends, with Mary Taylor and Charlotte Brontë at Roe Head school in 1831, noticed that Mary and her sister Martha

> were not dressed as well as other pupils, for economy at that time was the rule of their household. The girls had to stitch all over their new gloves before wearing them, by order of their mother, to make them wear longer. Their dark blue cloth coats were worn when *too short*, and black beaver bonnets quite plainly trimmed, with the ease and contentment of a fashionable costume.[5]

Clearly, the events of 1825-26 had brought a measure of social decline to the Taylors, but it was not on the scale of family disasters which produced so many Victorian distressed gentlewomen; the Taylors, after all, retained their property and business and were able to send all their children to school. But combined with other influences the experience was to make Mary, the eldest daughter, acutely aware of the value of money, and to reinforce her desire for economic independence.

A much greater influence on Mary's future was the long Taylor history of religious dissent and political radicalism. The secluded position of Gomersal had made it a safe haven for persecuted noncomformists, and it provided a major birthplace for Yorkshire Moravianism and Wesleyanism in the eighteenth century. John Wesley had been a close acquaintance of John Taylor, and lodged at the Red House when he preached at Gomersal in 1776 and 1789.[6] Despite this connection John Taylor remained aloof from the Wesleyan sect and preached in the family's own chapel nearby known as 'Taylor's Chapel'. His independent following had more in common with the Quaker-like, quietist Moravians, who were most firmly established in the contiguous area between Leeds and Halifax.[7] Mary's father, Joshua, whom Charlotte Brontë described as 'not irreligious but a member of no sect', may have lost interest in the chapel, for around the time of his death in 1841 it was converted into cottages, and his widow subsequently held religious services in the Taylor kitchen, conducted by men from Bradford.[8]

Mary Taylor inherited her father's inclination for a personal religion and contempt for organised church hierarchies.[9] She also inherited those common bedfellows of religious dissent: political and social radicalism, and ultimately a forthright feminism. The surviving accounts of Joshua Taylor suggest that he combined all the qualities of the laconic, straightforward and iconoclastic Yorkshireman with those of the cultivated and well-travelled English gentleman. Charlotte Brontë claimed that he varied his speech from a broad Yorkshire dialect to the purest educated English as the mood or company dictated.[10] Looking back, in 1850, Mary clearly valued his honest individualism and contempt for social convention. Commenting on the description of her family in *Shirley*, she approved of Charlotte's characterisation of all but her father, complaining:

> But my father is not like. He hates well enough and perhaps loves too, but he is not honest enough. It was from my father I learnt not to marry for money nor to tolerate anyone who did and he never would advise anyone to do so, or fail to speak with contempt of those who did.[11]

As a schoolgirl, Charlotte Brontë, the clergyman's daughter and loyal Tory, frequently clashed with Mary and Martha Taylor on subjects of religion and politics. Her visits to the 'Red House' invariably resulted in indignant lectures on the virtues of republicanism and the evils of the monarchy and the established church. The timid conservative was, Mary told Elizabeth Gaskell,

> always a minority of one in our house of violent Dissent and Radicalism. She used to hear over again, delivered *with authority*, all the lectures I had been used to give her at school on despotic aristocracy, mercenary priesthood etc.[12]

Mary's popular radicalism seems to have intensified with age. She wrote from New Zealand to berate Elizabeth Gaskell for presenting too mild a picture of the Yorkshire gentry in her biography of Charlotte Brontë:

> You give much too favourable an account of the black-coated and Tory savages that kept the people down, and provoked excesses in those days. Old Roberson said he 'would wade to the knees in blood rather than the then state of things should be altered,' — a state including Corn Law, Test Law, and a host of other oppressions.[13]

The combination of a radical background and constant need for family economy produced in Mary a fiercely persistent desire for financial independence and a determination not to be bound by conventional restrictions on female behaviour. With her closest friends, Charlotte Brontë and Ellen Nussey, she frequently adopted the role of mentor, encouraging them to join her in her most recent venture of independence — with notably little success. Charlotte ignored Mary's suggestion that she teach with her in a German boys' school, and Ellen, always conscious of her 'family duties', never responded to Mary's call to join her in rewarding work and freedom in New Zealand.[14] Mary's rebelliousness contrasted with Charlotte's patient submission during their early schooldays. Both top pupils who had learnt all their instructors could teach them, they were each given Blair's *Belles Lettres* to memorise; only Mary stubbornly refused to degrade herself with such seemingly useless activity, preferring instead to accept punishment.[15] In later years the difference expressed itself in contrasting attitudes on the feminist issue. Mary took Charlotte to task for her mild position on the need for female employment:

> I have seen some extracts from *Shirley* in which you talk of women working. And this first duty, this great necessity, you seem to think that some women may indulge in, if they give up marriage, and don't

make themselves too disagreeable to the other sex. You are a coward and a traitor. A woman who works is by that alone better than one who does not; and a woman who does not happen to be rich and who *still* earns no money and does not wish to do so, is guilty of a great fault, almost a crime – a dereliction of duty which leads rapidly to all manner of degradation. It is very wrong for you to plead for toleration for workers on the ground of their being in peculiar circumstances, and few in number, or singular in disposition. Work or degradation is the lot of all except the very small number born to wealth.[16]

Charlotte Brontë was certainly no anti-feminist, but her moderate position on women's work, close to the sentiments of many mid-Victorian feminists, illuminated Mary Taylor's more uncompromising and aggressive opinion.

Very soon after her father's death in 1841 there were clear signs that Mary intended to live by her philosophy. With Joshua Taylor gone there was little to hold the family together, since it seems that none of the children could tolerate their cantankerous mother.[17] Immediately after Taylor's death Charlotte Brontë accurately predicted the break-up and dispersal of the family. She was convinced that they were all 'restless, active spirits, and will not be restrained'. But Mary especially, she maintained, 'has more energy and power in her nature than any ten men you can pick out in the united parishes of Birstall and Haworth. It is vain to limit a character like hers within ordinary boundaries – she will overstep them'.[18] Within three months of her father's death Mary had decided that the boundaries of England itself were too limiting and she resolved to emigrate with her brother, Waring, to New Zealand. Charlotte Brontë summarised her reasons most succinctly. Mary had made up her mind, Charlotte told her sister Emily, that 'she cannot and will not be a governess, a teacher, a milliner, a bonnet maker nor housemaid. She sees no means of obtaining employment she would like in England; so she is leaving it.'[19] In the event Mary did not leave for New Zealand until 1845, four years after her brother's departure, but from 1841 she seems to have been determined not to stay in England.

It is not entirely clear what caused the Taylors to choose Wellington, New Zealand for their destination. The colony was, after all, only two years old in 1841. Charlotte Brontë's comments suggest that they considered several alternatives. 'Their destination unless they change', she told Emily, 'is Port Nicholson [i.e. Wellington] in the northern island of New Zealand ! ! ! . . . I cannot sufficiently comprehend what her views and those of her brother's may be on the subject, or what is the extent of their information regarding Port Nicholson, to say whether this is a rational enterprise or absolute madness.'[20] Probably their decision to go to New Zealand at this particular time reflected the considerable publicity which accompanied the organisation of the New Zealand Association[21] and the initial settlement at Wellington from 1839. Not all the publicity was favourable. The Evangelical missionaries, who opposed New Zealand colonisation, found a powerful ally in *The Times*, whose editors were consistently hostile to emigration schemes, but acrimonious debates like those between the Wakefieldian *Spectator* and *The Times* usually enhanced the popularity of new settlements without the taint of convictism. Since the publication of Wakefield's *England and America* in 1833 the Colonial Reformers had laid constant stress on the need for middle-class emigration, and this was a persistent theme in the New Zealand publicity. Furthermore, all the excitement and controversy of a new colony — the first ship for Wellington, the *Tory*, had only sailed in May, 1839, without Government approval and before British annexation of New Zealand — would no doubt be attractive to the adventurous Taylors.[22]

Although, for reasons unknown, Mary waited four years before following her brother to Wellington, she did not in the meantime languish in England.[23] She did, apparently, consider filling a governess's position in Ireland, but, as Charlotte Brontë put it, she was 'so circumstanced that she cannot accept it' since her brothers had 'a feeling of pride that revolts at the thought of their sister "going out".'[24] Genuinely impecunious gentlewomen were painfully aware of the stark dilemma posed by such attitudes, but despite her relatively greater affluence Mary Taylor found such restrictions equally unbearable, and her first instinct was to quit the country. Escape offered the attractive combination of foreign travel, freedom from the more socially restrictive atmosphere of English society and some useful preparation for an independent future. She made several trips to Brussels, some in company with her sister Martha, her brothers John and Joseph, and on one occasion with Charlotte Brontë. Like her trip to New Zealand, these visits were eased by the presence of relatives, in this case her cousins from Birmingham, the Dixons, who currently lived in Brussels. The connection encouraged both Mary and Martha in 1842 to attend a Brussels boarding school, the Château de Koekelberg, where Mary conveniently improved her French, German and music, qualifications which later proved useful during her early years in New Zealand. Her sister's sudden death from cholera in October disrupted these arrangements, and in her desire to quit Brussels she turned, not back to England, but farther afield to Germany. Now, for the first time, she went alone, and after a period of further instruction in German she began to teach at a school in Hagen (near Iserlohn). This was conventional enough, but what startled her peers was that she took a position in a boys' school.[25]

Characteristically Charlotte Brontë took alarm at her friend's 'resolute and intrepid proceedings'. She recognised, as she told Ellen Nussey, that such a step proved 'an energetic and active mind' as well as courage, independence and talent, but she condemned it on grounds of imprudence. Perhaps, she added, genius like Mary's might surmount every obstacle without the aid of prudence,

> but opinion and custom run strongly against what she does, that I see there is danger of her having much uneasiness to suffer. If her pupils had been girls it would all be well; the fact of their being *boys*, or rather young men, is the stumbling block.[26]

Mary, it seems, was willing to risk any amount of social disapproval to meet her need for constructive activity. Immediately after Martha's death she told Ellen Nussey that she was torn between a desire to return to Yorkshire and another to go to Germany. Finally she chose Germany, 'activity being in my opinion the most desirable state of existence both for my spirits, health and advantage'.[27] A few months later she wrote from Germany to confirm that she was 'cheerful and active', and within four months was advising Ellen that she was earning more than she needed to live.[28] A clue to her attitude can be seen in her later comments on her decision to learn algebra — 'I like it partly I believe because it is odd in a woman to learn it, and I like to establish my right to be doing odd things.'[29]

Mary's right to do 'odd things' had rarely been established in England, but by mid-1844 it was clear that she was feeling restless and dissatisfied with her teaching routine in Germany, and by September had revived her plan to emigrate to New Zealand.[30] The reaction of Charlotte, to whom it was 'something as if a great planet fell out of the sky', suggests that the idea might have lapsed since Waring's departure. Indeed, although Charlotte admitted frankly that Mary would be 'in her element' in New Zealand with 'a toilsome task to perform, an important improvement to effect, a weak vessel to strengthen', her general reaction was understandably one of regret.[31] For this reason her frequent comments to Ellen Nussey, while an important source for tracing Mary's activities, do not always accurately reflect Mary's true attitude and outlook in New Zealand. She was quick, for example, to interpret Mary's momentary expressions of depression as sure signs that she was 'more homesick than she will confess'.[32] In fact, Mary, who finally sailed in March, 1845, adjusted to the primitive environment of the infant Wellington colony with unusual rapidity, as her own letters, filled with the details of business dealings and plans, amply demonstrate.

Mary spent her first four years in Wellington at a variety of occupations without becoming fully committed to any single one. Unquestionably her adjustment was eased by the presence of her brother, with whom she lived at first. She was far from being wealthy, nor was she one of the leisured ladies of the administrative class of New Zealand like Charlotte Godley of Canterbury or Mrs H.S. Chapman of Wellington,[33] but unlike many distressed gentlewomen who were forced to take any available employment, she could afford to experiment. Consequently she was not confined to the traditional outlet of teaching, although she did teach during the first four years, and managed to astonish Wellington society by teaching a widower's daughter at his own home without any intention of marrying him.[34] At the same time she continued to establish her right to do 'odd things' for a woman. Most important was her dealing in cattle, which she purchased with money borrowed at five per cent interest from her brothers, John and Joseph, in England. By July, 1848, she had spent £100 in this way and anticipated a total expenditure of £500, with an eventual profit of fifty per cent.[35] She also bought land and built a house, which she rented at twelve shillings a week.[36] In addition she began to write, something she had never been inspired to do in England. Her New Zealand letters make frequent reference to her 'novel', which in the event was not published until 1890.[37] She wrote one article for *Chambers's* magazine on a New Zealand earthquake, and talked of writing more.[38]

Her various occupations made for 'an active, happy and joyous life' from which she was moved to pity for Charlotte Brontë's 'comparatively dull, uneventful, and unoccupied existence'.[39] Still, she had a more grandiose ambition: to establish an independent business or school, although she was reluctant to take the initial steps for such a venture alone. The problem was solved with the news that her younger cousin, Ellen Taylor, was to join her in 1849. Actually Mary's letters give no indication that she had any specific occupation in mind either before or for at least three years after she emigrated. Her only certainty had been that she would find it easier to earn her living independently and without degradation in the colonies than in England. But with the prospect of a partner she began to form more concrete plans, and after Ellen's arrival the pair decided to establish a women's clothing and drapery shop. By 1849 Mary had become closely acquainted with many potential customers and business associates among the tiny but growing Wellington population — in 1845 when Mary arrived the population totalled only 2,667, of whom 1,145 were children under 14 — and with the local retailing experience of her brother and no prospect of serious competitition she could be assured of reasonable success.[40]

The surviving evidence on Mary's cousin, Ellen Taylor, suggests that her short life approximated much more closely to the familiar distressed gentlewoman pattern than did that of Mary. Ten years younger than Mary,[41] it is probable that she lost her parents at an early age, since all the efforts to assist her education and employment appear to have been made by her cousins. In 1843 Abraham Dixon, who frequently accommodated Mary in Brussels, wrote that a recent business setback had forced him to abandon the idea of helping to finance Ellen at Madam Heger's school (the same school attended by Charlotte Brontë, both as a pupil and English teacher, in 1842 and 1843). As late as June, 1848 Mary's brother, Joseph, and Ellen's brother, Henry, made further enquiries about the same school on Ellen's account, although it is unclear whether they wished her to go as a pupil or teacher.[42] This suggests that Ellen's future had become something of a problem, for only seven months later she emigrated to New Zealand with her brother. Her decision, however rational, seems to have been taken reluctantly, was not planned far in advance like Mary's and was probably due to the absence of reasonable alternatives in England.[43] Her action certainly lacked the independent determination and overtones of feminist ideology so prevalent in Mary's. She did, as Mary wrote, 'come out with just the same wish to earn her own living as I have, and just the same objection to sedentary employment',[44] but, unlike Mary, she would not have emigrated without a large network of relatives to accompany, welcome and assist her. Despite this, Mary's influence and a more egalitarian colonial environment seem to have produced a rapid transformation in her attitude, for she soon came to share Mary's disregard for convention. She told Charlotte Brontë that most Wellingtonians laughed at her shopkeeping, and commented 'Before I left home I used to be afraid of being laughed at, but now it has very little effect on me.'[45] Her experience in New Zealand was a short one — she died from consumption in December, 1851 after only two and a half years — but it was long enough to illustrate the liberating effects of a colonial environment on women who had been bound by more rigid conventions in England.[46]

By all accounts the Taylors' shop prospered from the beginning. As with Mary's cattle dealing, success was partly due to the substantial help provided by her brothers in England. They lent her £100, gave her a further £300, and assisted Ellen on a slightly smaller scale, so that they began 'with as large a capital as probably any in Wellington'.[47] Their shop occupied an advantageous site, and being among the first in town was free from the threat of competition. They also benefited from the sales experience of Waring Taylor, who taught them book-keeping and assisted in wholesale purchasing.[48] There is no record of their actual profits, but in 1850 they anticipated returns as high as £400 a year. By 1854, over two years after Ellen's death, Mary had prospered sufficiently to add a twenty foot extension to her shop, and by 1857 she found wholesale purchasing 'not near such an anxious piece of business now that I understand my trade and have, moreover, a good "credit"', and could afford to hire an assistant, who eventually purchased the business when Mary returned to England.[49] Such a career, obviously, was radically different from that of most middle-class female emigrants; in the first place few women who could command so much capital without working would ever bother to emigrate. But the Taylors' experience does suggest how much greater scope for women's ambitions and enterprise could exist in the colonies than in Britain. They appear to have encountered virtually no social prejudice, and their relative boldness apparently caused more amusement than disapproval in Wellington.[50]

It is precisely in this area — the opportunities for work and the attitude towards it — that the parallels between the lives of Mary Taylor and other middle-class emigrants are so striking. Despite all her special advantages and her unconventional ideas her attitude towards work in New Zealand was characteristic of that adopted by many others when exposed to a colonial environment. In her case she was simply behaving as she had always wished to do, to the point of ideological commitment; for others — including Ellen Taylor — it was a matter of adjusting to an altered psychology in a social environment where it was considered less of a degradation to perform many forms of ungenteel work and to tolerate primitive living conditions. The extent of the required adjustment was expressed in Charlotte Brontë's astonishment to hear that 'Mary Taylor sits on a wooden stool without a back, in a log house, without a carpet, and neither is degraded nor thinks herself degraded by such poor accommodation.'[51]

Mary was, indeed, fully conscious that she was neither a typical middle-class woman nor a typical emigrant; even the New Zealanders raised their eyebrows at her eccentricities. 'To be sure', she wrote, 'I pass here for a monkey who has seen the world, and people receive me well on that account.'[52] But she was no less certain that emigration would provide the same escape for others from frustration, worry and genteel poverty. She tried, unsuccessfully, to persuade Ellen Nussey, a thoroughly conventional and self-sacrificing woman,[53] to join her in New Zealand. A woman could only earn her living in England by teaching, sewing or washing, she argued.

> The last is the best. The best paid, the least unhealthy, and the most free. But it is not paid well enough to live by. Moreover it is impossible for anyone not born to this position to take it up afterwards. I don't know why but it is.

This state of things she described as a 'nightmare' from which one could only escape by making a 'desperate plunge, and you will come up in another world'.

> The new world will be no Paradise, but still much better than the nightmare. Am I not right in all this? *and don't you know it* very well! Or am I shooting in the dark? I must say I judge rather by my own history than from any actual knowledge of yours. Still you yourself must judge, for no one else can. What in the world keeps you? . . . You could get your living here at any of the trades I have mentioned, which you would only die of in England. As to 'society' position in the world, you must have found out by this time it is all my eye seeking society without the means to enjoy it. Why not come here then and be happy?[54]

Mary and Ellen Taylor's letters are filled with enthusiastic descriptions of their endless tasks, from the building of their shop to the division of domestic chores which in England had been performed by servants. The result, far from being degradation, was satisfaction and freedom from the familiar frustrations of the respectable English social routine, as illustrated by Mary's revealing statement: 'We have been moving, cleaning, shop-keeping, until I was tired every night — a wonder for me. It does me good, and I had much rather be tired than ennuyée'.[55]

The Taylors' attitude to work was a natural effect of their integration into a more homogeneous society. Class distinctions certainly existed — the great majority of mid-century New Zealanders of all classes were, after all, only recently transplanted from Britain — but in such small, closely knit communities as existed in New Zealand some predominant social forces fostered the development of egalitarianism. Most important of these was the frequent necessity for men to marry 'beneath their station' because of the lack of single women, and this induced a large degree of social mixing.[56] In these conditions, while the Taylors were clearly distinguished from the administrative class, which played the part of a Wellington aristocracy, Mary could appreciate the fact that their social status was higher than it would have been in the same circumstances in England. Her own analysis was shrewd: 'Classes are forced to mix more here, or there would be no society at all. This circumstance is much to our advantage, for there are not many educated people of our standing.'[57] For Ellen Taylor, a decade younger and apparently more attractive to men than Mary, it was 'quite new to be of such importance by the mere fact of her femininity'.[58] Ellen's popularity involved Mary in a succession of dances and other social events at the new Mechanics' Institute. The class of people involved in their own circle were, according to her,

> not *in education* inferior though they are in money. They are decent well-to-do people. One grocer, one draper, two parsons, two clerks, two lawyers, and three or four nondescripts. All these but one have families to 'take tea with' and there are a lot more single men to flirt with.[59]

Such an unlikely mixture of occupations would have been rare in Britain, and the implications for middle-class women could be far-reaching. The majority, like Ellen Taylor, regarded the very need for emigration as a confession of social decline, but instead of 'coming woefully down in the world'[60] as she anticipated, a middle-class background alone earned them new status, causing Ellen, for example, to find herself 'better received than ever she was in her life before'.[61] The social value to the colonies of single women, and more especially of educated women, was too great for them to lose caste simply by performing menial work.

A more tolerant attitude to the performance of menial work extended in various degrees to all classes in the settlement colonies for most of the nineteenth century. The shortage of women, common to all the colonies, implied not only a dearth of prospective wives, but a chronic scarcity of domestic servants for the middle and upper classes. Consequently even women of the administrative class in New Zealand were soon faced with the need to perform unfamiliar domestic chores.

Catherine Chapman, wife of the Wellington judge, was initiated into such tasks during the voyage when her only maid was disabled by sea-sickness.[62] Those fortunate enough to find well-trained and efficient servants invariably lost them on short notice to new husbands. Until replacements could be found there was no alternative but to soil one's fingers. After one such interlude Lady Barker, on a sheep run in Canter-bury with her husband in the 1860's, wrote 'in the meantime we had to do everything for ourselves, and on the whole we found this picnic life great fun'.[63] Comments such as these abound in the memoirs of well-to-do women accustomed to large retinues of servants. Sarah Greenwood, whose husband later became headmaster at Nelson College, wrote that she had become expert in household work and cooking, and, far from feeling degradation, 'I never was happier or better in my life.' Shortly afterwards she remarked 'I am now complete maid-of-all-work, and very fully my time is occupied; all I regret is the want of more time for the education of my children.'[64] The experience was common to colonial women, whether they settled in the towns or country.[65] Lady Barker's observation was illuminating:

> The mothers are thoroughly domestic and devoted to their home duties, far more so than the generality of the same class at home. An English lady, with even an extremely moderate income, would look upon her colonial sister as very hard-worked indeed.[66]

For middle-class wives the new situation could soon prove to be a dubious blessing, implying, as it did for Sarah Greenwood, the sacrifice of intellectual functions to the requirements of rough domestic chores. But for the middle-class spinster changed circumstances brought changed attitudes which could only lead to relatively greater freedom, since she no longer had cause to fear loss of caste by stooping to work which had been considered ungenteel in England. Mary Taylor, who could proudly exclaim 'How we work! and lift, and carry, and knock boxes open as if we were carpenters by trade; and sit down in the midst of the mess when we are quite tired', was perfectly at home in this environment.[67]

In 1859, at the age of 42, Mary Taylor returned to England after almost fifteen years in New Zealand. Her letters give the impression that she had never intended to stay permanently, although her friends in England remained uncertain.[68] Mary's literary ambitions and her longing for the intellectual life she had known in England, but could not find in New Zealand, prevented her from ever integrating fully into Wellington society. In a sense she lived a double life, and, for different reasons, could feel at home in neither country.

I can hardly explain to you the queer feeling of living, as I do, in two places at once. One world containing books, England, and all the people with whom I can exchange an idea; the other all that I actually see and hear and speak to. The separation is as complete as between the things in a picture and the things in a room. The puzzle is that both move and act, and [I] must say my say as one of each. The result is that one world at least must think me crazy.[69]

Her yearning for intellectual companionship, which she rarely found in Wellington, was partly satisfied when Ellen joined her, but even then the two of them talked of returning to England when they had earned enough money. They planned at one time to send wholesale goods to New Zealand after gaining four or five years' experience in shop-keeping.[70] Mary's letters, preoccupied as they eventually became with future plans to return, give the impression that the advantage of New Zealand to her was that it offered the only means by which she could provide for an independent and prosperous future in England. Exactly how prosperous she became is unknown. But after selling her shop to her assistant, Miss Smith, and investing £400 in land in Wellington, she was wealthy enough to return to Yorkshire, build a secluded house of her own — *High Royd* at Gomersal — and live a life of cultured leisure devoted to writing and travel.[71]

This is not the place for a detailed exposition of Mary Taylor's later life in England,[72] but her published writings do much to illuminate both her own behaviour and the position of women in Britain. Fortuitously, her return coincided with first moves towards an organised 'women's movement' dedicated to improving female education and employment prospects.[73] She was quick to capitalise on the new climate. Between 1865 and 1870 she published a series of articles in a new feminist journal, the *Victoria Magazine*, all of which were later collected and republished as *The First Duty of Women* in 1870. Written with the avowed object 'to inculcate the duty of earning money' for all women,[74] the essays repeat many of the stern admonitions already seen in letters to Charlotte Brontë and Ellen Nussey. Read in the context of other feminist writings of the 1860's, the essays sound radical and uncompromising. Her concern went beyond the immediate employment needs of impecunious gentlewomen to all women, insisting that it was an act of duty for everyone to have an alternative to marriage to forestall humiliating dependence or starvation. Married women, even mothers, she argued, had an obligation to earn money and contribute to the well-being of their families, especially when their time was left idle by an army of servants.[75] She dismissed the notion of the feminine civilising mission and female self-sacrifice as a contemptible sham invented to deprive women of their rights.

> It is an offer that those who make it would not take were the case their own, and the frequent repetition of it when women are in question, suggests the suspicion, that those who urge it are not thinking of the women's interests but of their own; and more than that, that they do not believe the two to be identical.[76]

Her novel, *Miss Miles*,[77] which was finally published in 1890, three years before her death, develops similar arguments with object lessons in the responsibility of women — to themselves and to society — to be financially independent.[78] *Miss Miles* also betrays a clear sympathy with the radicalism of virtuous working-class dissenters against a callous ruling-class.[79] There was little here to suggest that the independent outlook of her Belgian, German and New Zealand days had moderated. Her writing suggests that if she lived during the Edwardian years of militant feminism she would have been likely to share the socialistic and anti-autocratic outlook of Sylvia Pankhurst.

As her advice to Ellen Nussey indicates, Mary viewed emigration as one of the rare avenues of escape for middle-class women in Britain without prospects. Significantly, though, she joined other feminists in the 1860s in opposing female emigration simply as a means to find husbands. In his widely read article of 1862, 'Why Are Women Redundant?', William R. Greg had proposed a massive scheme of middle-class female emigration in order that surplus women in England would be able to marry in the colonies.[80] Mary Taylor, the returned emigrant, replied indignantly.

> The men who emigrate without wives, do so because in their opinion, they cannot afford to marry. The curious idea that the women, whom they would not ask in England should run after them to persuade them would be laughable if it were not mischievous. Those who adopt it must dispense with that cultivated forethought that makes both sides wish for some provision for the future before entering into matrimony. It is true there is a certain number who have attained their object, and have the means to marry, but the

greater number are intentionally single, as are the corresponding class in England.[81]

Her reply drew as much on her New Zealand experience as on her ideological conviction. Emigration, she knew, could offer a path to independent activity unfettered by many of the chains of social convention, but it must not be abused in a less worthy cause. It was a message that was slow to reach thousands of distressed gentlewomen.

Few of the middle-class emigrants encountered in this study returned home to write feminist tracts, and fewer still began with the financial advantages enjoyed by Mary Taylor. But her experience is no less illuminating for that. The very attraction of New Zealand for both Mary and Ellen Taylor was a greater tolerance towards the performance of ungenteel work by middle-class women. Precisely the same factor, as we saw in the previous chapter, could enable less exceptional emigrants to adjust to a colonial environment and seek a wider range of work opportunities without drastic social decline. The opportunities 'outside the cage'[82] were not unlimited, but as Mary insisted to Charlotte Brontë and Ellen Nussey, they were a marked improvement on the Hobson's choice available in Britain. The 'desperate plunge' necessary to escape, could, indeed, lead to a new world much better than the British 'nightmare'.[83]

Notes

1. To some extent the choice of Mary Taylor for close study is dictated by the relative abundance of sources. Her close friendship from adolescence with Charlotte Brontë produced a voluminous correspondence, much of which was destroyed, but the surviving letters provide a rare insight into her background, motivation and emigration experience. Most of the surviving Brontë correspondence has been published. The most thorough collections are T.J. Wise and J.A. Symington, *The Brontës: Their Lives, Friendships and Correspondence* 4 vols (Oxford, 1932); C.K. Shorter, *Charlotte Brontë and her Circle* (London, 1896); C.K. Shorter, *The Brontës: Life and Letters*, 2 vols, (London, 1908). Since my initial research based largely on these sources Joan Stevens has edited an extremely useful collection of the Mary Taylor correspondence, *Mary Taylor, Friend of Charlotte Brontë: Letters from New Zealand and Elsewhere* (Auckland, Oxford, 1972). Wherever possible, therefore, I have referred to the Stevens book.
2. C. Brontë, *Shirley* (first published London, 1849), ch. 4.
3. H.A. Cadman, *Gomersal Past and Present* (Leeds, 1930), pp. 55-7.
4. Ibid., p. 59. Ellen Nussey's impressions of Mary Taylor written to Elizabeth Gaskell, Stevens, pp. 10-11.
5. Nussey impressions, ibid.
6. Cadman, pp. 58, 61, 185.
7. The Moravian leader, Count Zinzendorf, preached his first English sermon in

Gomersal. Ibid., p. 181; *Cleckheaton Guardian*, 15 June, 1894, p. 6. On the Moravians and Methodists in Yorkshire see E. Langton, *History of the Moravian Church* (London, 1956), pp. 98-129. In Charlotte Brontë's time the character of the Taylor services may have changed, for the scene she described at the 'Briar Chapel' in *Shirley* approximated more closely to the emotional spontaneity of Primitive Methodism.

8. Brontë, *Shirley*, chs. 4, 9; Cadman, p. 61; see also J.A.E. Stuart, *The Brontë Country, its Topographies, Antiquities and History* (London, 1888), pp. 144-5; Ellis H. Chadwick, *In the Footsteps of the Brontës* (London, 1914), pp. 30-1.

9. See her comment to Elizabeth Gaskell, 18 Jan. 1856, Stevens, p. 160. She shocked her devout sister-in-law in New Zealand by claiming that she (Mary) only went to chapel 'for amusement'. M. Taylor to C. Brontë, Wellington, 24 July 1848, Stevens, p. 77.

10. Taylor spoke French and Italian, and took pride in his collection of Continental paintings; even allowing for Mary's reservation, the best description of him is in *Shirley*, chs. 3, 4, 9. See also E.C. Gaskell, *The Life of Charlotte Brontë* (first published 1857, London, 1958), pp. 100-1.

11. M. Taylor to C. Brontë, 13 Aug. 1850, Stevens, p. 97.

12. M. Taylor to E. Gaskell, 18 Jan. 1856, ibid., p. 160.

13. M. Taylor to E. Gaskell, 30 July 1857, ibid., p. 133.

14. C. Brontë to E. Nussey, Brussels, 13 Oct. 1843, M. Spark, *The Brontë Letters* (London, 1954), pp. 108-9. M. Taylor to E. Nussey, 9 Feb. 1849 and 15 Aug. 1850, Stevens, pp. 80-4, 100-3. She urged Charlotte Brontë to look upon her writing as a means to financial success and 'influence and power'. M. Taylor to C. Brontë, 5 April, 1850, Stevens, pp. 87-8.

15. Nussey impressions, Stevens, p. 10.

16. M. Taylor to C. Brontë, 29 April 1850, ibid., pp. 93-4. For the relevant passages in *Shirley* see ch. 22. For similar comments on *Jane Eyre* see M. Taylor to C. Brontë, 24 July 1848, Stevens, pp. 74-5. Taylor's later collection of articles entitled *The First Duty of Women* expressed similar sentiments.

17. The fullest account of Mrs. Taylor is given in *Shirley* as Mrs. Yorke, chs. 9, 23. Her hostile reaction to the characterisation suggests that it was not far wrong. M. Taylor to E. Nussey, 11 March, 1851, Stevens, p. 105.

18. C. Brontë to E. Nussey, 3 Jan. 1841, Shorter, *Brontës*, I, pp. 198-9.

19. C. Brontë to E. Brontë, 2 April 1841, ibid., p. 208. See also W. Gerin, *Charlotte Brontë, The Evolution of Genius* (Oxford, 1967), p. 174.

20. C. Brontë to E. Brontë, 2 April 1841, Shorter. Stevens, pp. 20-1. speculates that the choice of Wellington may have been influenced by the early commercial interest in New Zealand shown by the Birmingham banker, John Dixon, a probable Taylor relative, and by an extensive publicity campaign for settlers in Yorkshire by the New Zealand Company.

21. Reformed as the New Zealand Company in 1838.

22. On the founding of Wellington and accompanying publicity see P. Bloomfield, *Edward Gibbon Wakefield* (London, 1961), pp. 144-71; *The Times*, 25 April 1840, p. 4; 4 May 1840, p. 4; H.S. Chapman, 'Emigration: Comparative Prospects of our New Colonies,' *Westminster Review*, XXXV, Jan. 1841, 131-87; Chapman, himself an ardent Wakefieldian, emigrated to Wellington in 1844 to become the first judge. A. Drummond (ed.), *Married and Gone to New Zealand* (London, 1960), pp. 66-7.

23. Her delay may have been due partly to Charlotte Brontë's strong advice in 1841: 'I counselled her to go to France . . . and stay there a year before she decided on this strange unlikely sounding plan of going to New Zealand, but she is quite resolved'. C. Brontë to E. Brontë, 2 April, 1841, Shorter, *Brontës*, I, p. 208.

24. C. Brontë to E. Nussey, 10 June, 1841, Shorter, *Brontës*, I, p. 212.
25. Cf. Gerin, pp. 174, 181, 211-13; C. Brontë to E. Nussey, 7 Aug. 1841: joint letters from Mary and Martha Taylor and C. Brontë to E. Nussey, Koekelberg, March, 4 and 5 April 1842; M. Taylor to E. Nussey, Brussels, 30 Oct. 1842, Shorter, *Brontës*, I, pp. 218-19, 234-6, 243-4. .
26. C. Brontë to E. Nussey, Brussels, 1 April 1843, and Nov. 1843, Shorter, *Brontës*, I, pp. 263-5, 273-4.
27. M. Taylor to E. Nussey, Brussels, 1 Nov. 1842, Stevens, p. 40.
28. M. Taylor to E. Nussey, 16 Feb. 1843, 25 June 1843, ibid., pp. 43, 45.
29. M. Taylor to E. Nussey, n.d. (Winter, 1843), ibid., p. 50.
30. Cf. M. Taylor to E. Nussey, n.d. (1844), ibid., pp. 54-5; C. Brontë to E. Nussey, 16 Sept. 1844, Shorter, *Brontës*, I, p. 284.
31. C. Brontë to E. Nussey, 16 Sept. 1844 Shorter.
32. C. Brontë to E. Nussey, 5 June 1847, ibid., p. 352.
33. Cf. J.R. Godley (ed.), *Letters from Early New Zealand by Charlotte Godley*, (Christchurch, 1951); Drummond, pp. 66-7.
34. M. Taylor to C. Brontë, June to 24 July 1848, Stevens, p. 77; cf. Stevens, pp. 66-9.
35. M. Taylor to C. Brontë, ibid., p. 76. The optimistic estimates of profits were not fulfilled; two years later she wrote to say that she would just escape loss on her cattle, but she avoided hardship when her brothers converted their loan into a gift. M. Taylor to C. Brontë, 5 April 1850, ibid., pp. 91-2.
36. M. Taylor to C. Brontë, June to 24 July 1848, ibid., p. 76.
37. See below, note 77.
38. *Chambers's* did not print her article and 'three or four articles' sent to *Tait's Edinburgh Magazine* were not acknowledged. M. Taylor to C. Brontë, 10 April 1849, June to July 1848, Stevens, pp. 86, 76.
39. C. Brontë to M. Wooler, 28 Aug. 1848, Wise and Symington, II, pp. 248-9.
40. M. Taylor to C. Brontë, 10 April 1849, 5 April 1850; Ellen Taylor to C. Brontë, 13 Aug. 1850, Stevens, pp. 85-92, 97-100. The Wellington census of 31 Aug. 1845 was published in the *New Zealand Journal*, 9 May 1846; the total for Wellington and surrounding districts was 4,897.
41. In 1850 Mary was 33 and Ellen 23. M. Taylor to C. Brontë, 13 Aug. 1850, Stevens, pp. 98, 1.
42. A. Dixon to his daughter Mary Dixon, Brussels, 24 July 1843, *Dixon Letters*, Leeds City Museum; C. Brontë to E. Nussey, 26 June 1848, Shorter, *Brontës*, I, pp. 426-7.
43. C. Brontë to E. Nussey, 16 Feb. 1849, Shorter, II, p. 28 mentions the imminent departure of Ellen and Henry Taylor from London. Ellen's disappointed resignation to her fate is suggested in Mary's remark that 'She thought she was coming wofully down in the world when she came out, and finds herself better received than ever she was in her life before.' M. Taylor to C. Brontë, 5 April 1850, Stevens, p. 91.
44. Stevens, p. 88.
45. E. Taylor to C. Brontë, 13 Aug. 1850, ibid., p. 100.
46. Ibid., p. 106.
47. M. Taylor to C. Brontë, 5 April 1850, ibid., p. 88.
48. E. Taylor to C. Brontë, 13 Aug. 1850, ibid., p. 99.
49. M. Taylor to C. Brontë, 5 April, 1850; M. Taylor to E. Nussey, 24 Feb. to 3 March 1854, and 4 to 8 Jan. 1857, ibid., pp. 88, 121, 131.
50. Ellen Taylor told Charlotte Brontë that their shopkeeping 'astonishes everybody here' and that many thought it only a temporary whim, but noticed that when Mary bought merchandise 'the people are always civil to her'. 13 Aug. 1850, ibid., pp. 99-100.

51. C. Brontë to E. Nussey, 28 Sep. 1846, Shorter, *Brontës*, I, pp. 338-9.
52. M. Taylor to E. Nussey, 9 Feb. 1849, Stevens, p. 82.
53. Cf. Stevens, pp. 12-13.
54. M. Taylor to E. Nussey, 9 Feb. 1849, ibid., pp. 80-1.
55. M. Taylor to C. Brontë, April 1850, ibid., p. 94.
56. In 1847 the Wellington population included 528 bachelors and 248 spinsters. J. Miller, *Early Victorian New Zealand* (London, 1958), p. 164.
57. M. Taylor to E. Nussey, 11 March 1851, Stevens, p. 105.
58. M. Taylor to C. Brontë, 5 April 1850, ibid., p. 91.
59. Ibid.
60. Ibid.
61. Ibid. As Mary noted Ellen was also better received because of her femininity, but in male dominated colonies the value of such middle-class women as sex-objects was inseparable from their social value as a means of status advancement.
62. Drummond, pp. 66-7.
63. Lady M.A. Barker, *Station Life in New Zealand* (Christchurch, 1950, first pub. 1870), p. 67; see also pp. 35, 40-3, 67-9, 104-7 and Barker, *Station Amusements in New Zealand* (Christchurch, 1953, first pub. 1873), pp. 154-64, 169-73.
64. Letters of Sarah Greenwood, Nelson, Aug. 1843; Motueka, 31 March 1844 in Drummond, pp. 73-7.
65. Jessie Campbell, the wife of a settler at Wanganui, had similar experiences, and argued that the greater physical activity of colonial women made childbirth a much easier ordeal than for women in England. Ibid., p. 63.
66. Barker, *Station Life*, p. 57.
67. M. Taylor to E. Nussey, 11 March 1851, Stevens, p. 104.
68. C. Brontë, to E. Nussey, 16 Sep. 1844, Shorter, *Brontës*, I, p. 284. In 1844 Charlotte Brontë predicted that Mary would return before long unless she married, yet was unconvinced enough in 1849 when she wrote *Shirley* to conclude her description with the question 'Will she ever come back?' *Shirley*, ch. 9.
69. M. Taylor to C. Brontë, 24 July 1848, Stevens, p. 77.
70. M. Taylor to E. Nussey, 15 Aug. 1850, ibid., pp. 101-2.
71. Cf. ibid., pp. 71-2; E. Nussey, *The Story of the Brontës* with mss. notes (Bradford, 1885-9, British Museum, suppressed before publication).
72. Cf. Stevens, pp. 141-8.
73. Notably the extensive activity of women at the National Association for the Promotion of Social Science congresses from 1857, the founding of the *English Woman's Journal* in 1858 and the establishment of the Society for the Promotion of the Employment of Women from 1859. See ch. 5 below.
74. M. Taylor, *The First Duty of Women* (London, 1870), pp. iii-iv.
75. Ibid., pp. 86-110.
76. Ibid., pp. 13-14.
77. M. Taylor, *Miss Miles, or, A Tale of Yorkshire Life Sixty Years Ago* (London, 1890).
78. Sarah Miles's parents 'would have laughed at the notion of losing dignity by work of any kind. If dignity could not take care of itself they would let it go'. Sarah's identical attitude is contrasted to the classic experience of genteel female distress produced by the ruin of the Turner family. Ibid., pp. 182, 203-23.
79. Ibid., pp. 168-9.
80. First published in *National Review*, XXVIII, April 1862, 434-60, see ch. 5 below.
81. Taylor, *First Duty*, p. 43.
82. Mary's phrase to Ellen Nussey referring to the 'pent-up' atmosphere in

England. Sep. 1842, Stevens, p. 38.
83. See note 54 above.

4 EMIGRATION AND RESPECTABILITY, 1849-1853

Successful emigrants like Mary Taylor did much to illustrate the potential of emigration for middle-class women — providing the message could reach them in Britain. But there were persistent obstacles which prevented the wider exploitation of this outlet, and in the 1840s the obstacles seemed insurmountable. Most obvious was the simple lack of demand in young settlement colonies for the occupations of middle-class women; a governess who might not be prepared to turn to less genteel employment could quickly become a colonial liability. An equally pervasive obstacle was the continuing unsavoury image attaching to emigration. As we have seen, women intending to emigrate often had to defy social convention, public opinion and bureaucratic barriers. The old view of emigration simply as a cure for pauperism died hard, as did the association of Australia with the evils of convict transportation. Until these attitudes changed, and female emigration could be seen to be safe and respectable, the departure of any significant number of middle-class women would be inhibited.

The second of these obstacles — the unsavoury image of emigration — underwent a dramatic change during the early 1850s. A series of largely unrelated developments which kept public interest in emigration, and Australasia especially, at a sustained high pitch, came together to transform the image of emigration for the middle-classes. The Wakefieldian Canterbury Settlement in New Zealand in 1850, the proliferation of philanthropic emigration societies at mid-century and discussion of the Australian gold-rush in 1852 all played a vital part in this minor revolution. Significantly, in each of these developments female emigration assumed a unique importance and prompted a serious discussion on the role of women in the founding of new societies. In the process the issue of female emigration itself became instrumental in revolutionising the appeal of emigration to the middle classes, but more importantly the changes in attitude laid the foundation for more ambitious and enduring ventures to assist educated women to emigrate. The transformation constituted a watershed with long-term consequences for women, and thus deserves close scrutiny.

As early as 1841 Wakefieldian propagandists, anxious to attract respectable settlers to their new colonies in South Australia and New Zealand, were claiming that a radical shift had occurred in middle-class attitudes to emigration. Henry Samuel Chapman, an enthusiastic reviewer of Wakefield's *England and America*, maintained that colonisation

> has taken the place of mere emigration; the removal of society, that
> of mere masses; and men of refinement and education may now
> emigrate, without any material disturbance of their previous habits.
> . . . As to the change itself, it is impossible to go into intelligent
> society without meeting some evidence of it. People to whom the
> idea of severing themselves from their native country was insuperably repugnant, now speak familiarly of emigration as a possible
> contingency, either not to be dreaded, or to be desired. Among the
> educated portion of the middle-class, where families are numerous, it
> is now not unusual to find some one or more of the sons seeking
> fortune in our distant possessions. Young women, too, of refined
> education, no longer object to emigrate if circumstances favour that
> step.[1]

Chapman's description probably contained as much wishful thinking
and propaganda as objective social observation; it was often hard for
Wakefieldians to see beyond the enthusiasms of their own pressure
group. But by 1850 other interested publicists were beginning to notice,
and promote, the phenomenon of the genteel female emigrant. A writer
in the *Colonial Magazine and East India Review* described the hard
working but happy lives of English gentlewomen in colonial kitchens,
dairies and farms. 'Such is the life', he wrote,

> led by hundreds of young ladies who once figured as belles in
> crowded ball-rooms, and are now the happy, industrious and prosperous wives of Colonists, and mothers of healthy children, but who,
> had they remained in England, would too probably have become,
> like thousands and thousands, jaded, listless, unhappy women, unable to marry, and in many instances useless members of society. We
> say such a state of things was not intended, it is contrary to all the
> beneficent ordinances of Heaven, and it is only through the ignorance, the folly, the weak fears, the want of energy of society that it
> exists.[2]

Once again the feminine civilising mission was enlisted in the cause of
female emigration, but practical action soon began to accompany the
rhetoric. Certainly by the end of the 1840s philanthropists and other

private organisations were beginning to show an interest in emigration beyond its customary association with pauperism.

The first attempts to establish a system of emigration specifically for distressed gentlewomen came in 1849 when some officials of the Governesses' Benevolent Institution approached the Emigration Commissioners with a plan to organise an emigration scheme for governesses. In the same year Hyde Clarke laid plans for the National Benevolent Emigration Fund for Widows and Orphan Daughters of Gentlemen, Clergymen, Professional Men, Officers, Bankers and Merchants.[3] Both schemes proved abortive, partly because the Australian colonies could offer no prospect of a steady demand for educated women simply as governesses, and partly because of the Colonial Office's habitual nervousness about adequate protection for genteel female emigrants. Despite their failure, though, the proposals indicated an awareness of the relevance of emigration for educated women, and a growing willingness to promote it.

Hyde Clarke's proposals to the Colonial Office certainly revealed a close understanding of the problem of distressed gentlewomen in Britain, where a preoccupation with status narrowed the range of work opportunities. His analysis led naturally to the conclusion that emigration alone could permit such women to take any form of work without humiliating loss of caste.

A clergyman, or professional man leaves a widow, and two or three daughters, with no other endowment than their talents or education, and absolutely destitute of the means of changing their place of residence. A young lady engaged in tuition finds herself after sickness deprived of employment, and forced to struggle against the competition of an overstocked profession. A family brought up in competency, by some sudden stroke of misfortune are deprived of their property, obliged to seek a subsistence; their delicacy would rather find it among strangers than among neighbours.

Widespread impoverishment of this kind in Britain, Clarke argued, was matched by the pressing deficiency 'of a higher class of feminine society in the colonies' and their need for a higher moral tone, which could be provided only by respectable women. But relief for the women and civilisation for the colonies were obstructed so long as potential emigrants were 'debarred by want of means, and want of friends, protectors and advisers, to aid them in undertaking voyages to distant and strange lands'. Clarke's society, financed through charitable contributions, intended to provide this aid to well-recommended women by means of loans in Britain and superintendence and protection by ecclesiastical authorities in the colonies, and he asked the Colonial Office to request full co-operation from each colony.[4]

The Emigration Commissioners thought the project might be worthy of encouragement 'under proper restrictions', but feared that the greatest obstacle, as with the GBI's scheme, was 'the mode of affording adequate security and protection to the younger females who may be sent out'. They were, at least, sanguine enough to anticipate sufficient demand for governesses in the colonies to justify the project.[5] But the Australian reaction was more discouraging. From South Australia the Lieutenant-Governor wrote that there were already 'more respectable and educated females seeking employment in that capacity than there are families requiring their services', and few settlers were yet in a position to hire governesses or any kind of upper servants.[6] Similar replies came from officials in Van Diemen's Land and New South Wales, each acknowledging that while the objects of the enterprise were laudable, and a few women might find suitable positions as governesses, there was little scope for regular shipments of educated women.[7] The New South Wales agent added the familiar, stock response that the only certain prospects of female employment were in domestic service, the same work performed by shiploads of assisted working-class immigrants.[8] Hyde Clarke no doubt had this contingency in mind when he assured Grey that 'candidates will be made fully aware the career open to them is one of industry; and it is to be expected the ordinary household education, in town or country, will fit them to become useful members of society in the colonies'.[9] But in 1849 the time was not yet ripe in Britain for Clarke to pursue his logic further by urging middle-class women to turn to domestic service, if only as a stop-gap, and the luke-warm responses from both the Colonial Office and the colonies caused the scheme to lapse.

By 1850, admittedly, the outlook did not seem promising for middle-class emigration. Once again public attention was being directed to the abuses of Government assisted emigration to Australia. In 1848 the Colonial Secretary, Earl Grey, yielded to domestic pressure to rid Irish workhouses of large numbers of female orphans and reinstated the long abandoned system of mass shipments of young women to Australia.[10] Again, as in the 1830s, the critics condemned the system, often un-reasonably,[11] but there were enough real abuses to fuel a long press campaign in Britain against the system and against Government involvement in emigration generally. In 1850 Lord Mountcashell questioned

Grey about a report of assaults by drunken crew members on female emigrants aboard the *Indian*.[12] The *Illustrated London News* later discussed the same report, remarking that without guarantees against such treatment 'it were idle to expect virtuous females, or indeed any persons, to leave their native land'.[13] *The Times*, which had become favourable to well-organised emigration by mid-century, rebuked the Government for shipping out 'the refuse of our great towns and villages'.[14] Wakefieldian interests and other colonial lobbyists, who actually favoured more complete Government management in emigration, criticised the half-measures and alleged that Irish orphans 'have done nothing but to spread vice, together with the hellish doctrines of popery which sanctify vice — as a means to an end'.[15] As late as 1852 an Australian emigrants guide, designed to encourage respectable emigrants, repeated the warnings to young women of Caroline Chisholm, the 'emigrant's friend'.[16]

'Who has not been shocked' writes Mrs Chisholm, 'by the frightful details we have read in the public papers, how orphan after orphan has been victimised on board emigrant ships, by men calling themselves Christians; how modest maidens have been brutalized over and insulted by those whose peculiar duty it was to protect them.'[17]

It was in this highly unfavourable setting for the popularity of middle-class emigration that private and philanthropic efforts began to effect a change from about 1850. The misfortunes of the Colonial Office system enhanced the popularity of voluntary efforts, which were, in any case, far more in keeping with the prevailing ethos of self-help. The superior propaganda value of independent emigration schemes gave them a unique opportunity to promote a new image of middle-class emigration, and the fortuitous episode of the Australian gold rush reinforced the trend.

The most determined and self-conscious agent in the movement for respectable emigration was the old Colonial Reformer, Edward Gibbon Wakefield. His last major work, *A View of the Art of Colonization*, published in 1849, resurrected all his earlier arguments in favour of middle-class, and especially female, emigration, and included an attack on Grey for his emigration policy. He blamed Grey for a situation in which 'contempt for the colonies, a sense of their inferiority or lowness, pervades society here', so that the 'gentry class', by which he meant the middle class, came unconsciously to associate emigration with shame and failure, with hardened convicts, wretched paupers and

black sheep who had forfeited their good names at home. The key to
successful colonisation was the emigration of the respectable and educated, who

> lead and govern the emigration of the other classes. These are the
> emigrants whose presence in a colony most beneficially affects its
> standard of morals and manners, and would supply the most bene-
> ficial element of colonial government. If you can induce many of
> this class to settle in a colony, the other classes, whether capitalists
> or labourers, are sure to settle there in abundance.[18]

As in *England and America* in 1833, Wakefield deplored the plight of
women of the 'uneasy' or 'anxious' classes, the very women most
needed in the colonies. Great Britain was 'the greatest and the saddest
convent the world has ever seen' with thousands of educated women
condemned to a reluctant barren spinsterhood. The argument was
familiar, but in 1849 Wakefield carried it a step further. A vital element
in any civilised colony, he insisted, was religion; without it, whatever its
form, any society must decline into barbarism, as had all the male-
dominated British colonies except for that of the devout French
Canadians. Because women were the natural transmitters of religion
Wakefield argued that they were vital to the building of a civilised
religious community and indispensable in every phase of colonisation.
There were more religious women than religious men, and in every class
the best female colonists were those to whom religion was 'a rule, a
guide, a stay, and a comfort'. A colony founded with religious men
might in time degenerate in morals and manners, 'but if you persuade
religious women to emigrate, the whole country will be comparatively
virtuous and polite'.[19] Here was the Victorian feminine civilising
mission, a concept born of bourgeois leisure at the domestic hearth,
carried to its ultimate and logical conclusion. The question remained
whether it could be used to entice single women from their not so
leisurely homeland to pioneer colonies.

Wakefield's sudden interest in religion stemmed from deliberate cal-
culation. He was never noted for his piety. He showed few religious
scruples when abducting an heiress in 1826[20] and had not undergone a
sudden religious conversion. His plea in 1849 for new sectarian colonies
'with the strong attraction for superior emigrants of a particular creed
in each colony'[21] was based on far more practical considerations. Wakefield was planning a new colony in New Zealand and needed influential
support and patronage. Traditionally at odds with most members of the

establishment, he now courted them with a blueprint for an exclusively Church of England, Tory settlement in Canterbury, complete with a Bishop. His attempt was eminently successful.[22] The Archbishop of Canterbury accepted the presidency of the Canterbury Association, and the committee included prominent clerics, peers and politicians.[23] The Canterbury Settlement constituted a meticulous application of Wakefield's theories down to the last detail. For once he achieved his ideal of transplanting an exact cross-section of society, an extension of the English class hierarchy.[24] Gentry, women and children all formed their due proportion in a model of patrician emigration which put the Government's 'pauper-shovelling' to shame.[25]

Certainly this was the impression conveyed in the Canterbury publicity, with its persistent stress on the respectability of the venture. The press unanimously welcomed the prospect of a truly respectable colony and stressed the hierarchical character of the new community, drawing odious contrasts with the Government's own activity. For *The Times* the new scheme was a piece of heroic patriotism, for by transplanting a complete 'slice of England' it ensured that the colony would remain British; it was therefore essential that the mass of emigrants 'should not be mere heaps of pauperism, shovelled from our shores, but fairly selected portions of British society'.[26] The sustained publicity had a rapid impact on the image of emigration. *Fraser's* comment, only a month after the first departures, may have been as much a self-fulfilling prophecy as a true estimate of events, but at least it reflected a genuine shift of attitude:

> In ecclesiastical, then, as well as civil institutions, Canterbury bids fair for the revival of the colonizing art. She seems by her first appeal to have struck a chord of sympathy in the heart of this nation; and we can scarcely yet accustom ourselves to the novelty she has already realized in her speedy conquest of what Mr Wakefield almost despondingly laments over, as the indisposition of respectable people to emigrate.[27]

The Canterbury project overshadowed a host of minor schemes to foster emigration. It was a major colonisation scheme, sanctioned by the Government, which captured the imagination of the public. In fashionable news value it often competed favourably during 1851 with the Great Exhibition, and must have done much to soften many of the social taboos which placed fetters on the exodus of middle-class women. At the same time other influences were at work transforming the image of emigration, some with a more direct and exclusive concern for women. Each of them was less grandiose than the Canterbury scheme, but they exerted a powerful collective impact. From 1849 the rising interest in emigration gave rise to a multitude of charitable and commercial ventures, some regional, some occupational, some comprehensive, but all actively competing for public support.[28] Hyde Clarke's abortive scheme for orphaned gentlewomen in 1849 was a product of the general enthusiasm and appropriately reflected the temper of mid-century opinion. The British Ladies' Female Emigrant Society, also formed in 1849, regretted the need for female emigration, but attempted to render the procedure more safe and palatable for the women. Its members recruited matrons to supervise single women, especially on Government ships, they visited emigrants on board before departure to distribute bibles, tracts and work materials, and they organised colonial committees to assist women after their arrival. Less spectacular than most contemporary projects, it endured longest until 1888 when it became the basis for a more ambitious scheme to assist middle-class women.[29]

The mid-century 'rage for emigration'[30] was confined to no single class, group or sex, but the organisations which attracted the most sustained interest in Britain were either exclusively or substantially devoted to assisting unmarried women. Certainly the two societies with the greatest influence on public opinion were Caroline Chisholm's Family Colonization Loan Society and Sidney Herbert's Fund for Promoting Female Emigration. Both societies, which overlapped in aims and management, achieved a fashionable popularity in Britain for about four years, and initiated a sustained and influential discussion on the merits of female emigration.

Caroline Chisholm had a lifelong interest in the welfare of female emigrants.[31] The wife of an Indian army officer, she already had some experience of philanthropic work when she moved with her husband to Sydney in 1838, having organised and run a school for the unoccupied daughters of Indian soldiers in Madras. Historically she has been most remembered for her early rescue work in Sydney in 1841 and 1842, when, without official help, she gathered abandoned and friendless female immigrants, set up a 'Home' for them, established an employment registry, and conveyed the women to their employers. Her legendary trips into the bush with bullock-drays full of young women delighted farmers seeking servants for their wives and wives for their sons. In 1841 and 1842 the 'emigrants' friend', as she became known, placed about 2,000 emigrants. Among them were some complete families, but she devoted most of her time to the interests of single women.[32]

Chisholm's rescue work in Sydney certainly had a romantic appeal, but her later activities in London exerted a more dramatic and lasting effect on British opinion. She returned to England in 1846 after successfully obtaining a series of improvements in immigrant reception, and immediately besieged the Colonial Office with proposals for more humane and efficient methods of female and family emigration. After a succession of anxious enquiries from intending emigrants she decided, by 1848, to form her own emigration society, and with the active support and membership of Lord Ashley and Sidney Herbert, organised her Family Colonization Loan Society.[33] As its name implies, the society was neither wholly philanthropic nor designed expressly for single women. Chisholm insisted that the best method of emigration was that of complete family units, which, as far as possible, should be self-supporting. She organised groups of families in England before their departure, allowing them to become acquainted at regular meetings at her Islington home. Each family contributed the maximum possible amount to the cost of its emigration, and the Society provided the balance as a loan to be repaid in the colony, a popular gesture stressing the virtues of self-help. Single women without relatives were introduced and assigned to family groups for protection, and shipboard accommodation, all of a single class and divided into small cabins of families, single women and single men, was scrupulously designed to provide the maximum possible protection and superintendence.[34]

Chisholm's Society claimed a wide measure of success. It enabled several thousands with skilled working-class or lower middle-class backgrounds to emigrate without provoking colonial hostility.[35] It also received widespread and unqualified praise in Britain. The press used the society to expose the glaring deficiencies in Government emigration. The *Westminster Review*, eager to demonstrate the virtues of *laissez-faire*, saw in Chisholm's work 'lessons for the lovers of legislation . . . The State beaten by a woman!'[36] An article in *Household Words* stressed the society's great improvement over the Government's standard of shipboard conditions, especially the scrupulous care taken to avoid indelicate sleeping arrangements;[37] *The Times* drew the same distinction, noticing that the scheme was unique in catering to the feelings, and especially the modesty, of the working class.[38] A *Times* correspondent, critical of bureaucratic obstructions in the Government's procedures, thought Chisholm, in enabling persons of all ages and sexes to emigrate, 'follows the laws of nature, while the Commissioners act up to

their own restrictions'.[39] Although the society's first ship did not sail
until September 1850, when the news media and colonial interests were
monopolised by the Canterbury Settlement scheme,[40] the novelty and
excitement of Chisholm's work kept publicity at a high pitch.

The publicity was nowhere more sustained and influential than in
Charles Dickens's popular middle-class periodical, *Household Words*.[41] It
was logical that Dickens, habitually inclined to seek solutions to social
and industrial problems outside the socio-economic system, should be
attracted to the simple safety valve of emigration.[42] After meeting
Caroline Chisholm he discussed her society in the first issue of *Household Words*, and frequently described in detail the careful procedures
she followed to secure a reliable system.[43] An article written during the
Australian gold rush suggested that family colonisation was the only
remedy for colonial society against 'the curse of gold' which threatened
to attract hordes of unattached males.[44] Dickens's interest was reflected
in his current novel, *David Copperfield*, which began serialised publication in 1849, and ended with the emigration to Australia of two
problem families, the Micawbers and Peggottys. The choice of destination is significant, for Australia was becoming a new emigrants *El
Dorado* well before the gold rush. Dickens's description of the actual
departure bore a striking resemblance to the detailed accounts of
Chisholm's procedures in *Household Words*. Micawber's unlikely rise to
the magistracy and Peggoty's return visit to England as a successful
sheepfarmer illustrated the wisdom of prudent family emigration. Both
men had faced ruin and family disintegration in England, but by emigrating they achieved prosperity, preserved family solidarity, which
incidentally saved Little Emily from further moral corruption, and
demonstrated the infallibility of the Chisholm method.[45]

Chisholm's most serious biography gives the misleading impression
that she viewed female emigration as little more than a fortuitous by-
product of her system of family emigration. It is misleading because all
of her writing and practical work was concerned ultimately with the
moral efficacy of respectable female emigration. A devout Roman
Catholic convert and a devoted wife and mother, she believed
passionately in the ideal of the feminine civilising mission, and saw in
Australia an opportunity to translate this abstract concept into practice.
When she talked of the 'social wants of the people' in Australia she
stressed that even sorely needed schools and churches would yield few
benefits without ' "God's police" — wives and little children — good and
virtuous women'.[46] Ann Summers[47] has rightly pointed to the ideological implications of the term 'God's Police', for Chisholm's intention

was to give an upper-class Victorian ideal of womanhood practical relevance across class lines. Bachelors in the bush, she argued, would never be loyal subjects, but 'Give them help-mates, and you make murmuring, discontented servants, loyal and happy subjects of the State.'[48] An article she wrote for *Household Words* related the details of her visit to an Australian farm run by five bachelors. Despite all the outward comfort and prosperity she noticed a certain vacuum.

> Yes, this spot of beauty, to make it a delightful happy home, required, what one of our favourite poets, and the poet of nature, calls nature's 'noblest work' — women. 'Tis but too true — John Witney wanted a wife to make his home a fit habitation for man. What is John Witney without her? . . . It was this hope alone, warming and clinging to his heart, that some day he could call himself the father of a family, that inspired him to gather all these beauties and comforts around him.[49]

The moral regeneration of Australia, and its loyalty to the Empire were, she insisted, dependent on the influence of virtuous women. This attitude stemmed naturally from her Australian experience of 1841 and 1842 and remained the basic objective of her society.

Familiar with the potential hazards of poorly administered or ill-conceived female emigration, Chisholm was convinced that only well-organised family emigration could guarantee the complete success of such a delicate operation. Responsible families afforded the best possible protection for single women, and the only certain means of avoiding the 'brutalisation' suffered by the Irish orphan victims of Government policy. Under proper guidance she expected her system to improve to the point where 'our young women can be sent into a ship with the same confidence with which females now enter our trains and mail coaches'.[50] Her scheme was not unlike that followed by the Government after 1836, and claimed success largely because of her insistence on mutual acquaintance of family groups before departure. She took special pains to make the married men feel the full burden of their responsibility, and extracted a lofty pledge from them as a last reminder.

> That we pledge ourselves, as Christian fathers and heads of families, to exercise a parental control and guardianship over all orphans and friendless females of good repute for virtue and morality, proceeding with the family groups; to protect them as our children, and

allow them to share the same cabins with our daughters.[51]

After the gold rush, when Australia generated its own stimulus to emigration, Chisholm increasingly dwelt on the need to provide for 'a speedy emigration of women',[52] But this had been the rationale behind the Family Colonization Loan Society from the beginning.

Chisholm's work was of a practical and straightforward character, which detractors of the Government system never failed to exploit, but the high-toned rhetoric of the press and other admirers – and sometimes Chisholm herself – gave it the semblance of a moral and matrimonial crusade. Female emigration was an issue highly charged with romanticism and sentimentality, and well suited to long-winded moralists eager to expatiate on the visible manifestation of the feminine civilising mission. The politician Robert Lowe, who had seen Chisholm's work in Australia, dubbed her in a poem 'The guardian angel of her helpless sex.'[53] *The Times*, in a laudatory leader written just before her return to Australia, asserted 'There never was a more vigilant or efficient protector of female virtue, and thousands of happy wives and mothers in Australia owe it to her that they are living in peace, honour and competence, instead of vice, infamy and poverty.'[54] Chisholm herself was careful to choose the most sentimental anecdotes to illustrate her point. She told of a worried Australian father who travelled a hundred miles to see her, ' "If" said he, "you could only get me a good girl; if I could see my son married to a good woman, then I should die in peace" '.[55] It was natural, when marriage was deemed the only respectable occupation for women, that the propaganda in praise of female emigration should stress the favourable matrimonial prospects.[56] What the rhetoric failed to point out was that it was applying a middle-class ideal to working-class emigrants for whom it had never had much relevance.

Closely associated with Caroline Chisholm's society, and at times confused with it, was a charitable organisation devoted wholly to the emigration of single women known as the Fund for Promoting Female Emigration, organised and run by Sidney Herbert with Lord Ashley. This society's original aim was to finance the emigration of London's distressed needlewomen, but Herbert's decisive shift of interest over a period of three years from destitute needlewomen to the lower middle class and educated women of some gentility reflects the parallel shift in attitudes to emigration. By 1853, when Herbert turned to women of a 'superior class', middle-class emigration had become a more respectable proposition. The evolution of his society should help to illustrate the process by which a more favourable climate for the emigration of middle-class women emerged during the early fifties.

Herbert's society was born from the conjuncture of a rising interest in emigration with a sudden flurry of attention to the conditions of the most depressed class of needleworkers and slopworkers in the metropolis, publicised by Henry Mayhew's famous articles on the London poor in the *Morning Chronicle* of 1849. Herbert and Ashley, immediately after some dramatic enquiries in East London,[57] organised an emigration scheme which lasted for nearly four years, and quickly turned its attention to women other than needleworkers. Like similar previous ventures it occasionally gave offence to some colonists, who disapproved of the moral standards of some of the women. But in contrast to the criticism of the Government's scheme during the thirties, criticism of Herbert's work was absent from the British press, and it remained popular and fashionable in Britain, where its favourable publicity contributed to the changing image of emigration.

The most novel feature of the new scheme was the provision for a 'Home', a lodging house in Hatton Garden, to lodge prospective emigrants before departure.[58] It was furnished to accommodate over forty women, and the society provided for careful supervision by appointing a permanent matron and a ladies' committee in authority. Apart from serving as a quasi-convalescent home for the most destitute and under-nourished women, the 'Home' seems to have been designed with two key functions in mind, one moral, the other occupational. Herbert stressed in his report that the most careful selection procedures could still not prevent some morally corrupted women from obtaining a free passage, but several weeks in the 'Home' under the 'gentle discipline' of the matron, Mrs Batkin, served as a weeding-out process. A small proportion of women admitted to the 'Home' were regularly denied a free passage, and others were kept there beyond their original sailing date until their characters could be 'more thoroughly determined'.[59] More importantly, residence in the 'Home' provided an opportunity for rigorous training in domestic service in order to ensure rapid and satisfactory employment in the colonies.[60] These functions underscored Herbert's and the ladies' committee's sensitivity to the demands of colonial employers; they were not likely to forget the experience of their heavily criticised predecessors.[61] Their reaction affirmed that respectability and a capacity for domestic service were the decisive elements in successful female emigration.

The routine press accounts of the society's ships' departures were accompanied by glowing editorial comment long after the initial novelty had worn off early in 1850. *The Times* concluded from a report of the society in 1852 that the Australian bush 'must be a perfect Arcadia' for British women, and warmly commended Herbert's efforts.[62] Spokesmen for colonial interests continued to use the society to demonstrate the shortcomings of Government emigration, and viewed Herbert's scheme as the prelude to a potential massive project of female emigration.[63] The society's theme of emigration for distressed needlewomen was reflected promptly in popular melodramatic periodical fiction.[64] Both *Punch* and the *Illustrated London News* depicted the society's operations in drawings of scenes of the women on board ship, in the Hatton Garden 'Home' and in an imagined domestic utopia in Australia.[65] The *Illustrated* saw the events on Herbert's ships as a 'striking characteristic of the season' in 1850.[66] For at least two years, and throughout the period of heightened interest in Australia, the Fund for Female Emigration remained one of the most fashionable charities on the London scene.[67]

Public discussion of Herbert's work, like that of Caroline Chisholm, soon took on the appearance of matrimonial propaganda. This was partly due to a sudden unprecedented interest in the disproportions between the sexes in Britain and Australia. In his original appeal Herbert had stressed the deplorable effects of too many women in Britain and too many men in the Antipodes.[68] Excessive male emigration was a cause, and increased female emigration an obvious solution to these reciprocal evils, and the point was quickly taken up by the press. *The Times* thought the 'disease' required an urgent remedy in the form of massive assistance to female emigrants, and blamed the shortsightedness of past policy.

> Just at the moment that colony after colony is threatening independence it strikes the British public, as a novel thought, that it has made the great mistake of creating a settlement at the Antipodes with twice as many men as women instead of that equality which Heaven has ordained. And this is the accumulated error of half a century. Year after year we have witnessed its development with stupid indifference.[69]

The conception of the problem in these terms led logically to an interest in husbands rather than employment. A poem in *Punch*, inspired by Herbert's work, saw the solution to the needlewomen's plight in Australia, 'Where in wedlock's tie, not harlotry, we shall find men to mate us.'[70] Samuel Sidney, an emigration promoter, welcomed Herbert's scheme, and argued in a pamphlet that women were needed in

Australia more as wives than as servants.

> It is perfectly possible that a shipful of emigrant girls might give dis-
> satisfaction to the fashionables of Sydney, Melbourne, and Adelaide,
> and yet be gratefully received and happily settled in the interior of
> those districts.

The grateful recipients would be 'the new solitary dwellers in the bush
of Australia, whose homes will be lightened, and civilized, and Christian-
ized, by "wives and little children" '.[71] The frequency of this rhetoric
had predictable effects on the expectations of the emigrants, and the
society soon began to warn the women against making imprudent
marriages too soon after their arrival in the colony. Not that marriage
was an unworthy ambition, but the women should first depend on their
own conduct and industry, and subsequently 'they might expect in due
time to get good and worthy men to marry them, and thus they would
ensure their future happiness'.[72] Herbert realised that the practical
exigencies of an emigration scheme were far more complex than the
rhetoric implied; the only emigrants welcome in the colonies were those
willing and able to perform hard unpleasant work, but with so few
respectable alternatives open to women it was natural that such a
popular project should be romanticised into an imperial marriage
bureau in Britain.

The matrimonial issue soon prompted a debate about the women's
social origins. The prospect of boatloads of brides for bushmen was not
universally welcomed. A writer in *Household Words* later recounted
that 'some very delicate people were shocked to think that wives should
be exported like so many bales of printed cotton'.[73] Part of the problem was a confusion over precisely what kind of women the society
meant to assist. Mayhew's famous articles had established a firm connection — if it did not already exist — between the themes of needlework and prostitution, and William Brown, MP for South Lancashire,
immediately questioned the wisdom of encouraging abandoned slopworkers, unqualified in domestic work, to emigrate; 'women,' he
remarked, 'who cannot be helpers will be destroyers'. Herbert quickly
replied that he expected the supervision of the 'Home' to operate as a
check on the character and qualifications of each candidate, and that
the society was less interested in professional needlewomen than ex-
domestic servants who had been forced into the lowest paid forms of
needlework. 'Nor do we wish by any means', he added, 'to confine
ourselves to that, or indeed any other class.'[74] Herbert's original stress

on distressed needlewomen, therefore, caused some perplexity about the purpose and function of the society. No total figures for the entire duration of the scheme have survived, but various reports indicate that needleworkers were never in a majority. The first report classified only 167 out of its 409 emigrants in 1850 as needleworkers or dressmakers of various kinds, and 169 as domestic servants. Herbert was careful to point out that many women designated as servants were in fact 'servants-out-of-place' who had temporarily resorted to the needle to eke out a living, but the majority could still obtain testimonials from previous employers and had at least some experience in domestic service.[75] Most of the women, regardless of their previous history, took work as domestic servants in Australia, so that the proportion of them with relevant experience was a measure of their immediate suitability for the colonies.[76] The needlewomen controversy provided the necessary impetus to launch Herbert's venture, but in practice a much wider social range of women obtained assistance.

The most unexpected feature of Herbert's appeal to a broad cross-section of women was the slow but increasing facility it provided for middle-class women to emigrate. In his response to Herbert's initial appeal for a society Samuel Sidney anticipated hopefully that 'many young ladies of narrow means would benefit Australia by their education and refinement, and secure themselves better establishments than England can afford them, who are now deterred, by the want of maternal protection, from venturing on the voyage'.[77] The society at first made no specific appeal to 'young ladies', but its records show that it regularly accommodated substantial numbers of middle-class women. The 409 women sent out in 1850 included only six who might be identified as middle-class by occupation, i.e. three governesses and three teachers, but Herbert's first report indicates that larger numbers of impecunious middle-class women were quick to exploit the new opportunity. The report described 38 case histories of the 1850 emigrants, of which 16 had suffered the familiar experience of steep class decline following the death of a father, loss of family fortune or other causes usually identified with genteel poverty. E.H., for example, a 27-year-old daughter of a newspaper editor, was left without support after her father's death, and subsisted for ten years on the declining proceeds of her needlework; once admitted to the 'Home', however, she lent responsible assistance to the Matron and was appointed Sub-Matron during the voyage.[78] Some complaints from Victoria against educated women unqualified for domestic service suggest that their numbers amounted to more than a trickle. Lt-Governor La Trobe told Herbert after the first

arrival with 39 women that the most unsuitable women for the colony
was the type

> who possesses no resources and but ordinary education and accom-
> plishments, and who neither can nor will make up her mind to
> descend to what she has been led, from previous habit or associa-
> tion, to consider an inferior grade or servile occupation.[79]

In 1853 the Victorian Immigration Agent, Edward Grimes, again complained that governesses ignorant of domestic service were not only
useless but a moral liability to the colony while they remained unemployed.[80] Despite these warnings the press reports of ships' departures
gave increasing attention to well-educated emigrants whose 'manners
gave evidence . . . that they had seen better days'.[81] In 1851 the society
began to provide for 'protected cases', middle-class women who could
afford to pay their own passage but preferred to travel under the
society's protection.[82] Like the London Emigration Committee in the
thirties, the society was increasingly drawn into the problem of distressed gentlewomen, and responded by opening its facilities to them,
despite the meagre demand for educated women in the colonies. The
gradual shift of attention stemmed largely from the unrelenting pressure
from desperate educated women for assistance, but it was facilitated by
a generally more tolerant attitude to emigration induced by three years
of well-publicised voluntary activity.

In 1853 the character of the society changed to a programme of
emigration assistance exclusively for middle-class women. Since 1851
the *Australia and New Zealand Gazette*, a mouthpiece in Britain for
colonial interests which seems to have developed close contacts with
Herbert's managing committee, had been urging Herbert to organise a
scheme of emigration for educated women. Originally it suggested an
extraordinary plan to send out genteel women on specific orders as
wives for 'well-to-do bushmen'.[83] In 1853 it began more frequently to
expose the anomalous position of thousands of cultivated London
women forced into 'the degrading position of governess' who, married
and settled in Australia 'would completely change the face of society
among the half-million male bipeds already there'.[84] Soon afterwards it
argued for an emigration society for accomplished women 'solely with a
view to marriage', and reported that since the society's funds were
almost depleted Herbert had proposed to send out a higher class of
women, paying their own fares, under the society's name and protection.[85] On June 18 it reported a committee meeting of June 10, at

which the society officially resolved to confine its operations to taking up and fitting out first-class ships for respectable women who could pay a fare of £22 — a sum £10 less than the current intermediate cabin fare to Australia — and to providing all the customary protection, complete with experienced matron and surgeon, during the voyage and on arrival.[86]

Further indication of Herbert's thinking appeared in the *Morning Chronicle* in July.[87] It insisted that the new scheme would be directed more towards lower middle-class women than to the 'matrimonial necessities of Australia'. They should be neither 'fine ladies nor untaught paupers' but women of respectable parentage with some experience in housework. This class, the *Chronicle* maintained, was in greatest need of emigration 'for the drudgery which married life involves to the lower section of our middle-classes — the grade above servant-hood — is only known to those most experienced in our social organization'.[88] The new approach went beyond the earlier spasmodic assistance to distressed gentlewomen and foreshadowed some of the later female emigration schemes which made a special point of helping lower middle-class women. The last reference to the plan was on 16 July, when the *Gazette* reported that most of the first party of forty middle-class women had been accepted, and that the ship was expected to leave for Sydney in mid-August. The society's protection, it reported, was

> felt to remove the difficulties and objections which have hitherto stood in the way of unprotected female emigration. For a payment of £22, the friends of a young woman who has sufficient moral and physical energy to encounter a colonial life, may now, through the instrumentality of this society, make almost a life provision for her, without apprehension as to her safety, and with the almost certainty of her success.[89]

The new scheme was gratifying to the *Gazette*, since it was close to what it had been advocating for two years. Declining funds, and the outbreak of the Crimean War, must have cut the new project short, however, for there is no further reference to its existence after the departure of the first ship in August.

Despite the persistent agitation of the *Australia and New Zealand Gazette* it is hardly likely that such a remote specialist journal was the prime force in the society's change of policy; the new plan bore the clear stamp of Caroline Chisholm's influence in its emphasis on self-help principles and its concentration on respectable and educated women.

Since the onset of the gold rush in 1852 Chisholm had hoped to organise a large-scale project of female emigration. Her husband told a Victoria Select Committee on Immigration in 1852 that she was ready to organise such a system with the help of Herbert, Shaftesbury and their wives, and that she was already touring the United Kingdom to establish village emigration societies.[90] When she spoke of the need for 'a speedy emigration of women' in January, 1853, she stressed that if the women were unable to pay their own passage, their independence must be preserved by a system of loans rather than charity.[91] Furthermore, in June, 1853, when Herbert announced the change of policy, he also replaced Ashley (now Lord Shaftesbury) as Chairman of the Central Committee of Chisholm's Family Colonization Loan Society.[92] A Melbourne paper later noted that her society had under consideration 'a plan of female emigration suggested by Mrs Chisholm'.[93] The strong implication is that the two societies arranged some form of amalgamation at this time, although there is no concrete indication that it actually occurred. There is sufficient evidence, however, to confirm that both Herbert and Chisholm had shifted their focus to middle-class women. The society had moved a long way from the pathos of Mayhew's needlewomen.

The reputation of Herbert's society has fared less well in the hands of historians than it did among enthusiastic mid-Victorian contemporaries. Conclusions from a few unfavourable colonial reports that it 'was forced to disband'[94] and that it failed 'chiefly from the poor character of the women and girls it introduced'[95] simply do not stand up to the evidence. Victoria, the only colony to complain persistently of Herbert's emigrants, noted a marked improvement in the women's respectability from 1852.[96] The major reason for its gradual disappearance in 1853 was simply depletion of funds, and one factor in the shift to the middle-class project was a feeling that there was much less suffering among working-class women in 1853 than three years earlier.[97] Clearly Mayhew's journalism had prodded the philanthropic conscience in 1849, but with its cessation the fickle attentions of 'Society' soon wandered. Conditions would have been ripe for the middle-class plan in 1854, but the outbreak of the Crimean War in March hampered shipping arrangements and diverted Herbert's philanthropic energies; Chisholm, who might have supervised the scheme, left for Australia in April, 1854. The Victorian Immigration Agent, far from discouraging the society, recommended in 1853 that its request for a grant of £10,000 from the colony's emigration fund should be granted 'provided certain restrictions are imposed upon the Society'.[98] The 'restrictions', particularly those confining assistance to domestic and farm servants, were hardly consistent with Herbert's new project, and the grant was obviously not made, for in December, 1853 Chisholm wrote to *The Times* praising the society's work and regretting 'that the funds of the Society should be nearly exhausted'.[99] Subsequent comments in the press referred to the society, in the past tense, as having found wives for many deserving bachelors during a time of severe need.[100] In numbers alone the society's achievement was relatively small; in over three years it enabled more than 1300 women to emigrate.[101] But its favourable reception in the press popularised the idea of female emigration and had a marked effect on public attitudes, helping to ease the way for the acceptance of a feminist sponsored project six years later.[102]

An important reason for Chisholm's intensified interest in female emigration from 1852 was the sharp increase in male emigration to Australia prompted by the gold rush. The gold fever coincided with the voluntary operations of the early fifties, and enhanced public support for them by further underlining the need for an equilibrium of the sexes in emigration. The first gold discoveries were in 1851, but it was in 1852 that the 'national epidemic' of emigration to the gold-fields began to rage,[103] causing Australasian emigration to leap from 21,532 in 1851 to 87,881.[104] The gold rush probably did more than any other single development to extinguish, or at least overshadow, the old identification of emigration with paupers, poverty and, to Australia, transported criminals. For once members of the middle class who were not faced with starvation or ruin at home began to emigrate, often, it seemed, imprudently. *The Times* welcomed the polite tone of the new movement, but began to take alarm when it estimated that

at least half of the 15,000 persons who last quarter left London for the gold-fields had already a position more or less settled of their own. Many large establishments are now, in fact, like regiments after a battle, with young hands unexpectedly promoted to the duties of seniors, and vacancies in abundance still.[105]

The gold rush emigration contained a premature embryo of the elite emigration from Britain which set in more steadily during the late-Victorian period.[106] The main restriction to its acceleration at mid-century, after the excitement of gold discoveries subsided, was the simple fact of the limited capacity of Australian urban society to accommodate large numbers of professionals and white collar workers. The elite nature of the movement was substantial enough, though, to convey a quite unprecedented theme of middle-class respectability.

Gold-rush emigration maintained its romantic appeal for numerous middle-class men, women and whole families, despite protests from the colonies that it was a mistake for genteel people to emigrate unless they, were prepared for a life of hard physical labour. Few educated city-dwellers were suited to the rough life of the gold-fields and there was a continual surfeit of men seeking white collar work in Melbourne, the last resort of the disappointed gold seeker. In a land where high wages were the real basis of emigration even the aspiring gentleman farmer was unable to escape hard manual labour. Throughout the gold rush Lt-Governor La Trobe complained about the

> multitude of decent men of small means and large families, decayed or unfortunate tradesmen, half-educated clerks, young men of no decided calling or character, professing their willingness to do anything, with the power of doing nothing well.[107]

The Emigration Commissioners in their annual reports reproduced and restated all the warnings against middle-class emigration, but with little immediate effect.[108] It is no exaggeration to describe the mid-century change of attitude towards Australia and emigration as a minor revolution. The new enthusiasm even penetrated artistic circles. The pre-Raphaelite sculptor, Thomas Woolner, joined the exodus to the gold-fields in 1852, and inspired his colleague, Ford Madox Brown, to paint *The Last of England*, in which he probed the mixed emotions of an educated middle-class couple taking final sorrowful leave of their country.[109]

The sudden urge to emigrate did not solve the continuing social problem: the shortage of women in Australia. The excess of males in the population increased still further with the gold rush, and the colonies stepped up their demands for more women to redress the worsening sex disproportion.[110] In 1853 John Loch, the Immigration Agent for Van Diemen's Land, a colony immune from the vast inrush of gold-diggers, but affected by the increasing scarcity of women emigrants, complained that ladies 'of the highest respectability' were being forced to perform 'the most menial offices in the hosuehold' and many were unable to leave their houses because they had no one to care for their children. He urged that more funds should be expended on Government emigration to attract superior servants, but, hoping to tap a potential source, suggested that daughters of persons of a somewhat higher sphere, but in difficult circumstances, who are unwilling to go to service where they are known, would gladly undertake the duties of nursery-maids, house-maids, parlour-servants, needlewomen, and nursery governesses in this colony, were they aware of the advantages which would here attend them, and could they be brought out free of expense not being themselves able to contribute.[111]

This argument was becoming familiar in Britain, but its appearance in Australia, where colonial officials normally discouraged the emigration of middle-class women, indicates how urgently colonists saw the need for women.

The Australian emigration propaganda of the early fifties was not-able for the candid nature of its appeals to middle-class women. No longer were they advised to pursue the same unmarketable occupation of the governess to which they were restricted at home. Demand for female teachers in Australia lagged far behind the supply. Educated women, the argument went, were certainly needed as colonial house-wives, but if they must work before marriage they should enter domes-tic service, and they would be treated as partners by their equally hard-working mistresses. In this vein an emigrants' guide warned that few Australians could afford to employ governesses who would not stoop to housework, as the employers themselves would 'have to become the servants of those they employed'. An attractive alternative remained, however.

But it is in the power of any female to become practically acquain-ted with domestic duties or dressmaking, and by this knowledge, after emigrating, find herself released from the painful dependence, bondage, and trying position of 'the young person' in this country. There they would at once take a respectable position in society, have their own home; and instead of begging for bread, their industry would be begged of them, and handsomely rewarded.[112]

Appeals like these — seemingly a prescription for Mary Taylor's New Zealand career — suited the changing climate of opinion which acknow-ledged that the externals of the British social hierarchy had been shaken in Australia. A pillar of orthodoxy like *The Times* was now able to wel-come the persuasion of a Melbourne paper exhorting 'gentlemen and ladies to throw off at once the pride of a condition they can no longer support, to bow to the necessity of the times, and to seek menial employment at the present rate of wages in whatever capacity they may be fortunate enough to find it'. *The Times* went on to note that the new employers were affected by the change as much as the new employees.

> Extreme modesty is not a prevailing fault among the inhabitants of new colonies; but we can imagine an old convict rather embarrassed by finding that he has engaged a 'senior optime' for his valet, and a maid of all work a little discontented at being assisted in her toilette by a baronet's daughter.[113]

After allowing for the flippancy genteel women could draw the implication that menial work need bring no loss of caste provided it was not done in Britain.

The new tolerance towards 'educated menials' for Australia was consistent with Victorian moralists' concept of the feminine civilising mission. Elizabeth Eastlake had argued in 1845 that the Englishwoman's particular suitability for foreign travel stemmed from her special domesticity, a unique characteristic which distinguished the Englishwoman from her European contemporaries. The Englishman was highly mobile and adaptable to foreign countries simply because 'he takes his *home* with him; and has more within it and wants less beyond it than any other man in the world'. The peculiar English taste for travel and colonisation, she maintained, was due 'to nothing less than the *domesticity* of the English character'.[114] Eastlake was thinking of women like Mrs Louisa Meredith — whose book she went on to review — who as emigrants appeared to combine the duties of the all round domestic help-mate with the culture of the poet and author. In a later book Meredith herself berated urban middle-class colonial women for being ashamed of their domestic role. In the cities, too many women tried to hide the fact that they performed hard manual work at home, and tried to give a false impression of fashionably dressed idleness. Meredith shared the candour of emigration propagandists: she considered the neat working attire, which, she claimed, pleased her husband, quite fit for greeting casual visitors.

> And it seems to me far more pleasant to imagine one's ladyfriends notably busy in a morning, as good country housewives must be and are, than to conceive such useless impossibilities as ladies (some of whom, in this place, I know, keep no female servants) dressed in new silks or muslins at noon, and seated on a sofa doing nothing![115]

Cultured idleness, it seemed, ceased to be a virtue when separated from the domestic assistance more easily available in Britain, and it was easy for moralists and emigration propagandists to claim that cultivated domestics like Meredith were performing a more noble and truly English function than the idle ladies of Britain's genteel 'Society'.

The effect on some women of the new appeals to the respectable to emigrate during the gold rush can be seen in the publications of an emigrant who married in Australia, Mrs Charles Clacy. Clacy had accompanied her brother, who 'discarded his Homer and Euclid' for 'Guides' to the Diggings of Victoria, and emigrated in 1852. She described her experiences in a best selling book, *A Lady's Visit to the Gold Diggings of Australia in 1852-3*, published in England in 1853.[116] Clacy herself was an exceptionally articulate and independent middle-class emigrant. Her book describes several encounters with less fortunate middle-class women who had emigrated in desperation, and prospered and eventually married in Australia. In an appendix headed 'Who Should emigrate?' she summarised her experiences, repeating the familiar advice that only the less fastidious women who were prepared to work hard should emigrate. 'The worst risk you run', she continued, no doubt thinking of her own rapid marriage within a year of arrival,

is that of getting married, and finding yourself treated with twenty times the respect and consideration you may meet with in England. Here (as far as numbers go) women beat the 'lords of creation,' in Australia it is the reverse, and there we may be pretty sure of having our own way.[117]

The rapid success of Clacy's book, which appeared at the height of the 'gold fever', encouraged her to write a second work, a two volume collection of short stories, all avowedly 'founded upon facts that have occurred in real life — the greater portion of them having fallen within the personal knowledge of the author'.[118] Each of her sixteen melodramatic tales recounts the fortunes of middle-class families, and most often middle-class women, in the setting of Australian emigration. The details and underlying themes of these stories are significant for their capsule description of the educated woman's response to a different social milieu, and for the influence they were bound to exert on readers. One heroine, a young governess, summarises in a single passage all the striking 'social wonders' for the uninitiated middle-class woman in Australia:

Ladies are at a premium, and have no lack of suitors; using your hands is not considered debasing; those that were the poorer classes are richer than the fine gentlemen who land here, and servants are accustomed to have the upper hand of their masters and mistresses.[119]

Clacy's stories are replete with themes of love and marriage, but in each case the final successful match is achieved through the agency of emigration and the unique social conditions prevailing in Australia. All the familiar Victorian clichés of Australian life are present; bushrangers, bush fires, convictism, gold discoveries and extreme social mobility abound, but each serves as a catalyst to cement a relationship between a once forlorn spinster and a bachelor who needs only a wife to ensure his honest prosperity. In 'The Bush Fire' Julia joins her brother in Australia and soon learns to conquer her English prejudices against menial work.

Instead of wandering beneath the gum trees like a forsaken maiden in romance, she exerted all her energies to impart to her brother's home that air of comfort which a true Englishwoman disseminates wherever she goes. There was always something to be done, and she entered into the rough life with a hearty good will, and at length found herself absolutely enjoying it.

Her brother's partner, Hugh Clements, impressed with Julia's dignified domesticity, falls in love with her, but feels it would be 'an act of profanation', because of his humble origins, to declare himself. Their mutual love is revealed during a bush fire, and their marriage, which would have been considered a mesalliance in England, happily assured.[120] In almost every story the dismal prospect of celibate poverty in overcrowded England is exchanged for a future of married prosperity in Australia. Besides affording a valuable record of comparative social history for England and Australia, Clacy's stories provided some of the most effective pieces of propaganda for middle-class female emigration, and reflected the considerable change in attitude over five years. The popular themes of female emigration had shifted dramatically from the plight of Herbert's needlewomen to a preoccupation with problems of the genteel.[121]

Emigration statistics make it impossible to quantify the extent to which single middle-class women turned to emigration during the early fifties. Greater numerical precision would indeed be helpful, but the numbers are probably less important than the certainty that the general image of emigration had changed decisively, and that by 1854 the ground had been prepared for more ambitious ventures organised by women to assist middle-class emigrants exclusively. The colonies continued to be associated with hard work, and to some extent for the middle-class with social decline,[122] but rarely, as Wakefield had complained, with crime, degradation and pauperism. Technical improvements in communications, too, began from mid-century to erase prejudices against a long and fearsome voyage, especially to the Antipodes.[123] For middle-class women the changes meant that emigration no longer involved the traumatic ordeal experienced by early-Victorian women who had braved the rigours of working-class emigration schemes, often in steerage conditions. By 1859 the early feminists, anxious to exploit every possible outlet for women of their own class, recognised the potential value of the changed climate. Henceforth female emigration would be a respectable and serious business.

Notes

1. H.S. Chapman, 'Emigration: Comparative Prospects of Our New Colonies,' *Westminster Review*, vol. XXXV, Jan. 1841, p. 132.

2. *Colonial Magazine and East India Review*, vol. XXI, April 1851, p. 344.

3. Emigration Commissioners to H. Merivale (Permanent Undersecretary), 14 July 1849, and H. Clarke to B. Hawes, 23 June 1849, *PP* 1850, XL [1163], pp. 98-101. The Colonial Land and Emigration Commission was formed in 1842 as a sub-branch of the Colonial Office to administer affairs relating to Colonial lands and emigration; T.F. Elliot was the first Chief Commissioner; see F.H. Hitchins, *The Colonial Land and Emigration Commission* (Philadelphia, 1931).

4. H. Clarke to B. Hawes, with prospectus, 23 June 1849, and Clarke to Grey, 10 Aug. 1849, *PP.* 1850, XL [1163], pp. 98-102.

5. Commissioners to Merivale, 14 July 1849, ibid., pp. 100-1.

6. Lt Gov. Sir H.E.F. Young to Grey, Adelaide, 26 Jan. 1850, *PP* 1851, XL (347-II), p. 15. Elliot to Clarke, 27 May 1850, CO 385/24.

7. Fitzroy to Grey, 23 April 1850, *PP* 1851, XL (347), pp. 42-3. Lt Gov. Sir W. Denison to Grey, 18 July 1850, *PP* 1851, XL (347-II), pp. 140-2. Not all the colonists agreed with the official assessment; Denison's despatch included a letter from Walter A. Bethune, a leading grazier, JP and Legislative Council member, who, in applying for one of the society's governesses, claimed that many Van Diemen's Land families would willingly hire such women at double the salaries paid in Scotland, then £30 to £40.

8. F. Merewether's report in Fitzroy to Grey, ibid.

9. Clarke to Grey, 10 Aug. 1849, *PP* 1850, XL [1163], pp. 98-102.

10. Commissioners to H. Merivale (Permanent Undersecretary), 14 Jan. 1848 and 17 Feb. 1848; Grey to Fitzroy, 31 Jan. 1848 and 28 Feb. 1848, *PP* 1847-48, XLVII [986], pp. 83-4, 88-90; cf. Madgwick, pp. 193-9.

11. The scheme raised the familiar spectre of popery and religious sectarianism in Australia. Fitzroy to Grey, 16 June 1849, *PP* 1850, XL [1163], pp. 48-50.

Therry, pp. 412-13. Significantly, Australian colonists later requested more Irish orphan girls to counteract the massive influx of single male gold diggers; Young to Newcastle, 27 Oct. 1853, *PP* 1854, XLVI (436-I), pp. 21-2. The Permanent Undersecretary, Herman Merivale, later asserted that the orphan emigration had enabled Victoria to remain 'free from the worst features of the turbulence, vice and insecurity, which attended the height of the gold fever in California'. *Lectures on Colonization and the Colonies* (London, 1861), pp. 472-3.

12. Hansard, *Debates*, 3rd Ser., vol. CVIII, Lords, 15 Feb. 1850, cc. 809-813.

13. *Illustrated London News*, 16 Feb. 1850, p. 115.

14. *The Times*, 24 Sept. 1851, p. 4.

15. *Australia and New Zealand Gazette* (London), 5 Feb. 1853, pp. 130-1., *Spectator*, 8 and 29 Dec. 1849, pp. 1158-9. 1232.

16. See the discussion of Caroline Chisholm below.

17. E. Mackenzie, *Mackenzie's Australian Emigrant's Guide* (London, 1852), p. 2.

18. E.G. Wakefield, *A View of the Art of Colonization* (London, 1849), pp. 135-6, 140-7.

19. Ibid., pp. 72, 152-8.

20. Cf. Bloomfield, pp. 1-14.

21. Wakefield, *Art of Colonization*, pp. 158-61.

22. Cf. Bloomfield, pp. 292-324, and C.E. Carrington, *John Robert Godley of Canterbury* (London, 1950), pp. 47-94.

23. The committee boasted 18 prominent clerics, 16 aristocrats and eleven members of Parliament, including Archbishop Whately of Dublin, Bishop Blomfield of London, Lord Ashley, Sidney Herbert, the Earl of Lincoln and Lord John Manners. Bloomfield, Appendix G, pp. 352-3.

24. The first of four ships for Christchurch, which sailed in September, 1850, carried 127 cabin passengers at £42 a berth, 85 intermediate passengers at £25 a berth, and 534 steerage passengers at £15 a berth. Carrington, pp. 94-95.

25. Bloomfield, p. 318.

26. *The Times*, 18 April 1850, pp. 4, 8; 5 July 1851, p. 8. At a well publicised shipboard banquet for the Canterbury gentry on 30 July 1850, the bishop-designate, the Rev. Thomas Jackson, set the tone by proclaiming that Canterbury would not be a colony 'where men drink and do not dress for dinner'. Carrington, p. 87.

27. 'Canterbury, New Zealand', *Fraser's Magazine*, vol. XLII, 1850, p. 468.

28. A guide to London charities in 1850 observed that emigration was now so universally recognised 'as the panacea for destitution and distress' that 'no opportunity is lost of advertising into notoriety various schemes of private interest, and advocating peculiar measures'. S. Low, *The Charities of London* (London, 1850), p. 152.

29. Low, pp. 160-1. D. Fraser, *Mary Jane Kinnaird* (London, 1890), p. 65. *Emigrant's Penny Magazine*, vol. I, no. 2, June, 1850, pp. 25-29, vol. II, no. 11, March 1851, pp. 71-4. *The Times*, 17 April 1850, p. 6, 24 April 1852, p. 7. *Australia and New Zealand Gazette*, 23 Aug. 1851, pp. 373-374. Ellen Layton, 'On the Superintendence of Female Emigrants,' NAPSS, *Transactions*, 1863, pp. 616-18. Other charitable societies not expressly designed to assist emigration, such as the Governesses Benevolent Institution and the Jewish Ladies Benevolent Loan and Visiting Society looked to emigration at this time as a means of relief for middle-class women. Report of Commissioners, 14 July 1849, in Grey to Fitzroy, 30 July 1849, *PP* 1850, XL [1163], pp. 100-1; M.S. Oppenheim (Hon. Sec. of Jewish Ladies Society) to Newcastle and Commissioners, 10 June 1853, CO 384/91.

30. The large number of letters on emigration received by *Chambers's Edin-*

burgh Journal prompted a writer to claim that it was currently the subject with the strongest hold on the public mind. 'A New Emigration Field', vol. XII, 20 Oct. 1849, p. 249. Five months later an article began, 'Never was there a period at which the public mind was more deeply stirred by the question of emigration than at the present moment.' 'Mrs Chisholm', vol. XIII, 30 March 1850, p. 201. As late as 1855 an emigrants guide claimed that emigration 'rages as a national epidemic'. E. Mackenzie, *The Emigrant's Guide to Australia* (London, 1852), p. 3.

31. Despite her contemporary reputation Chisholm's importance was neglected until the publication of a biograpy by Margaret Kiddle, *Caroline Chisholm* (Melbourne, 1950).

32. Ibid., pp. 21-62. Therry, pp. 418-22. C. Chisholm, *The A.B.C. of Colonization* (London, 1850), p. 22. E. Mackenzie, *Memoirs of Mrs Caroline Chisholm* (London, 1852), pp. 43-68.

33. Lord Ashley was president of the society. Kiddle, p. 130.

34. Ibid., pp. 130-61. Anon., *What has Mrs Caroline Chisholm done for New South Wales?* (Sydney, 1862), pp. 5-12. Mackenzie, *The Emigrant's Guide*, pp. 27-8.

35. The receiving colonies were sufficiently convinced of the society's value, in contrast to the Government system, to vote substantial grants for its exclusive use, £10,000 from NSW and £5,000 from Victoria. Kiddle, pp. 180-1.

36. 'Over Legislation', *Westminster Review*, vol. LX, July 1853, p. 70.

37. 'Better Ties than Red Tape Ties', *Household Words*, vol. IV, 28 Feb. 1852, p. 532.

38. *The Times*, 24 Sept. 1851, p. 4.

39. Ibid., p. 8.

40. *What has Mrs Caroline Chisholm done for NSW?*, p. 6.

41. Cf. Coral Lansbury, *Arcady in Australia: The Evocation of Australia in Nineteenth-Century English Literature* (Melbourne, 1970), pp. 69-73.

42. Cf. Raymond Williams, *Culture and Society, 1780-1850* (London, 1963), pp. 104-8.

43. 'A Bundle of Emigrants' Letters', vol. I, 30 March 1850, pp. 19-24. See also 'Family Colonisation Society,' vol. I, 24 Aug. 1850, pp. 514-15; 'Safety for Female Emigrants,' vol. III, 31 May 1851, p. 228; 'Pictures of Life in Australia,' vol. I, 22 June 1850, pp. 307-10. Cf. Kiddle, pp. 140-54, and P.H. Fitzgerald, *Memories of Charles Dickens with an Account of Household Words* (Bristol, 1913), pp. 135, 299.

44. 'Three Colonial Epochs', vol. IV, 31 Jan. 1852, pp. 433-8.

45. *David Copperfield* (London, 1849-1850), chs. 51, 57, 63.

46. C. Chisholm, *Emigration and Transportation Relatively Considered* (London, 1847), pp. 21-2.

47. A Summers, *Damned Whores and God's Police: The Colonization of Women in Australia* (Ringwood, 1975), pp. 291-316.

48. Chisholm, *A.B.C. of Colonization*, pp. 30-1.

49. 'Pictures of Life in Australia', *Household Words*, vol. I, 22 June 1850, pp. 307-10.

50. Chisholm, *A.B.C. of Colonization*, pp. 7-11.

51. 'Safety for Female Emigrants', *Household Words*, vol. III, 31 May 1851, p. 228.

52. Report of Chisholm's address at Greenwich Mechanic's Institute, *The Times*, 5 Jan. 1853, p. 5. *What has Mrs Caroline Chisholm done for NSW?*, p. 6.

53. R. Lowe, 'Mrs Caroline Chisholm,' in *What has Mrs Caroline Chisholm done for NSW?*, pp. 20-1.

54. *The Times*, 8 Aug. 1853, p. 6.

55. Chisholm, *Emigration and Transportation Relatively Considered*, p. 20.

56. Chisholm admitted that 'I should not feel the interest I do in female emigration if I did not look beyond providing families with female servants – if I did not know how much moral good they may spread forth in society as wives', but she was careful to add that in all her matchmaking expeditions in NSW she allowed no immediate engagements or employment in bachelors' premises, instead placing the women with families in areas where wives were in the most obvious demand. Mackenzie, *Memoirs of Caroline Chisholm*, pp. 95-106. Mackenzie's emigrants guide included a lengthy warning to women not to accept immediate proposals on arrival without proper acquaintance and courtship. *The Emigrant's Guide to Australia*, pp. 127-8. J.F. Hogan gave the same warning 20 years later, and maintained that 99% of female emigrants were influenced by the hope of immediate marriage. *The Irish in Australia* (London, 1887), pp. 164-5.

57. For an account of the formation of the scheme see E.P. Thompson, 'Mayhew and the *Morning Chronicle*,' in E.P. Thompson and Eileen Yeo, *The Unknown Mayhew* (London, 1973), pp. 24-6.

58. The 'Home' was rented from the Society for Improving the Condition of the Labouring Classes at £130 a year. S. Herbert, *First Report of the Committee of the Fund for Promoting Female Emigration* (London, March, 1851).

59. 'A Rainy Day on the *Euphrates*', *Household Words*, vol. IV, 24 Jan. 1852, pp. 409-414.

60. The emphasis on domestic training foreshadowed a similar preoccupation of middle-class emigration societies later in the century. See below, ch. 6.

61. The Emigration Commissioners had greeted Herbert's original proposal with a warning against inherent evils in the scheme, and related a detailed history of the London Emigration Committee's experience in the 1830s. Commissioners to Herbert, *PP* 1850, XL (1163), pp. 166-9.

62. *The Times*, 2 Jan. 1852, p. 4. See also the similar praise during a Commons debate on female emigration. *Debates*, 3rd Ser., vol. CXI, 28 May 1850, c. 444.

63. *Australia and New Zealand Gazette*, 12 July 1851, pp. 324-5, 5 Feb. 1853, pp. 130-1.

64. 'Ellen Linn the Needlewoman' in *Tait's* described the heart-rending tale of an unemployed, starving needleworker, desperately seeking a character testimonial in order to join her lover in Australia. Her sudden madness from accumulated misfortunes, just before the arrival of long-sought help, implied, without much subtlety, that the cumbersome regulations of state emigration were inadequate to deal with the intimate personal needs of distressed needlewomen. *Tait's Edinburgh Review*, vol. XVII, Aug. 1850, pp. 465-70.

65. *Punch*, vol. XVIII, 5 Jan. 1850, p. 1. *Illustrated London News*, 17 Aug. 1850, p. 156.

66. Ibid., p. 156.

67. Herbert, like Chisholm, obtained valuable support and publicity from Charles Dickens. See especially the detailed description of one of the ships' departures in *Household Words*. 'A Rainy Day on the *Euphrates*', vol. IV, 24 Jan. 1852, pp. 409-14.

68. *The Times*, 6 Dec. 1849, p. 3.

69. Ibid., 2 Jan. 1850, p. 4.

70. 'The Needlewoman's Farewell', *Punch*, vol. XVIII, 12 Jan. 1850, p. 14. A leader in *The Times* commented on Herbert's annual report that the emigrants wrote 'above all of the perfect facility with which excellent husbands are forthcoming on the faintest inquiry, or indeed, without any inquiry at all. It is all *Acis* and *Galatea* in practice'. 2 Jan. 1852, p. 4.

71. 'The moral amendment of Australia', he added, 'lies in hearths and homes.' S. Sidney, *Female Emigration as it is – as it may be; A Letter to the Rt. Hon. Sidney Herbert, M.P.* (London, 11 Jan. 1850), pp. 1, 5, 14.

72. Address of Rev. B. Noel to emigrants on *Northumberland. The Times*, 3 Aug. 1852, p. 8.

73. 'The Iron Seamstress', vol. VIII, 11 Feb. 1854, p. 575.

74. Correspondence between Brown and Herbert dated 5, 12, 19 Jan. 1850 in *Liverpool Mercury*, 22 Jan. 1850, p. 53. Cf. W. Shaw, *An Affectionate Pleading for England's Oppressed Female Workers* (London, 1850), p. 20.

75. Herbert, *First Report*, p. 4.

76. Out of 90 emigrants to Victoria from 1 July, 1851 to 30 June 1852, 51 were domestic servants, 27 milliners and dressmakers and 12 not designated, while 64 of them took work as domestic servants in the colony. In 1853 there were 46 servants, 49 needlewomen and 25 others, of whom 91 entered domestic service. Reports of Victoria Immigration Agent, 30 June 1852, Appendix 16, in La Trobe to Pakington, 6 Aug. 1852, *PP* 1852-3, LXVIII (1627), pp. 139-45, 160; Lt Gov. Sir C Hotham to Sir Geo. Grey, 24 Oct. 1854, CO 309/27.

77. Sidney, p. 13.

78. Herbert, *First Report*, pp. 4, 35-8.

79. La Trobe to Herbert, 19 July 1850, in Fitzroy to Grey, 17 Oct. 1850, *PP* 1851, XL (347), pp. 52-4.

80. Report on Herbert's immigrants, 24 Oct. 1853, *Votes and Proceedings*, Legislative Council, Victoria, 1853-1854, vol. I, p. 472. See also F. Merewether's complaints of unqualified women sent to NSW in the *Jane Morrison*, letter to Herbert, 2 Nov. 1850, Herbert Papers.

81. Accounts of departures in *The Times* of 3 Aug. 1852, p. 8, 17 Aug. 1852, p. 8, 17 Sept. 1852, p. 5. See also letter from C.S. in 'A Rainy Day on the *Euphrates*,' *Household Words*, vol. IV, 24 Jan. 1852, pp. 409-14.

82. *The Times*, 1 July 1851, p. 5.

83. *Australia and New Zealand Gazette*, 12 July 1851, pp. 324-5.

84. Ibid., 5 Feb. 1853, pp. 130-1.

85. Ibid., 21 May 1853, pp. 490-1.

86. Ibid., 18 June 1853, p. 587.

87. Herbert had been one of the group of Peelite proprietors of the *Morning Chronicle* since February 1848. Thompson, p. 20.

88. *Morning Chronicle*, 8 July 1853, pp. 4-5.

89. *Australia and New Zealand Gazette*, 16 July 1853, pp. 684-5.

90. Evidence of A. Chisholm to Select Committee of Victoria Legislative Council on Immigration, 10 Aug. 1852, QQ 211-213, pp. 8-9, *Votes and Proceedings*, Legislative Council, 1852-3.

91. Report of address at Greenwich Mechanics' Institute, *The Times*, 5 Jan. 1853, p. 5.

92. Kiddle, p. 181.

93. *Argus*, Melbourne, 31 Aug. 1853, quoted, ibid.

94. W.S. Shepperson, *British Emigration to North America* (Oxford, 1957), pp. 124-5.

95. Kiddle, pp. 192-3. Kiddle reproduced one of the engravings of Herbert's emigrants 'between decks' from the *Illustrated London News*, 17 Aug. 1850, p. 156, implying that the illustration depicted Chisholm's emigrants. In fact the engravings accompanied a eulogistic article on Herbert's society, p. 154.

96. Report of Immigration Agent for 1852, Victoria, 9 June 1853, Appendix 4, *PP* 1854, XLVI (436), pp. 168-9.

97. *Morning Chronicle*, 8 July 1853, pp. 4-5. *Australia and New Zealand Gazette*, 21 May 1853, pp. 490-1.

98. Report on Herbert's immigrants, 24 Oct. 1853, *Votes and Proceedings*, Legislative Council, Victoria, 1853-4, vol. I, p. 472.

99. *The Times*, 8 Dec. 1853, p. 8.

100. 'The Iron Seamstress', *Household Words*, vol. VIII, 11 Feb. 1854, pp. 575-6; 'Employments of Women,' *Chambers's Edinburgh Journal*, vol. XX, 3 Sept. 1853, p. 156.

101. To the end of 1852 the society assisted 1071 women in 29 ships. In 1853 it sent six more ships on the old plan, three of which carried 120 women to Victoria. Assuming the customary average of 40 women in each ship the remaining three ships would have carried a further 120 women, bringing the total to 1311, not including the 40 middle-class women assisted in August 1853. *Illustrated London News*, 12 March 1853, p. 204; Report of Victoria Immigration Agent, 1853, in Hotham to Sir G. Grey, 24 Oct. 1854. CO 309/27.

102. See below ch. 5.

103. Mackenzie, *The Emigrant's Guide to Australia*, p. 3.

104. Ferenczi, vol. I, p. 627.

105. *The Times*, 4 Nov. 1852, p. 4. After the news of the first gold discoveries reached England *The Times* predicted that gold would cause the convict element to be swamped by the sudden influx of newcomers 'bringing with them the feelings and associations of English citizens' and forcing an end to convict transportation. 4 Sept. 1851, p. 4; 23 Sept. 1851, p. 4.

106. Cf. F. Musgrove, *The Migratory Elite* (London, 1963), pp. 17-28.

107. La Trobe to Pakington, 28 Oct. 1852, *PP* 1852-53, LXIV (1607), p. 261.

108. Reports of Colonial Land and Emigration Commissioners for 1851, 1852 and 1853, *PP* 1852, XVIII (1499), p. 28 and Appendix no. 27; *PP* 1852-53, XL (1647), p. 21; *PP* 1854, XXVIII (1833), pp. 10-11. Cf. W.P. Morrell, *The Gold Rushes* (New York, 1941), pp. 221-3; G. Nadel, *Australia's Colonial Culture* (Melbourne, 1957), p. 43.

109. H. Fleming, *Rossetti and the Pre-Raphaelite Brotherhood* (London, 1967), pp. 189, 206. L. Parris, *The Pre-Raphaelites* (Tate Gallery, 1966), plate 19 and comments, including Brown's discussion of the models for his emigrants.

110. See Report of Select Committee of Legislative Council of Victoria, 1853. *Votes and Proceedings*, Legislative Council, Victoria, 1852-3. p. 21. From March, 1851 to March 1854 the Victorian male population increased from 46,202 to 155,887, while the female population rose from 31,143 to 80,911, *Victorian Year Book*, 1874, p. 62.

111. Report from Immigration Agent, Van Diemen's Land, 31 Jan. 1853, in Lt. Gov. Sir W.T. Denison to Pakington, 1 April, 1853, *PP* 1854, XLVI *(436-I)*, pp. 51-64. See also the enclosed official pamphlet, 'Information Regarding the Colony of Van Diemen's Land,' pp. 99-100.

112. Mackenzie, *The Emigrant's Guide to Australia*, pp. 36-7; see also Mackenzie, *Memoirs of Mrs Caroline Chisholm*, p. 172.

113. *The Times*, 16 Aug. 1853, p. 8.

114. E. Eastlake, 'Lady Travellers' (reviewing Meredith's *Notes and Sketches of New South Wales* (1844)), *Quarterly Review*, vol. LXXVI, June 1845, pp. 98-136.

115. L.A. Meredith, *My Home in Tasmania* (London, 1852), vol. II, pp. 150-2.

116. The first edition sold out immediately, to be followed by a second edition in 1853; see pp. 7-9 of 1963 edition.

117. Clacy, p. 151.

118. Mrs C. Clacy, *Lights and Shadows of Australian Life* (London, 1854), vol. I, pp. v-vi. For a more blatant example of fiction serving as emigration propaganda see W.H.G. Kingston, *How to Emigrate: or the British Colonists. A Tale for all Classes* (London, 1850); Kingston's story was a model of multi-class emigration to Australia.

119. Clacy, 'Leaves from a Young Lady's Diary,' vol. II, p. 258.

120. 'The Bush Fire,' ibid., vol. I, pp. 165-84.

121. The propagandistic fiction, too, contrasted starkly with the grim lessons of 'Ellen Linn the Needlewoman' four years earlier. See above note 64.
122. Cf. Peterson, in *Vicinus*, pp. 16-17.
123. See the estimate in the *Illustrated London News*, 21 Aug. 1852, p. 125, of a 50-day journey in a fast mail steamer from Liverpool to Melbourne, a revolutionary prospect when compared to the old sailing voyage of 100 days.

5 FEMINISM AND FEMALE EMIGRATION, 1861-1886

'Lady Baldock is blooming', said Lord Fawn; 'certainly blooming; — that is, if evergreens may be said to bloom.'

'Evergreens do bloom, as well as spring plants, Lord Fawn. You come and see her, Mr. Finn; — only you must bring a little money with you for the Female Protestant Unmarried Women's Emigration Society. That is my aunt's present hobby, as Lord Fawn knows to his cost.'

'I wish I may never spend half-a-sovereign worse.'

'But it is a perilous affair for me, as my aunt wants me to go out as a sort of leading Protestant unmarried female emigrant pioneer myself.'

'You don't mean that', said Lord Fawn, with much anxiety.

'Of course you'll go', said Phineas. 'I should if I were you.'

'I am in doubt', said Violet.

'It is such a grand prospect', said he. 'Such an opening in life. So much excitement, you know; and such a useful career.'

A. Trollope, *Phineas Finn* (1869), Chap. 41.

Trollope's proposed career for Violet Effingham and his portrayal of enthusiastic benevolence by polite society gave some idea of the respectability accruing to female emigration by 1869, which had been flourishing for nearly a decade by the time he wrote. Not surprisingly, Trollope's fictional equivalent gave no hint of the feminist origins of the real organisation, the Female Middle-Class Emigration Society, formed in 1862 amidst controversy about the 'excess' of women in Britain, the dangers of promoting 'matrimonial colonisation' and the demand for governesses in the colonies. For this reason it would be easy to be misled by Trollope's optimistic impression. Certainly evidence presented in previous chapters should leave no doubt of the potential demand for emigration among single middle-class women, and of their ability to adapt to radical changes in their social environment. All that seemed necessary to tap the demand was a respectable organisation able to offer encouragement, assistance and protection; female emigration might then become a significant social and demographic force, and by the 1850s the climate seemed ripe for such a development. By the 1880s, with a new generation of female emigration societies, something of this sort actually occurred, but the emigration movement launched in 1860 could claim only modest success, at least in numerical terms. The middle-class feminist movement which developed in the late 50s soon found itself in conflict, theoretically at least, with some awkward implications of female emigration to new settlement colonies, and the resulting tensions acted to limit the operations of the FMCES to token proportions; it helped a mere 302 women to emigrate between 1862 and 1886. This chapter will be concerned mainly with the working out of those tensions, but will also draw on a valuable collection of letters from FMCES emigrants to illustrate the impact of emigration on those women helped by the society.

The encouragement of middle-class emigration did not lag far behind the first stirrings of the middle-class feminist movement in the late 1850s. With few exceptions the movement focused, from the beginning, on the educational and employment problems of single and widowed women of the middle class; time and again they were forced to confront the familiar problem of the distressed gentlewoman, and the logic of their work led naturally to an exploration of the utility of emigration as one of the many solutions. A search for fundamental remedies for inadequate education and restricted employment opportunities was evident in the earliest expressions of the new movement. In particular the founding of the first feminist journal,[1] the participation of women and sympathetic men in the annual congresses of the National Association for the Promotion of Social Science[2] and encouragement from prominent women such as Harriet Martineau[3] indicated the dimensions of the problem and stimulated the first practical ventures. But from the beginning the 'Ladies of Langham Place', as the first activists were nicknamed, faced some awkward questions of priorities. Feminist speakers at the early Social Science Congresses were mainly preoccupied with the need to find wider employment opportunities outside the overcrowded trades of teaching and needlework.[4] But there was general agreement that they must give female education priority before, in the long term, they could 'open a fair field to the powers and energies we have educed'.[5] In the meantime thousands of ill-educated women sought immediate work. Bessie Parkes, the editor of the *English Woman's Journal*, asked whether 'we are trying to tide the female population of this country over a time of difficulty, or are we seeking to develop a new state of social life?'[6] In fact most feminists worked vigorously toward both ends, so that the long-term campaign for higher education and professional qualifications co-existed with a search for short-term palliatives to alleviate pressing employment problems.

The search for new forms of employment available to young ladies, however, was beset with difficulties. The feminist Society for Promoting the Employment of Women, founded in 1859, recognised that teaching was becoming a more precarious occupation for untrained ladies.[7] By the 1860s it was more difficult than ever for a woman with a superficial education to become even a moderately paid governess. The new secondary schools for women founded after 1848 had quickly become prestige institutions catering largely to the upper middle class.[8] Many of their graduates took up teaching as a serious profession, and very soon their superior qualifications did much 'to raise the standard and improve the tone of education generally'; by the 1860s they had become the generally accepted standard for governesses.[9] Sarah Harland, a mathematics lecturer at Newnham College, observed later that 'the usual opening for impecunious gentlewomen, that of teaching, had been taken up by others with higher qualifications for the work, who are without the impulse of poverty'.[10] The Employment Society's initial policy, therefore, was to endow more suspect occupations with a new air of respectability and thereby open them to women of a higher social class. They concentrated on manual occupations from which many Victorian young ladies would shrink. The earliest openings came in telegraph offices, printing, lithography, hairdressing and various semi-menial vocations.[11] But with the exception of law-copying and book-keeping most of these new opportunities appealed primarily to upwardly mobile women from the working class and lower middle class. Bessie Parkes estimated in 1860 that these 'less refined' women constituted one third of the middle-class female work force. She added that most of the 'semi-mechanical employments' so assiduously promoted by the feminist employment societies were only suitable for this class; the salary of a telegraph clerk, after all, hardly allowed her to look and live 'like a lady'.[12] The mass of untrained distressed gentlewomen were consequently helped little by the first *ad hoc* measures to relieve the pressure for employment, and they were invariably forced back into some form of underpaid teaching.

Office work provided one of the few new outlets that would not compromise a lady's gentility, and significantly it was the overwhelming demand for such employment among gentlewomen that led the feminists to promote emigration. Maria S. Rye had these women in mind when she opened a law-copying office in Lincolns Inn Fields as a branch of the Employment Society. Recruiting women as copyists was a simple matter. Rye was inundated with applications and on one occasion 810 women applied for a single position paying only £15 a year. Faced with this situation, she quite independently advised and assisted the applicants to emigrate, and in 1861, without any formal organisation, she helped twenty-two educated women to reach various colonies by providing loans and arranging for their protection and reception.[13] Spurred by this success, the emigration idea spread rapidly among the feminist circle at the Social Science Association and the employment societies, who initially saw it as a panacea for women of a 'superior class' who were unemployable in Britain. At the Social Science Congress in 1860 Bessie Parkes argued that many women, unsuited to the 'semi-mechanical arts', required

> a wider field of intellectual and moral exertion than the compositor's case or the law copyists desk can afford; and seeing, as I do daily, how great is the comparative delicacy both in brain and in the bodily frames of women of the middle and upper class, of the bad effect on them of hours of sedentary toil, and of competitive employment, the more anxious I become to see the immense surplus of the sex in England lightened by judicious, well-conducted, and morally guarded emigration to our colonies, where the disproportion is equally enormous, and where they are wanted in every social capacity.

She hoped that large-scale emigration would allow the remaining gentlewomen in Britain to be trained 'in all those functions of administrative benevolence, which are in fact but a development of household qualities'.[14]

Encouraged by the general support, Maria Rye described her work at the 1861 Social Science Congress and appealed for help in establishing a formal society to promote the emigration of educated women. Like Bessie Parkes, she saw emigration as the basic solution to the problem of distressed gentlewomen in Britain, and she expected that the colonies would benefit equally from their civilising influence, 'an elevation of morals being the inevitable result of the mere presence in the colony of a number of high class women'. Significantly, though, her brief experience with female emigrants had already raised the troublesome question of domestic service in the colonies. She had communicated with interested persons in Australia, New Zealand and Natal who had impressed upon her their pressing need for domestic servants. To meet this need she suggested that a dual emigration system of gentlewomen and 'superior servants' might be established. The various colonial assisted immigration schemes strictly excluded all women above the working-class. She therefore advocated a system of loans to a wide range of middle-class women, with a network of representatives in each colony to receive the emigrants and arrange appropriate employment.[15] At the same meeting other speakers, including the General Secretary, G.W. Hastings, made enthusiastic reference to emigration as the 'best and natural solution' and the 'truest remedy' for educated women.[16] Rye's efforts culminated in the formation of the Female Middle-Class Emigration Society in May, 1862, but in the meantime the rapid publication of her paper as a separate pamphlet and its appearance in the *English Woman's Journal* publicised the subject beyond feminist circles, and a popular debate ensued, in *The Times* particularly, on the merits of female emigration.

Despite its unmistakeable tone of approval,[17] the press debate soon revealed that female emigration was unlikely to proceed without encountering practical difficulties and public controversy. The first difficulty was the familiar one which had already inhibited earlier efforts to send single gentlewomen to the colonies. It arose from frequent assertions that there was insufficient colonial demand for working gentlewomen, especially for governesses. 'J.K. A Returned Australian Governess' described to *The Times* how she was forced to do daily needlework in Melbourne because of the sparse demand for governesses, and finally returned to England on the proceeds of a subscription raised by her friends.[18] Other letters warned against sending governesses to Australia without prearranged employment, and 'S.G.O.' (Lord Osborne) suggested that the women most in need of emigration would be least qualified to fill the position of really competent governesses. To send out women who were useless to the colonies would be worse folly than to send convicts.[19] More ominously, Stephen Walcott, a member of the Land and Emigration Board, reported that the latest information from Australia indicated no demand whatever for such a 'superior class' of women as governesses; a few might succeed if they had friends in the colony to care for them indefinitely, but any large-scale project would only end in disappointment and disaster.[20] These forebodings failed to daunt Maria Rye, for she maintained that the experience of her own emigrants, who had all obtained well-paying situations, was exactly to the contrary. She insisted that there were openings 'for many hundreds of women vastly superior to the hordes of wild Irish and fast young ladies who have hitherto started as emigrants'.[21]

A second difficulty raised some particularly awkward questions for

a feminist society purporting to extend opportunities for women
beyond marriage and motherhood. The Christian Socialist, Charles
Kingsley, candidly praised Rye's venture on the ground that all attempts
to open new occupations to women were mere substitutes 'for that far
nobler and more useful work which Nature intends her — to marry and
bear children'.[22] His implication that the new society would be little
more than a colonial marriage bureau sparked an immediate controversy
over the merits of 'matrimonial colonisation'. Kingsley's brother-in-law,
Lord Osborne, protested at the mere hint that emigration for work
might become a masquerade for a degrading form of husband-hunting.[23]
A *Times* leader answered by asserting that the imbalance of the sexes in
Britain and Australia rendered female emigration a necessity, whatever
the pretext; and in any case a woman who emigrated under responsible
and respectable protection 'is guilty of no more indelicacy than a girl
who goes to a ball or an archery meeting'.[24] Again Maria Rye intervened
in the argument: if women were not so fastidious about whom they
married at home they could easily find unworthy (i.e. lower-class) husbands immediately; there was no reason to think they would be less
scrupulous in the colonies. Her society sought to find decent employment for women overseas, and marriage was a matter for individual
decision.[25] However circular the debate, the stress on marriage and
women's natural work contained important implications for the future
conduct of the society. As *The Times* argued, all prospective emigrants,
no matter what their destiny, must possess 'an industrial training and
domestic accomplishments even more than they are likely to want in
this country'.[26] These 'domestic accomplishments' might reasonably be
expected to predetermine, to some extent, a woman's future career
abroad, a realisation which was not lost on later female emigration
societies.

It was ironic, and perhaps unfortunate for the FMCES, that the controversy over its formation coincided with a heightened interest in the
problem of the disproportion between the sexes in Britain and the
complementary shortage of women in the colonies.[27] The interlocking
controversies over the 'redundancy' of women and the apparent panacea
of emigration raised sensitive issues for feminists and prompted some of
them to oppose emigration because it was a popular anti-feminist solution. It appeared all too readily as a device to confine women to their
'proper sphere' of the household and as an unjust safety valve to siphon
off pressure for progressive reform. The most irritating provocation was
William Rathbone Greg's frequently reprinted essay 'Why are Women
Redundant?'[28] For Greg, all the surplus women were 'redundant' only

in the sense that they lacked the opportunity to fulfil their 'natural' role in relation to men. Domestic servants, for example, were not redundant because they 'fulfill both essentials of a woman's being, *they are supported by and they minister to men.* We could not possibly do without them'. Greg blamed the heavier emigration of men for altering the balance, but female emigration could now create the 'natural rectification' by providing wives for the surplus men in North America and Australia. Only a massive emigration of up to 40,000 women a year, in the spirit of Caroline Chisholm's work, would suffice to eliminate the redundancy of 405,000 adult women in Britain. He estimated that the largest group of redundant women belonged to the class immediately above the labouring poor, 'the daughters of unfortunate tradesmen, of poor clerks, or poorer curates'. These women had all been disciplined 'in the appropriate school of poverty and exertion', and their education and refinement would insure their adaptability to new conditions in the colonies. The one thing to avoid was the feminist solution of making single life as easy, attractive and lucrative as it was for men, and thereby encouraging further 'redundancy' of women.[29]

In 1862, as we have seen, the feminists were by no means opposed to female emigration, but Greg's blatant association of emigration with anti-feminism, together with some discouraging reports from the colonies, caused many of them to change sides. Frances Power Cobbe thought Greg's remedy amounted to a sentence of transportation or starvation for all old maids. She favoured emigration to give women a free choice between marriage and profitable employment — a choice most women were still unable to exercise in Britain — but estimated that the colonial demand for educated women was so low as to render the proposal irrelevant to women's problems.[30] By 1863 there was further confirmation from some colonies that the demand for governesses was limited, and Jessie Boucherett, a founder of the Employment Society, regretted that this seemingly obvious solution to the quest for women's work would provide little relief while women lacked specialised occupational training.[31] A writer in the *Victoria Magazine*, a new feminist journal, thought that the colonial news could only disappoint those who,

> misled by the statistical accounts of the disparity of the sexes, which, of course, reveal nothing as to the *causes* of the disparity, took for granted that the whole question of the employment of educated women could be summarily disposed of by wholesale shipments to the colonies. It may be hoped that we shall now have no more

suggestions about making homes for settlers, as the only and the very easy solution of this troublesome problem.[32]

The re-publication of Greg's essay in 1868 and 1869 brought a further round of comment. Mary Taylor's indignant reply has already been quoted. Marriage, she argued, no matter where it might be contracted, was no panacea for the problem of 'redundant' women.[33] Most feminists actually continued to support the prudent and modest efforts of the FMCES, but they were united in rejecting promotion of the idea for Greg's wrong reasons.

Regular publicity, both critical and favourable, did not prevent the society from quietly pursuing its declared objective.[34] It could not, however, evade some of the basic questions raised in the continuing debate. In the face of colonial warnings against sending governesses, Maria Rye's insistence that her own emigrants all obtained decent employment, often with several alternative offers, did not always conform to facts reflected in early private letters from the emigrants to the society. In the 1860s, especially, women frequently reported from Australia, New Zealand and South Africa that governesses' positions were scarce or ill-paid, and many experienced difficulty at first in adjusting to a situation in which, materially at least, they were no better off than in Britain. Catherine Brough complained from Cape Town in 1863 that

> I am far worse off than ever I was in England; it is next to impossible to obtain employment and the pay is so low that though I have had two temporary engagements I have not earned enough to pay my board, lodging and washing.[35]

Others, while obtaining attractive employment themselves, warned that economic depressions and competition with new colonial government schools left the governess market no better than in England, and that without qualifications in music governesses might remain unemployed indefinitely.[36] Furthermore, the critics' insistence that the women workers most needed by colonists were domestic servants, and that even the most refined and accomplished governess must be prepared to do some plain housework on occasion, demanded the society's attention. An ex-Australian resident's paper at the 1862 Social Science Congress recommended that intending emigrants should 'undergo a short training on the theory, at all events, of household work and duties, and needle-/ work of the most useful kinds, and in medicine so far as to treat ord-/

inary diseases'.[37] However unpalatable the advice might have seemed, the society could hardly ignore it.

Together, the issues of indadequate colonial demand for governesses and the need for domestic training raised the question of exactly what kind of system the organisers intended. It could be a mere agency for placing well-qualified governesses in the colonies or a more comprehensive project to enable a wide range of middle-class women to find varieties of employment, including domestic service, abroad. The different approaches of Maria Rye, and her successor, Jane Lewin, on these issues epitomised two contrasting views on female emigration and employment. Maria Rye, in the tradition of Victorian philanthropy, was content to promote the emigration of women of all classes, whether for professional work, domestic service or eventual marriage. Jane Lewin, in the newer feminist tradition, made a clear distinction between the husband-hunting advocated by Greg and the professional career concept. Ultimately Lewin's approach prevailed, with paradoxically limiting effects on the scope of the society's activities.

Rye's approach showed a keen awareness of the need for domestic preparation and adaptability on the part of educated female emigrants, and while she directed the society the special requirements dictated by rougher colonial conditions remained the prime consideration.[38] She hoped to accommodate the colonies' particular needs by maintaining a two-tier emigration system. Two classes of women, both above the working-class but different in social origins and training, would receive assistance. First, 'a few really accomplished governesses, who command from £40 to £100 in England, and who could obtain situations in the colonies, equal in money value and superior in social position and comfort'. Second,

> a class beginning with the half-educated daughters of poor professional men, and including the children of subordinate government officers, petty shopkeepers, and artisans generally, who have been accustomed to domestic economy at home, and on whom the want of employment often pressed heavily.[39]

Besides well-trained governesses, Rye hoped to send out women from the lower middle-class who may even be willing to enter domestic service. But she insisted that regardless of their origins all of them must be prepared to stoop to domestic chores, and she inserted a clause in the society's rules to that effect: 'Every applicant is examined as far as possible, with regard to her knowledge of cooking, baking, washing,

needlework, and housework, and is required to assist in these depart-
ments of labour, should it be necessary.'[40] A governess employed in
Britain might regard such a requirement as an unacceptable compromise
of her gentility, but Rye viewed it as a simple concession to the
demands of colonial employers for the sake of extending female
employment. Given her understanding of the mutual social needs of
female emigration, Rye's plans contained the seeds, at least, of a large-
scale project.

Rye's management of the society, together with her policy, however,
was short-lived. Her intimate knowledge of colonial requirements led her
progressively to an exclusive interest in working-class emigration. Almost immediately after the society's formation in May, 1862, and quite
independently of her work with it, she began to foster the emigration of
Manchester cotton operatives and other working-class women. News of
a rising demand for servants – but emphatically not governesses – in
the young colony of British Columbia prompted her to help recruit
working-class women in co-operation with the newly formed Columbian
Emigration Society. At the same time the Queensland and New Zealand
governments asked her to recruit female domestic servants for their
assisted passages. Altogether in 1862 she independently helped four
hundred women to emigrate, of whom only forty were governesses, and
she decided to accompany one-hundred of them to New Zealand.[41] Her
basic reason for leaving was to investigate the demand for women
workers in Australia and New Zealand and to complete the society's
arrangements for reception facilities. Her experience confirmed her
view that there was ample room in the Antipodes for all classes of
women, provided they were hard-working and adaptable. After her
return in 1865, however, she left the society's work to others in order
to concentrate exclusively on working-class emigration.[42]

Rye's work as Honorary Secretary of the society was taken over by
her co-worker, Jane Lewin, who occupied the position until her retirement in 1881 and conducted most of the routine administration and
interviewing. Lewin shared Rye's conviction that the most refined
women must be prepared, when required, to help with household work;
the society, she stressed, 'requires education of the hands, as well as of
the head'. But she abandoned Rye's concept of a two-tier system of
female emigration in which women without formal teaching qualifications would play a major role. Under her direction officially eligible
emigrants ranged from the highly accomplished finishing governess to 'a
woman who can do little beyond teaching English correctly'.[43] But in
practice this came to mean that she reduced the society's function to

that of a colonial placement agency for governesses, and mostly well qualified governesses. It was this factor, more than any lack of overseas demand for governesses, which constricted the society's operation to token proportions during its twenty-three years and inhibited the growth of a larger project of female emigration from the middle classes until the 1880s.

The surviving records of the society indicate that Jane Lewin pursued her objective consistently. From the society's reports it is possible to determine the initial colonial occupations of 222 out of its 302 emigrants. Of these, 113 were either governesses or school-teachers, 34 joined friends or relatives on arrival, 16 were unemployed for reasons of health, age or misconduct, 9 returned to England and 8 were ladies' companions. Only 22 took occupations that might identify them as lower middle-class, such as milliners, dressmakers, cooks, nursery-governesses and singers.[44] Furthermore, the substantial correspondence sent by emigrants back to the society indicates that many women who failed to obtain immediate employment ultimately took up teaching. Out of 114 correspondents 98 eventually turned to some form of teaching or intended to do so, and only 5 entered menial or less respectable occupations.[45] Lewin was clearly insisting on teaching qualifications from her applicants, for a later report observed that the smaller numbers of actual emigrants had been out of all proportion to the large numbers who applied.[46] The society's capacity to provide loans was undoubtedly limited, but had it encouraged a wider social cross-section of women, its ability to attract further subscriptions should have increased accordingly.[47]

The society's records, like similar material encountered in chapter 2, need to be interpreted carefully, for a woman's colonial occupation would not necessarily be a reliable guide to her social position in Britain. Since governessing was a popular means of achieving upward social advancement among women of the lower middle and working classes, and since moderate teaching ability was the main qualification, Lewin might easily have admitted women from all classes with little teaching experience. Fortunately it is precisely on this kind of question that the letters written by the women themselves are most informative and revealing. Their content invariably suggests that the writers came from middle or even upper middle-class origins. Many complained condescendingly of the breeding of their colonial employers, like Annie Davis, who, when moving to a new position in Sydney, noted that 'in my new home I shall make acquaintance with a new class of people — "*the nouveaux riches*" but I may consider myself now "colonized" so it will be only viewing a new phase of life'. She found them 'very vulgar', however, and left them after only five months.[48] Similarly, Sarah Henderson 'was certainly not remarkably comfortable in my first situation, as the husband of the person I was living with was an exceedingly vulgar low-minded man'.[49] The women complained frequently of vulgar working-class emigrants during the voyage. Marion Hett found their presence unduly irksome.

> Certainly if one could choose one would not select a ship which carried Government emigrants. The girls were always on the poop with us, and often annoyed us extremely by their levity of conduct. They ought never to come out in a ship with mixed passengers, but if possible emigrants should have a ship to themselves . . . [50]

The tone of these letters, as well as the information, suggest a level of gentility rarely encountered among the lower middle or working class. Emigrants like the station master's daughter who had been an impecunious dressmaker in England and went to Colorado as a nurse and helper were rare exceptions to the general rule, in occupational background as much as destination.[51] Many of the society's emigrants may not have been distressed, but most of them were undoubtedly gentlewomen with teaching qualifications.

The society assisted some women for whom economic or psychological hardship had clearly played little or no part in their decision to emigrate. Caroline Haselton, who could afford to send regular donations back to the society, was able to move about freely. She taught for high wages in South Africa and Australia, and her last letter from Melbourne contained inquiries about the possibility of teaching in India or South America.[52] Annie Davis was delighted with her new circumstances in Sydney, but added that her English experience 'was a singularly happy one'.[53] Many of the society's most enterprising women had sufficient capital and qualifications to be able to establish their own school after arrival. Its greatest success story in this respect was Miss S.A. Hall. She emigrated to South Africa in 1868 and nine years later made persistent requests to Lewin to send out teachers for her thriving school at Graaf Reinet, where she hoped to encourage the 'right sort' of English people 'to absorb all and every element which is antagonistic to progress' in South Africa. She obtained highly qualified teachers, all of whom had commanded good salaries in Britain; three of them were honours students from prominent English educational institutions. The society recruited at least seven women of this stamp for Hall, and each obtained a high salary in the range of £100 to £150.[54] No doubt they proved a valuable addition to Hall's school and to the English community in Graaf Reinet, but they were hardly from the class most in need of emigration. In by-passing less qualified women who had been thrown out of employment by competition with the new generation of well-educated teachers, the society was ignoring the class with the greatest social need.

Like the women encountered in previous chapters, most of the FMCES emigrants were enterprising and adaptable, adjusting, in most cases, to their new social environments with surprising rapidity. This is certainly the dominant impression gained from a reading of the emigrants' letters, but it would be misleading to suggest that the society's 302 protegées all found a governesses' *El dorado*. Many, as already described, experienced hardship in finding initial employment. Others, regardless of their employment, simply failed to adapt to colonial society. Rosa Phayne wrote from near Melbourne in 1869 to complain of the passengers on board ship, 'so very low and horrid a set' and to stress the unsuitability of Australia for cultivated women.

> I do not use too strong a language when I say *no one* with the tastes, habits, or feelings of a lady should ever come out to Australia, it may do for mediocre governesses who can put up with roughnesses, or I should rather say vulgarity of mind and great want of intellect but I never would advise a lady to try it. I hate Australia and the Australians. I shall be with them but never of them; I would rather have £15 per annum in London than £50 here.[55]

Three years later Phayne found Australia equally uncivilised and appealed to Lewin, apparently in vain, for help in returning to England. 'I am so unhappy', she concluded, 'for my family are very poor, and I am wretched out here alone.'[56] Such extremes of discontent, though, were far from being representative of the FMCES correspondents. More common were tales of initial hardship followed by moderate success after some determined perseverance. Laura Jones went to Melbourne in 1868 and became an assistant schoolmistress in a bush school run by dissenters. She lived 'in a hut about six feet square' and soon found herself ostracised because, not being a dissenter, she refused to attend chapel. After being forced to leave she 'existed by doing needlework for the diggers' wives, when I managed to get money enough to come to town'. By 1869 she was teaching English in a Melbourne boarding-school 'and am getting along a great deal better'.[57] Similarly, Mary

Wilson was most unhappy in her first governess post at £50 near
Dunedin, New Zealand, but after several months moved to Wellington
to a more congenial position with kind employers, although required to
perform housework and paid only £40. She reflected that the early
difficulties were hard to bear,

> but now I am getting more reconciled to a colonial life in many
> ways, it is so different from home, but I endeavour to suit myself to
> the people and to the place.[58]

By the 1870s even the much publicised complaints about lack of
colonial employment for governesses came to be replaced by enthusiastic claims of multiple job opportunities. In 1873 Kate Brind, in a
'first-rate situation' at £90 in Nelson, New Zealand, reported that in
Nelson and throughout New Zealand there was a 'great demand' for
good governesses. She had received many attractive offers, the greatest
drawback to most being their isolation, 'but if you make up your mind
to rough it a little you can get on very well'.[59] Six years later the
society's New Zealand correspondent, Mrs H.H. Herbert, confirmed the
'great dearth' of good governesses, although she warned that new
arrivals may first have to take 'an inferior situation' at a lower salary,
and that 'Ladies requiring the excitement of town life had better stay in
England.'[60] Similar stories came from emigrants in South Africa and
Australia, though often qualified by the insistence that a sound training
was essential.[61] The results for most emigrants were probably best
summed up by Elizabeth Long from Hawke's Bay, New Zealand, who
admitted that while colonial life was 'undoubtedly the paradise of
servants, I am afraid the paradise for governesses has yet to be discovered'.[62] A nineteenth-century governesses' paradise — or a servants'
for that matter — would indeed have been hard to discover, but most of
the FMCES emigrants rarely doubted that the colonies provided more
tolerable working conditions than they had known in England.

Under Jane Lewin's direction the society clung to her policy of
governess emigration, despite consistent evidence from its own emigrants that the colonies offered relief to gentlewomen less because of
higher wages for governesses than because they were quick to adapt to a
social environment that exerted fewer social taboos on the kind of work
middle-class women could perform with some dignity. Some emigrants
did complain about low salaries but invariably felt compensated by
close companionship in a more egalitarian social atmosphere. Mary Long
took a governess's position in a clergyman's family in Canterbury at only

£30 and did a great deal of needlework and housekeeping besides teaching four children; in spite of all this she was content because 'kindly treated and quite one of the family', and she concluded that, regardless of salary, 'I would rather be a governess here than in England.'[63] Eleanor Blackith earned the same salary at Napier, New Zealand, but had no complaints, noting that she would 'help Mrs. Simcox in anything and she treats me exactly like a sister'; in a subsequent letter, still thrilled at being treated 'exactly as one of the family', she boasted that since arriving she had 'become quite clever in the art of cooking'.[64]

The tolerance toward household chores and delight at becoming 'one of the family' pervades almost the entire correspondence of the society's emigrants. Miss L. Geoghegan became a governess in the Australian bush and was soon impressed with the lack of social discrimination against governesses; bush life, 'a strange mixture of roughing and refinement', could be dull, but 'I can rake a hoe in the garden as I please and the freedom to please oneself more than compensates for the monotony'. The position of the rural governess, she observed, could be an exalted one, despite the need to light the schoolroom fire:

> It is a totally different life from what it is at home. In nearly every instance you are looked on as the Intellectual member of the Establishment; you are the constant companion and associate of the Lady, considered — I might say indulged in every way, and your only difficulty is to civilize the children.[65]

From Dunedin, New Zealand, Eliza Brook wrote that although the work was rougher than in England, 'where everyone works there is no occasion for pride', governesses were appreciated in Dunedin and could command from £30 to £60, 'but to those who object to be on an equality with the family and are afraid to render assistance when required I do not think there is such good promise'.[66] In case Jane Lewin missed the point, Mrs Herbert, the society's representative in Hawke's Bay, New Zealand, spelt out colonial requirements yet again. To ensure adaptability, she insisted, the accent must be on youth; ladies of forty were too old to be transplanted to the roughness of colonial life; household conditions for gentlewomen were different: 'there are fewer servants — sometimes the family is left for weeks without any — and a governess who stood on her dignity and refused to help would do a foolish thing'.[67] Probably the most telling illustration of adaptability came in Miss Barlow's letter from Melbourne; after opening her own school she boasted:

I am getting quite a Colonial woman, and fear I should not easily fit into English ideas again, can scrub a floor with anyone, and bake my own bread and many other things an English Governess and Schoolmistress especially would be horrified at.[68]

From the insistence that governesses must be prepared to help with the household chores it was a short step to suggest that the less well-qualified adopt domestic service or other less respectable, menial work as their permanent, or at least initial, colonial occupation. This step Jane Lewin refused to take, despite persistent evidence that it could have been a feasible proposition. The society's emigrants and colonial representatives urged repeatedly that only highly qualified intending governesses should be sent out; teaching standards were high, especially in the cities where government schools were beginning to supplant governesses, and the mediocre would fare much better as colonial servants.[69] Annie Davis, whose own qualifications gave her ample security as a governess, remarked

Were I in the position of the third or fourth rate Governess (I was about to say second) in England, I would unhesitatingly become a domestic servant in Australia in preference . . . I have no doubt it would require some common sense and humility for such a Governess to become a Servant, and she would find herself infinitely better off (salary apart). Servants are more considered, there is more freedom and independence here than at home. If my words could reach some of my toiling sisters at home I would say 'Be sensible, undergo a little domestic training and come out here to take your chance with others with a certainty of succeeding withal.'[70]

The available evidence reveals few actual domestic servants among the society's emigrants,[71] but the letters certainly suggest that many of the women soon came to share Annie Davis' strong views and were at least prepared to turn to other forms of less respectable work when teaching was unavailable. Annie Hunt, who had worked as a law-copyist in England, refused to mix with the freshly arrived dressmakers and needlewomen in Melbourne, but was quite content to become a 'milliner-dressmaker-machinist' with a family up-country.[72] In Brisbane, Agnes MacQueen knew of many instances where intending governesses were compelled 'to take situations in shops at a better rate of pay'.[73] Miss J. Merritt, who described her employers as 'rather low', was nevertheless well-conditioned in colonial ways, and admitted candidly that she would rather become a servant than a governess at £25.[74] There was ample precedent for successfully implementing Annie Davis' suggestions, but they were unlikely to appeal to a feminist-run emigration society.

In view of the controversy that accompanied the origins of the FMCES, it is hardly surprising that Jane Lewin shrank from the concept of genteel domestic service in the colonies.[75] In some respects her policy was a triumph for middle-class feminism against those familiar notions of women's 'proper sphere' so tenaciously upheld by moralising anti-feminists like Greg and the *Saturday Review*. Indeed, given the terms of the original controversy, Lewin had little real alternative. While a more flexible policy might have helped more of those distressed gentlewomen and lower middle-class women genuinely in need of emigration, the predictable charges of 'matrimonial colonisation' could easily have been seen as a threat to the entire venture. If feminists like Lewin were to promote emigration, therefore, both ideology and expediency required it to be a path to emancipation and independence rather than a mere supportive prelude and training period for the contingency of marriage. In these terms Lewin's policy was a clear success. At the opposite end of the spectrum Maria Rye had joined the feminists simply in order to further piecemeal efforts to improve the material conditions of unemployed women, and she saw no inconsistency in later helping whole families and abandoned children to emigrate. Characteristically, she withdrew from the Society for Promoting the Employment of Women when its members joined the women's suffrage movement.[76]

Significantly the society began slowly to change its policy back to Rye's original scheme after Jane Lewin's retirement as Honorary Secretary in 1881. None of her successors were particularly prominent feminists, and one of them, Julia Blake, was attracted to the FMCES through her previous work with other emigration societies rather than through feminism.[77] The last report of the society indicated a cautious return to Rye's policy:

> Half educated teachers must be warned to turn to any other means of living, (such as 'Mother's Help'), rather than face the just competition with the well-trained teachers, who, if holding a certificate from any of our Universities, can still command a good salary.[78]

This attitude reflected the more ambitious policies being pursued by newly established emigration societies in the 1880s. But the depleted funds and modest facilities of the FMCES prevented the implementation of a new policy on any large scale. Other societies had assumed the major burden of promoting female emigration, and the old society was eventually absorbed by them.[79] The paradox of the FMCES was that in twenty-three years it probably did more to inhibit than to encourage female emigration.

The FMCES attitude to domestic service was in many respects representative of the more general attitude of middle-class feminists. During the seventies a number of schemes were canvassed to promote 'domestic service for gentlewomen' in Britain. One of these schemes, devised by Rose Mary Crawshay, established a London placement office, offered cookery lessons and placed over a hundred gentlewomen as servants within eight months.[80] The success of these projects was, understandably, short-lived, but the impact and publicity was enough to draw a sharp response from feminist critics. The *Victoria Magazine* considered the 'new-fangled term "lady-help"' a tribute to a vulgar spirit that degraded the meaning of the word 'lady', and dismissed it as an attempt to glamorise 'the unpalatable idea of domestic service'. Domestic service was unfit for gentlewomen and in any case not practical.[81] Louisa M. Hubbard, proprietor and editor of the women's magazine *Work and Leisure*, argued that gentlewomen should accept domestic service only if they were willing 'to relinquish the social position accorded to persons belonging to the educated and cultivated classes'. If faced with charity or starvation, gentlewomen should certainly turn to domestic service, and would probably be respected for their refinement by discriminating persons. But a problem remained.

> The test of class seems to us to be very much one of education and culture . . . We only suggest that a line should be drawn somewhere, and that while a lady should be ready to accept any respectable employment which will support her when she needs it, she should not expect to enjoy the privileges of education and culture while relinquishing the exercise of both in a class possessing neither.[82]

In the same book Hubbard applied a similar standard to emigration. The qualities necessary for successful emigration seemed to be precisely those which would make a woman independent of it and able to choose her own career. Capability and training were required as much in the colonies as at home.

> The only hope, therefore, for those who do not possess them is to go where the mere fact of being a woman, and therefore able to cook or

wash, or do other feminine work, in however blundering a way, may stand them in some stead.

Furthermore, conditions on emigrant ships 'are still such as would be almost unendurable to a gentlewoman, and are trying enough, even to persons accustomed to roughing it'.[83]

The feminist attitude to domestic service betrayed a class-conscious preoccupation with the implied loss of gentility in outlets such as the 'lady-help' or emigration. For most middle-class feminists this attitude constituted a conflict that could easily inhibit their effective contribution to the cause. Some feminists were, indeed, beginning to scrutinise their notions of middle-class ladyhood, but they had not yet rejected the prevailing definition. Since the colonial demand for domestic servants clashed with the requirements of that definition, the feminists were naturally reluctant to interpret the colonies' need as their opportunity. Activities that might compromise a gentlewoman's social position conflicted at too many points with a middle-class feminism interested primarily in the well-being of a female elite. Colonial social conditions required a reordering of traditional British categories of class, status and female employment, a difficult task for women whose class-consciousness overshadowed their feminism. Not surprisingly, then, it was of little consequence to the feminists that the emigrants themselves found warnings like Hubbard's irrelevant.

Jane Lewin's retirement in 1881 heralded the end of the connection between feminism and middle-class female emigration. By 1886, when the FMCES was absorbed into the recently formed Colonial Emigration Society, middle-class emigration had returned to the charge of philanthropists, where it had begun. From the 1880s to 1914 a variety of more ambitious female emigration socities, in the mainstream of voluntary work, helped over 20,000 women to emigrate. Unlike the FMCES, they freely used genteel domestic service and potential marriage as incentives to emigration. Their detailed history forms the subject of the next chapter, but the numbers alone suggest the degree to which the uneasy relationship between feminism and female emigration had operated as an inhibiting factor. The greatest victim of that relationship was the distressed gentlewoman who lacked formal teaching qualifications, the very misfit the 'Ladies of Langham Place' had begun by trying to help. If the more fortunate FMCES emigrants were any guide, there was a large pool of enterprising and adaptable single women in Britain fully capable of making their own way in colonial societies. In Britain piecemeal educational reform had worsened their competitive position to the point where middle-class feminism could have little to offer genteel ladies without formal, marketable training. Feminism had failed to capitalise on the potential of female emigration; it remained to be seen whether philanthropy could exploit it more fully in the interests of the most disadvantaged groups of middle-class women.

Notes

1. The *English Woman's Journal*, founded by Bessie R. Parkes in 1858.

2. The annual congresses were notable for the number of papers given by women and the serious attention given to subjects on the position of women. The proceedings were published in the annual *Transactions* of the society (hereafter *TNAPSS*).

3. H. Martineau, 'Female Industry,' *Edinburgh Review*, vol. CIX, 1859, pp. 293-336. On the influence of Martineau's article see Josephine Kamm, *Rapiers and Battleaxes: The Women's Movement and its Aftermath* (London, 1966), p. 45.

4. See, for example, J.D. Milne, 'Remarks on the Industrial Employment of Women', *TNAPSS* (1857), pp. 531-8; B.R. Parkes, 'The Market for Educated Female Labour', (1859), pp. 727-8; J. Boucherett, 'The Industrial Employments of Women', (1859), pp. 728-9; J. Crowe, 'Report of Society for Promoting the Employment of Women', (1861), p. 685.

5. Martineau, p. 336.

6. *TNAPSS* (1862), pp. 808-9.

7. The society was headed initially by Jessie Boucherett and Jane Crowe, and its formation was soon followed by the establishment of branch societies in Edinburgh, Dublin and other provincial towns, all affiliated with the Social Science Association. Crowe, *TNAPSS* (1861), p. 685; SPEW, *Annual Report* (1879), pp. 3-4.

8. In 1865 Dorothea Beale observed that out of 100 fathers of her pupils at Cheltenham Ladies' College, 83 were military officers, 'private gentlemen', clergymen or medical men, and the rest were civil servants, lawyers, bankers, merchants and manufacturers. *TNAPSS* (1865), p. 275. Similar conditions prevailed at Queen's College, Miss Buss's North London Collegiate School and Bedford College, all secondary schools founded between 1848 and 1853. C.A. Biggs, *TNAPSS* (1879), pp. 442-4.

9. E. Davies, 'On Secondary Instruction as Relating to Girls', *TNAPSS* (1864), p. 403 (reprinted in a separate pamphlet (London, 1864), p. 23); see also her evidence to the Taunton Commission, 'Report of Schools Inquiry Commissioners', vol. V, *PP* 1867-68, XXVII (Pt. IV), p. 246, QQ 11293, 11370-1. See also ch. 1, above.

10. *TNAPSS* (1884), pp. 417-18.

11. J. Boucherett, *TNAPSS* (1861), pp. 685-6; A.B. Corlett, (1862), pp. 612-13; Corlett and P. Blyth, (1863), pp. 698-707. Emily Faithfull boosted women's opportunities in the printing industry by establishing the Victoria Press, run for and by women; it obtained orders for most feminist publications, especially the *Victoria Magazine*. By 1860 Faithfull had apprenticed nineteen female compositors and found that other printers were planning to admit women. Faithfull, *TNAPSS* (1860), pp. 819-20.

12. *TNAPSS* (1860), pp. 814-15. Louisa Hope thought that this class, too eager for the 'peacockism of education', would be better off 'as cottagers' or trademen's

wives and mothers, or as household servants'.*TNAPSS* (1860), pp. 399-401.

13. M.S. Rye, *Emigration of Educated Women* (London, 1861), pp. 3-5, 14; B.R. Parkes, *Essays on Women's Work* (London, 1865), p. 66.

14. *TNAPSS* (1860), p. 818.

15. Rye, pp. 2-14; U. Monk, *New Horizons: A Hundred Years of Women's Migration* (London, 1963), pp. 1-3. A summary of Rye's paper appeared in *TNAPSS* (1861), p. 686.

16. *TNAPSS* (1861), pp. xliii, 632, 686.

17. The formation of the FMCES in May, 1862 was accompanied by a stream of letters in *The Times*, mostly in support. In December, 1861 Emily Faithfull had publicised the aims of the proposed society, and in April Rye herself began to write regular letters acknowledging subscriptions and explaining the society's intentions. *The Times*, 4 Dec. 1861, p. 7; 6 Dec. 1861, p. 4; 7 April 1862, p. 6; 9 April 1862, p. 12; 25 April 1862, p. 5; 29 April 1862, p. 14; 21 June 1862, p. 12.

18. Ibid., 24 April 1862, p. 12.

19. Ibid., 23 April 1862, p. 6; 28 April 1862, p. 5; 30 April 1862, p. 7.

20. Ibid., 26 April 1862, p. 12.

21. Ibid., 29 April 1862, p. 14.

22. Ibid., 11 April 1862, p. 5.

23. Ibid., 28 April 1862, p. 5.

24. Ibid., p. 8.

25. Ibid., 29 April 1862, p. 14.

26. Ibid., 28 April 1862, p. 8.

27. For a full discussion of the problem see ch. 1, above. Interest in the problem in the 1860s was stimulated by the dramatic rise in the ratio of women to men in England and Wales in 1861 to 1,053 to 1,000, compared with 1,042 to 1,000 in 1851. The greatest 'excess', 209,663, occurred between the ages of 20 and 29. Between 30 and 39 it was 107,380, and between 40 and 49, 56,231. B.R. Mitchell, *Abstract of British Historical Statistics* (Cambridge, 1962), p. 6, Table 2; General Report, Census, England and Wales (1861), *PP* 1863, LIII, Pt. I (3221), Appendix, p. 115, Table 70.

28. First published in the *National Review*, vol. XXVII, pp. 434-60, in 1862, Greg's essay was reprinted in his collection, *Literary and Social Judgements* (London, 1868, 1869) and as a separate pamphlet in 1869. Greg was a moderate Liberal but by the 1860s he showed signs of increasing conservatism; see the 'Memoir' by his wife in Greg, *Enigmas of Life* (London, 1891).

29. Greg, 'Why are Women Redundant?'.

30. F.P. Cobbe, 'What Shall we do with Our Old Maids?' *Fraser's Magazine*, vol. LXVI, 1862, pp. 60-75; reprinted in *Essays on the Pursuits of Women* (London, 1863).

31. J. Boucherett, *Hints on Self Help: A Book for Young Women* pp. 42-8.

32. 'Social Science', *Victoria Magazine*, July 1863, pp. 282-3; see also Oct. 1863, p. 571, and A. Houston, *On the Emancipation of Women from Existing Industrial Disabilities, Considered in its Economic Aspect* (inaugural lecture as Whately Professor of Political Economy, Dublin University, 1862), pp. 30-4.

33. Taylor, *First Duty of Women*, p. 43. See above, ch. 3, note 76.

34. The society obtained some influential support and achieved the status of a fashionable charity. Both Lord Shaftesbury and Lord Brougham promoted it, and Shaftesbury became its first president. Shaftesbury to Barbara Bodichon, 25 July 1862; Bodichon to Shaftesbury, 26 Sept. 1862; Rye to Bodichon, 7 Oct. 1862, Fawcett Library, Autograph Collection, vol. II, Pt. A; FMCES, *First and Second Reports* (London, 1861-62), 1872.

35. C. Brough, Cape Town, 20 March, 1863, FMCES, *Letter Book No. 1*

(Fawcett Library), pp. 51-4. See also C.M. Heawood, Melbourne, 25 March 1862, and F.M. Cary, Dunedin, 18 Oct. 1863, Ibid., pp. 15-18, 101-4.
  36. See, for example, letters of E. Boake, Melbourne, 26 Feb. 1868; L.M. Scott, Christchurch, 1867 and M.A. Oliver, Horsham, Victoria, 2 Oct. 1871, Ibid., pp. 295-6, 286-7, 391-5.
  37. *TNAPSS* (1862), p. 812.
  38. Rye's early reading had included Susanna Moodie's famous account of her experiences as an immigrant's wife in the Canadian backwoods, *Roughing it in the Bush* (first published, 1852), which effectively illustrates the painful process by which a genteel woman adapted to the crude physical and social conditions of a primitive environment. See above, ch. 2, note 18. E.A. Pratt, *Pioneer Women in Victoria's Reign* (London, 1897), p. 23.
  39. Rye, *TNAPSS* (1862), pp. 811-12. This was an elaboration of her earlier plans proposed in 1861 in her *Emigration of Educated Women*, pp. 9-11.
  40. FMCES, *First Report* (1861-62), p. 3.
  41. Only eight of the one hundred women were governesses, a proportion deemed admirably suitable by Roger Therry, ex-judge of the NSW Supreme Court, who added that Rye had 'wisely and successfully extended her zeal and exertions to the introduction of a much more needed class in the Colony — domestic servants'. Therry, pp. 430-1.
  42. *The Times*, 3 Nov. 1862, p. 10; FMCES, *First Report* (1861-62), p. 7; Rye to Bodichon, London, 25 Sept. 1862; Redfern (Sydney), 20 May, 1865, Fawcett Library Autograph Collection, vol. II, Pt. A. After 1865 Rye made several trips to Canada, and from 1869 she organised a system of Canadian emigration for young 'waifs and strays', a scheme designed to thwart the growth of prostitution in Britain. Pratt, pp. 30-7; Monk, pp. 6-7, 119-21.
  43. J. Lewin, *TNAPSS* (1863), pp. 612-16.
  44. Compiled from lists of emigrants in FMCES. *Reports* (First, 1861-2; Second, 1862-72; Fifth, 1880-2; Sixth, 1882-5); there is no trace of surviving copies of the third and fourth reports covering December 1872 to 1879.
  45. FMCES, *Letter Books Nos. 1 and 2* (Fawcett Library). The letter books contain contemporary copies of 276 letters received from 114 emigrants. The basic incentive for most of the letters was to repay the society's loans, but most of the emigrants were informative and literate correspondents and revealed a good deal about thier colonial lives, although less about their former circumstances in Britain.
  46. FMCES, *5th Report* (1883), pp. 3-4.
  47. Maria Rye's initial collection in 1862 was £500, and by 1885 the society's capital was only £269. Once in full operation, however, a large working capital was unnecessary, for most emigrants repaid their loans and many paid all or part of their passage, requiring only the protection and facilities of the society. FMCES, *6th Report* (1886), pp. 3-6.
  48. A. Davis, Sydney, 20 Jan. 1865, 21 Feb. 1867, *Letter Book No. 1*, pp. 172-7, 257-62.
  49. S. Henderson, Tongaur, Natal, 28 Sept. 1863, *Letter Book No. 1*, pp. 83-5; see also M. Atherton, Brisbane, 2 Sept. 1862; M. Richardson, Port MacQuarie, NSW, 13 Feb. 1863; M. Wyett, Wairapapi, NZ, 10 Feb. 1866, A.M. Hunt, Melbourne, 11 Oct. 1869; L. Phillips, Melbourne, 12 Aug. 1873, Ibid., pp. 34-9, 47-51, 216-20, 349-52, 420-2.
  50. M. Hett, Christchurch, NZ, 23 June 1870, Ibid., pp. 366-8; see also R. Phayne, Melbourne, 13 Aug. 1869, Ibid., pp. 341-6.
  51. FMCES, *5th Report* (1883), No. 219.
  52. C. Haselton, Graaf Reinet, 9 May and 15 Aug. 1877, Melbourne, Nov. 1879, *Letter Book No. 2*, pp. 7-8, 24-5, 83-5.

53. A. Davis, Sydney, 17 June 1864, *Letter Book No. 1*, pp. 123-7.
54. S.A. Hall, Cape Town and Port Elizabeth, 17 Jan. 1868, 21 April, 1870; Graaf Reinet, 18 Aug. 1876, *Letter Book No. 1*, pp. 289-92, 360, 407, 502-4; Graaf Reinet, 4 Feb. 1877 to 25 March 1882, *Letter Book No. 2*, pp. 2-150, *passim*; see also the letters from S.E. Evans, C. Haselton, A. Hart and M.E. Jenvey in *Letter Book No. 2*.
55. R. Phayne, Melbourne, 13 Aug. 1869, *Letter Book No. 1*, pp. 341-6.
56. R. Phayne, Melbourne, June 1872, Ibid., pp. 407-9. Phayne's persistence, and a few similar cases, give the impression that Lewin sternly discouraged any talk of return to England and that she dismissed any appeals for financial help. Ibid., pp.379-82.
57. L. Jones, Rushworth, Victoria, 7 Nov. 1868; Melbourne, 13 Aug. 1869, Ibid., pp. 315-16, 339-41.
58. M. Wilson, Wellington, 25 Sept. 1871, Ibid., pp. 414-16.
59. K. Brind, Nelson, 1 June 1873, Ibid., pp. 436-7.
60. H.H. Herbert, Hawke's Bay, 8 May 1879, *Letter Book No. 2*, pp. 55-9.
61. See, for example, A.M. Hunt, Melbourne, 3 Dec. 1871, *Letter Book No. 1*, pp. 396-400; E. Mitchinson, Bedford, South Africa, 16 Aug. 1879, *Letter Book No. 2*, pp. 64A-6.
62. E. Long, Hawke's Bay, 20 May 1880, *Letter Book No. 2*, pp. 104-7.
63. M. Long, Waipakarau, NZ, May 1880, Ibid., pp. 108-9.
64. E. Blackith, Napier, n.d. (ca. Aug. 1881), 2 Nov. 1881, Ibid., pp. 122-4, 130-1, E. Glen, who received only £24 for teaching in a South African Mission School, nevertheless felt that 'the dark cloud that has hung over my life is fast disappearing'. Verulam, 27 Oct. 1866, *Letter Book No. 1*, pp. 238-40.
65. L.A. Geoghegan, Apsley, Victoria, 18 Oct. 1867,17 May and 12 Aug. 1868, *Letter Book No. 1*, pp. 254-7, 285-6, 302-4, 310-12.
66. E. Brook, Dunedin, 20 Jan. 1869, Ibid., pp. 331-3.
67. H.H. Herbert, Waipakarau, NZ, 8 Nov. 1879, *Letter Book No. 2*, pp. 76-80.
68. Miss Barlow, Melbourne, 24 June 1863, *Letter Book No. 1*, pp. 76-8.
69. See, for example, L. Dearmer, Sydney, 1 June and 14 Dec. 1868; Mrs E.C. MacDonell, Dunedin, 27 July 1870, Ibid., pp. 304-9, 318-24, 268-71. Mrs. I. White, Bowral, NSW, 27 April 1881, *Letter Book No. 2*, pp. 137-45. On the development of Government schools and female education in Australia and New Zealand see A. Clayden, *A Popular Handbook to New Zealand* (London, 1885), p. 126; N.I. MacKenzie, *Women in Australia* (Melbourne, 1963), p. 21.
70. A. Davis, Sydney, 17 June, 1864, *Letter Book No. 1*, pp. 123-7.
71. One of the few exceptions was 'Emigrant No. 267 – Converted Jewess; cast off by her family; took situation as cook in Canada'. FMCES, *Sixth Report* (1883-1885), pp. 9-12.
72. A.M. Hunt, Melbourne and Wangaratta, Victoria, 11 Oct. 1869, 9 May 1870, *Letter Book No. 1*, pp. 349-52. See also FMCES *Second Report* (1873), pp. 6-12, especially emigrant numbers 107 and 120.
73. A.B. MacQueen, Brisbane, 18 April 1866, *Letter Book No. 1*, pp. 222-5.
74. J. Merritt, Auckland, 31 July 1863, Ibid., pp. 73-6.
75. Lewin was a niece of the Utilitarian-Radical historian, George Grote. Pratt, p. 30. In practice her approach adhered closely to the more uncompromising principles on women's employment argued by feminists like Mary Taylor. There is little evidence to determine whether Lewin was more partial to applicants who shared her own views; S.A. Hall, the schoolteacher at Graaf Reinet, reported that one emigrant's (Miss Jackson's) 'great idea is to educate women that they shall be what she calls "emancipated" and placed on an equality with man; that they may be thoroughly independent of them'. Hall did not share Jackson's 'great idea'. 18 July 1878, *Letter Book No. 2*, pp. 40-1.

76. Kamm, *Rapiers and Battleaxes*, p. 102; *D.N.B. Supplement* (1901-11), pp. 245-6.

77. Both Rye and Lewin remained on the society's committee, but the working secretary exercised final control over the selection of applicants. Miss Strongitharm succeeded Lewin in 1881 and in 1884 was succeeded by Julia Blake from the Colonial Emigration Society, and Alice Bonham-Carter. FMCES, *Sixth Report* (1883-85), pp. 3-6, Monk, p. 23.

78. FMCES, *Sixth Report* (1883-85), pp. 3-6.

79. Monk, pp. 10-13.

80. The idea was discussed initially at the Social Science Association. Mrs Browne, *TNAPSS* (1869), pp. 609-10; Mrs E.M. King, *TNAPSS* (1874), p. 947. R.M. Crawshay, *Domestic Service for Gentlewomen . . . With Additional Matter* (London, 3rd. ed., 1876; first published 1874). Crawshay recommended large households for her scheme so that at least two gentlewomen could be employed and keep each other company, and regular servants could be retained for the heaviest and diertiest work. The fact that domestic service was becoming increasingly unpopular with the traditional servant class may explain both the origin and short life of the scheme.

81. *Victoria Magazine*, April 1876, pp. 510-12, 562-3; June, 1876, pp. 185-6.

82. L.M.H. (Louisa M. Hubbard), *The Hand-Book of Women's Work* (London, 1876), pp. 41-5.

83. Ibid., p. 131.

6 EMIGRATION PROPAGANDA AND THE DISTRESSED GENTLEWOMAN, 1880-1914

Jane Lewin's work illustrated the difficulties inherent in promoting female emigration under middle-class feminist sponsorship. The tensions created by the notion of genteel domestic service and Greg's spectre of 'matrimonial colonisation' inhibited Lewin's willingness and ability to encourage a wider cross-section of middle-class women to emigrate. The policy of Lewin's successors was in marked contrast to her approach. From 1880 to 1914 a variety of female emigration organisations came into being, whose leaders, although women, emphatically were not feminists. Consequently they found no inconsistency in using genteel domestic service and the prospect of marriage as incentives to female emigration. By 1914 the propaganda of these societies was highly sophisticated, and deserves close analysis. The various schemes attracted a larger number of educated women than any of their predecessors and helped women of diverse social backgrounds. Yet while the bulk of the propaganda was aimed at distressed gentlewomen, it is by no means clear that these women were the chief beneficiaries of the new organisations. The emigration rhetoric, so heavily reliant on the language of the feminine civilising mission, and apparently unresponsive to important social changes in Britain and the colonies, seemed to mask the rapidly changing social origins and occupations of the women who emigrated. How successful, then, was the new propaganda, who benefited from it, and how did it affect the fortunes of distressed gentlewomen?

The facts about the formation of the late-Victorian emigration societies may be stated briefly. In 1880 a meeting of several like-minded philanthropists launched the short-lived Women's Emigration Society, a scheme designed to encourage women of all classes to emigrate. It resulted mainly from the cooperation of two prominent women, Mrs Caroline (E.L.) Blanchard and Miss Louisa M. Hubbard. Blanchard had already gained substantial experience in emigration work as an official selection agent for the New Zealand and Queensland governments' assisted emigration schemes. Louisa Hubbard, proprietor and editor of the women's magazine, *Work and Leisure*, had, by the 1880s, come to support emigration as one among many schemes to alleviate the condition of women. By 1883 two well established branches of the WES were operating, one in the East End of London run by the wife of the vicar

of St Philip's, Stepney, Adelaide Ross, and a Northern Branch in Marylebone run by Caroline Blanchard. The society's central organisation was
never placed on a sound footing, however, and by 1884 it had disinte-
grated. The two regional branches continued in operation, Blanchard's
Northern Branch becoming the Colonial Emigration Society, which
concentrated mainly on recruiting working-class emigrants for the
colonial governments' assisted passage schemes.[1] This left a situation,
coincident with the declining activity of the FMCES, in which innumerable individuals prosecuted their own local emigration work without the
facilities or finance of a central parent society. Louisa Hubbard was
responsible for bringing together some of the most prominent workers,
particularly Adelaide Ross of Stepney and Ellen Joyce, a clergyman's
widow who had organised an emigration department for members of
the Girls' Friendly Society, and had helped families to emigrate
through the Winchester Emigration Society at her home in Winchester.
In 1884 these women organised a register of emigration workers, and
then consolidated the independent workers, into a single United
Englishwomen's Emigration Association ultimately renamed the British
Women's Emigration Association. It was this society, again catering to
all social classes, which directed the bulk of protected female emigration for the next thirty years. It absorbed Blanchard's CES in 1892, and
in 1902, after the Boer War, its special sub-committee to direct South
African emigration detached itself as a sister organisation, the South
African Colonisation Society. Finally, in 1910, some of the members of
these two societies formed the Colonial Intelligence League to promote
the emigration of educated and professional women exclusively.[2]

All these societies benefited from the trial and error of their
predecessors. For one thing their organisation was far more elaborate,
extending well beyond the confines of London. The BWEA had
separate Scottish and Irish branches, county branches for Staffordshire,
Wiltshire and Somerset, and individual workers in practically every provincial town in the country, from Aberdeen to Worcester to Winchester.
Many local workers were schoolmistresses or clergymen and their wives,
and the society was publicised extensively in parish magazines and at
girls' schools and clubs.[3] From 1902 the BWEA and SACS published
their own monthly journal, the *Imperial Colonist*, which discussed the
most promising colonies and openings for women and the safest
methods of travel.[4] The main aim behind most of the organisers'
painstaking work was their ambition to achieve a reputable and safe
method of female emigration. Adelaide Ross and Ellen Joyce, the two
foremost workers, were acutely conscious of the manifold dangers in-

herent in the emigration of single women, and repeatedly stressed the
need for them to travel under the society's auspices.[5] They took
meticulous precautions to safeguard each step of the process. They
established hostels in Liverpool and London where women from the
provinces could reside before departure. The largest of these was the
Wortley Hostel in Paddington, founded in 1902, which 'combined the
unusual advantages of a house for lady boarders of a superior class, with
a locality equally suited for approaching the various railway stations'.[6]
The next step was the actual voyage, and the BWEA eventually took
charge of the responsibility for providing matrons to supervise each
'protected party' of women. By 1897 matrons on the Canadian voyage
were accompanying the emigrants across the continent to Vancouver
and Victoria; one of these matrons, Miss Mary Monk, accompanied
thirty-five separate parties to Australia, New Zealand and Canada over a
period of twenty years.[7] Finally, in the colonies the societies established
an intricate network of cooperative 'correspondents' who informed
them of local demand for female emigrants and arranged for the
women's safe reception, lodging and respectable employment. Emigration workers like Blanchard and Joyce travelled through each colony to
recruit responsible helpers. By 1900 there were 'welcoming hostels'
with reception committees in all the major cities of Canada and South
Africa, and in some cases, notably Vancouver, the YWCA took over the
same function. The societies were thus able to boast, with some justice,
that theirs was a near foolproof system of 'protected emigration'.[8]

With the exception of Louisa Hubbard, whose work was largely
organisational, none of the new emigration workers were notable
feminists. Women like Adelaide Ross, Ellen Joyce and Caroline
Blanchard extended their sympathy to all unemployed women, including impoverished gentlewomen, and were determined to help them,
but, like Maria Rye, their sentiments derived from philanthropy rather
than feminism. They were attracted to middle-class female emigration
either through more general emigration work or through wider charitable efforts quite unrelated to the women's movement. Joyce was characteristic in doing her first emigration work for the Girls' Friendly
Society, an offshoot of the Church of England whose leading workers
were primarily clergymen's wives and, according to Ray Strachey, some
of the most bitter anti-feminists in Britain.[9] In 1912, at the height of
the female suffrage controversy, the BWEA was quick to disassociate
itself from the suffrage activities of one of its members.[10] It is significant that after the initial organisation of the UEEA was completed in
1884, Louisa Hubbard left emigration work for other causes within the

women's employment and education movement which she deemed more important.[11] Her action exemplified the typical and, at the time, necessary single-mindedness of the feminists. Most of them, preoccupied with the fortunes of middle-class women, would have regarded the UBWEA decision in 1889 to extend their assistance to men and families as an irrelevant diversion from the aims of the women's movement.[12] With the abandonment of Lewin's more restrictive policy, the implications of female emigration necessarily began to attract workers whose philanthropy was unlikely to include a feminist outlook.[13]

All the new emigration societies made much of their intention to devote most of their energies to middle-class women, either refined ladies or at least women with some education. They applied their various loan funds strictly towards the emigration of a 'superior class', those seen to be in the greatest need of help, and never towards domestic servants or other working-class women. When the UBWEA took over the remains of the moribund FMCES loan fund in 1886 they promised to administer it, like their own, 'for the emigration of educated women only'.[14] Unlike the FMCES, however, all the new societies, with the exception of the Colonial Intelligence League formed in 1910, also gave aid, short of financial assistance, to working-class women. Frequently this meant offering their protective umbrella to women who had already decided to emigrate. By offering their advice, providing their facilities and enforcing their rules, the societies could encourage the orderly conduct of female emigration, and forestall colonial strictures against the quality of British womanhood. The BWEA frequently protected, and occasionally selected, working-class women for the state-assisted passages provided by such colonial governments as Queensland and Western Australia, and more than half of its emigrants were consistently working-class.[15]

This expansion from the narrower policy of the FMCES came at a potentially opportune time for many women whose social origins ranged dowards from the lower middle class to the upper levels of the working class. It was these women, rather than the more familiar distressed gentlewomen, distinguished by their social decline, who began to fill the new female employment outlets created during the last quarter of the nineteenth century. They were an indeterminate social group, barely distinguishable by occupation at the lower level from most working-class women. Clara Collet attempted to analyse this group in 1892; she placed a 'second group' above the first group — the lowest paid women workers.

From the second group of working women are drawn our better-paid factory girls, our tailoresses, domestic servants, and a large number of our dressmakers and milliners, shop assistants, barmaids, clerks and elementary teachers. A considerable number of dressmakers and milliners, shop assistants and clerks are, however, drawn from the lower middle-class, and a few from the professional class. Although this second group is the largest group in London, and probably in England, it is the one about which we have least information. They have hardly been made the subject of industrial inquiry, do not regard themselves as persons to be pitied, and work in comparatively small detachments. They are nevertheless of more industrial importance than the working women of the first group . . . Their work is skilled and requires an apprenticeship. They are in the majority of cases brought into direct contact with the consumer, and education, good manners, personal appearance and tact all raise their market value.[16]

Collet's intention here was to discuss skilled working-class women, but in the process she recognised that many of these women shared a large employment field with the lower middle class. Later she noticed that lower middle-class women also joined the upper middle class as teachers and civil service clerks.[17] The meaning of all this was that the old accepted social classifications for women were becoming obsolete. By the end of the century a new generation of aspiring suburban women of varied backgrounds had joined the more refined but no better qualified group of middle-class women in a search for employment on equal terms.

The results of this turbulent social mobility were compounded by the fact that, even at the beginning of the twentieth century, the majority of educated working women still turned to the overcrowded teaching profession for respectable employment. The hospital, the shop counter and the typewriter attracted increasing numbers of late-Victorian women, but the school-room still appealed to the majority. The 1891 census revealed that out of 328,393 'professional' females, there were 146,375 teachers, 70,650 students over 15 and 54,392 in medicine (including nurses); furthermore the teachers continued to show a greater increase than any other occupation, having jumped from 123,995 in 1881.[18] These teachers constituted a vast number of women with varying qualifications, and with steadily increasing standards of education only those best trained could expect good salaries. The highest qualification, a university degree, commanded only £105 to

£150 in 1890, and Clara Collet noticed that out of the 800 to graduate so far — of whom she herself was one — the great majority turned to some form of teaching. For the rest the competition was even more intense than it had been among mid-Victorian governesses, and the demands more intellectually rigorous; teaching was still 'the only brain-work offered them, and badly paid as it is, it is better paid than any other work done by women'.[19] Emigrationists, in particular, were in a unique position to understand the process by which so many women were reduced to a situation where emigration might provide the best alternative:

> While governesses, all but those of exceptional attainments, and many teachers who once passed muster, find their occupations gone with our greater demands, there are more 'unemployed' than ever of the educated classes, to whom emigration offers the best solution of the struggle for life.[20]

The new societies, therefore, catered to a wide cross-section of women, even within the group they defined as 'educated'. The larger numbers attracted through this policy, combined with the colonial shortage of domestic servants, caused them to encourage openly middle-class women to turn to some form of domestic service in the colonies. This shift from Jane Lewin's policy was dictated primarily by the occupational needs of the various colonies, but it also reflected a shift of opinion in Britain on the subject of employment for gentlewomen. Already, during the seventies, as we have seen, some women had advocated and encouraged domestic service in Britain as a field of employment for gentlewomen.[21] Predictably, the proposal met with a mixed reaction and limited success, but it was sufficiently acceptable for its chief enthusiast, Rose Mary Crawshay, to place over a hundred women in 'genteel service' within eight months from her 'Office for Lady Helps' in Portman Square; only six of her clients were reported to have been failures.[22] But significantly, while feminists, including Louisa Hubbard, were united in reacting strongly against the whole idea,[23] the new emigration promoters like Ellen Joyce and Adelaide Ross were quick to turn it to their advantage. Neither opposed the notion of the British 'lady-help', and they did not hesitate to recommend the occupation as a means for educated women to begin a life abroad. Like Crawshay, they felt it essential to cater first to the practical needs of women rather than to their genteel susceptibilities, and they assumed that most women were sufficiently resilient to withstand any culture-shock which might ensue. For them the basic situation was simple. All the settlement colonies needed women, both as wives and domestic servants; Britain had the surplus women to supply their deficiency, but the surplus occurred primarily among women above the traditional servant class; hence their task was to make it possible and palatable for these women to become first colonial servants and ultimately competent wives and mothers.

Partly because of the new stress on domestic skills, the emigration societies soon became markedly sensitive to the charge that they encouraged much needed domestic servants to leave the country. As charitable organisations dependent on public goodwill they could not afford to alienate potential subscribers by urging emigration upon women who were wanted as servants by the upper and middle classes. In 1886 Adelaide Ross regretted the frequent criticism of female emigration made on the grounds that England was threatened with a failure in the supply of good domestic servants.[24] The societies' natural reaction was to discourage the traditional servant class from emigrating, and to offer protection only if servants insisted on leaving. Their strict refusal to extend loans to domestic servants stemmed partly from this policy.[25] Most often, however, their defence rested simply on the argument that domestic servants were sufficiently well off in Britain not to wish to emigrate, and that the class of women most in need of help had little scope at home.

> The 'superfluous women' of the United Kingdom are not the 'good cooks', 'house-parlour maids', and 'capable general-servants', for which there is everywhere an insatiable demand; but the sensible, useful girls who are practised in the necessary duties of their own homes and who desire to earn their living in some such active employment, without losing caste by having to associate with those who are less educated than themselves.[26]

Their distinction was an important one, and they adhered quite literally to the policy of discouraging the 'regular servant class', but the misfortune of having to work in an atmosphere of increasing servant shortage bedevilled all the societies up to the outbreak of the World War, and probably operated as a permanent check on the size of their funds.[27]

To dissuade qualified servants from emigrating solved one problem for the societies, but it created two others. First, the persistent colonial demand for trained domestic servants had to be satisfied by sending a class of women not previously accustomed to the duties and social position of domestic service. Ellen Joyce sent a circular to Western Canada in 1906 explaining that the British servant shortage was as severe as that in Canada, and that emigrant servants had to be drawn from a higher class.[28] More important was the need to reconcile educated women to the idea of doing domestic service overseas. Rose Crawshay had successfully induced a few gentlewomen to become servants in Britain, but it was by no means certain that significant numbers would be prepared to do the same abroad, notwithstanding the advantages of a greater degree of egalitarianism in the colonies. Many FMCES emigrants had perceived the advantages of this very possibility, but only after a time of colonial experience; women in Britain, lacking that experience, might be difficult to persuade. It was, then, necessary to convince potential emigrants first that only in domestic work 'is the newcomer certain of finding instant employment on landing', and, secondly, that

> no domestic who is any good remains a domestic in the Colonies. They prosper, rise in life, set up establishments of their own, and require domestic help for themselves.[29]

The effort to popularise the notion of genteel domestic service in the colonies, to bring to it an air of polite respectability and to link it with the prospect of marriage constituted a major theme in the emigrationists' propaganda for over thirty years, and embodied a novel application of the feminine civilising mission.

In encouraging educated women to become colonial servants, the emigration societies had to tread carefully to avoid offending the sensitivities of both colonial employers and the women themselves. Colonial housewives wanted helpers who would not be ashamed to perform the roughest chores to which they themselves were accustomed, and middle-class women who hesitantly consented to such a drastic step needed assurances that they would receive treatment due to a 'lady' and social equal. The various euphemisms used to describe the genteel servant reflect the delicate position of emigrationists in trying to please both sides. The women were variously known as 'home-helps', 'lady-helps', 'companion-helps' and 'help-companions'. The 'home-help' was the most enduring title, and eventually replaced the more pompous 'lady-help', 'to prevent Canada thinking that those we send are fine ladies'.[30] After a South African complaint that many 'companion-helps' 'seem to think too much of the Companion part and not enough of the Help', the UBWEA characteristically inverted the title to 'help-companion'.[31]

The emigrationists were determined to make a virtue out of some of the most potentially distasteful aspects of colonial life for the home-help. They warned women that the emigrant, whatever her class, must be prepared to 'rough it' and to work long and hard at tasks she would disdain at home. Adaptability and youth were pre-requisites to success-ful emigration, but given these advantages a woman could expect to be rewarded with success.[32] The colonial environment was a fertile field for applying the Victorian moral that success inevitably follows hard work, and nowhere was it used with greater effect than on the educated woman. A Canadian argued that her country had no room for idle and thriftless women, but great promise for the industrious.

> You must be a worker, you must know how to do *something*, and be able to turn your hand to *anything* . . . On your powers of adapta-bility will depend your progress and success . . . I often tell friends in the Motherland that we live on hard work and hope in Canada.[33]

The educated woman ennobled menial domestic work by bringing her greater intelligence and dignity to bear on it and by combining the chores of the kitchen and wash-tub with the social graces of a companion-hostess at visiting times. In Canada all women were working women, but as compensation 'one perceives mental culture to be a weapon as well as a defense in every condition of life, and for that reason Canada should be the Mecca of that ever-increasing body of Englishwomen who, on this side of the Atlantic, come under the cate-gory of the "working gentlewoman"'.[34] The *Imperial Colonist* wel-comed the tenor of an article in *The Times* which argued that intending female colonists must not be afraid to soil their hands. A little learning, it pronounced, often distorted the outlook of the working class, but those above them had no such qualms; a well-bred girl undertaking gardening, cooking or nursing was proud enough to perform 'every preparatory stage which leads up to the final triumph'. An educated woman could perform all the usual work of the poor far better than they because she used brains as well as hands. 'If any work is menial it is so because of the worker, not because of the work'.[35] With these argu-ments the gentlewoman was persuaded that her simple labour would be a dignified blessing overseas.

Another disadvantage for the cultivated home-help was that most of the colonial openings, whether in Canada, South Africa or Australia,

were 'up-country' or in the 'bush'. The societies warned gentlewomen
that in large colonial towns, such as those of Eastern Canada, class distinctions flourished as strongly as in England, and employers treated the
servant accordingly, regardless of her social origins. By the twentieth
century, with the growth of large colonial cities, this process was
impossible to ignore, and emigration propaganda directed women
instead to sparse and primitive settlements in the Canadian West, the
Transvaal and Orange River Colony and the Australian bush.[36] The
great drawback here for the educated woman was isolation and bore-
dom, but all this, the emigrationists claimed, was compensated by the
easier social mobility and the greater respect and distinction given to
the culture of a gentlewoman. In country districts respectable housewives were anxious to have intelligent companions rather than mere
'ignorant and uneducated' servants, and the ideal home-help combined
dignified service with companionship. The household chores were
shared equally between the mistress and help, 'and they hardly ever put
their hand to anything the squatter's wife would not do herself'.[37]
Above all, the colonists acknowledged the social position of home-helps
by treating them willingly 'as members of the family'.[38] This was a
constant factor in female emigration propaganda after 1880. The
societies repeatedly drew attention to the letters of contented emigrants
who were 'very happy and comfortable, treated quite as one of the
family, and dine at the same table'.[39] It was the most effective appeal
possible to the sensitive gentility of the 'young lady'.

Most emigration promoters recognised that home-helps came from a
wide range of differing class backgrounds. In 1897 the UBWEA asserted
that it was the class 'above the servant class, rising up to the highly
cultivated woman of our day, that the Association most desires to
help'.[40] At one extreme they described, somewhat resentfully, working-
class women who had been forced, Viscountess Strangford argued, out
of their 'natural station' by 'over-education' into overcrowded competition with distressed gentlewomen;[41] barely above them were the
daughters of tradesmen and small farmers whose mothers had frequently been 'superior domestic servants, but they will not let their
daughters go to service, and prefer, as more genteel, the comparatively
unhealthy and inactive lives of the shop and office'.[42] Finally, at the
other extreme, were the impecunious but 'well-born ladies, who belong
to the collateral branches of well-connected families, or who are the
daughters of men who have been in the services or in the medical profession'.[43] All these women made successful home-helps, but Ellen
Joyce insisted that one type formed the most ideal woman for colonial

service:

> She is country bred and born; it is in the country villages she thrives;
> she is the useful eldest daughter of the large families of the poorer
> clergy. She lives in the riverside homes of the retired officers of both
> services; she gets her education and some knowledge of the world at
> the High School . . . In many of these households no servant is kept.
> Indeed we have sent so many to South Africa it is difficult to get any
> and thus we are forced to make Home-Helps for ourselves.

This model of the Brontë-style country girl — providing she had done 'a great
part of the household work' herself[44] was an ideal home-help only because
she was well qualified to take up the rough domestic work of a colonial
home; the rest, and notably the more gently nurtured women, were invariably ignorant of household work. Confronted with their situation, the societies soon turned to the question of preparation and training for colonial
service, or, in Joyce's words, began 'to make Home-Helps for ourselves'.[45]
The home-help enthusiasts soon came to insist that some previous
training in domestic work was an essential pre-requisite for most emigrants. The untrained, incompetent gentlewoman, no matter how
willing, was certain to be shocked when faced with a sudden unfamiliar
round of rough domestic chores in a colonial farmhouse, with unfortunate results both for herself and her employer. To send women abroad
'without an idea of lighting a fire or sweeping a room would be, as
everyone knows, a cruel kindness'.[46] After four years' experience of
this kind the BWEA acknowledged the problem by establishing, in
1890, a 'Colonial Training Home' at Leaton in Shropshire. For a payment of ten shillings a week for three months, middle-class women in
residence received a thorough training from a farmer's wife in all the
essential duties of colonial housework. They were instructed in 'house-
wifery', cooking, baking and washing, together with milking, dairy work,
poultry-care and bee-keeping. Furthermore, the 'Home', an old
fashioned manor house, contained neither modern household conveniences nor domestic servants so that the trainees were forced to do all
the work, including the heaviest and dirtiest, for themselves. In this
way, the managers claimed, Leaton secured the rejection of the unfit as
well as the training of those likely to succeed. They also claimed that
the wholesome atmosphere of the 'Home' improved the women's health
and increased their adaptability. Most important the comradely atmosphere bred a new attitude towards work, which would be a crucial advantage abroad, since 'the frame of mind generally supposed to be

ratlivi common among girls of this class, of considering domestic work menial, does not exist'.[47]

The Leaton 'Home' served its intended purpose impressively. It catered to a depressed class of women who, by virtue of their genteel backgrounds, would be least prepared for any form of colonial life without some prior orientation. It occasionally accommodated some working-class women, but the regular reports indicate that the majority of trainees came from the middle and occasionally the upper classes. A Leaton officer remarked that the women's social status often differed, but her examples suggest that in most cases it stopped just short of the lower middle class:

> With the present fierce struggle for bread, we have had women glad to be prepared for colonial life whose names are written in 'Burke' and 'Walford' and whose fathers have been sheriffs or deputy-lieutenants for their counties, whilst other pupils have been the daughters of professional men, farmers, or small business-men.[48]

The constant demand for training from such women invariably filled the 'Home' to capacity; in 1907 it was transferred to larger premises at Stoke Prior, near Bromsgrove, Worcestershire, and renamed the Colonial Training College.[49] The 'Home's establishment in 1890 coincided with the beginning of an upsurge in emigration — and especially female emigration — to the Canadian West and South Africa, and most of the trainee home-helps emigrated to those regions. The institution became so well known in British Columbia that many employers there refused to accept 'ladies who have not been trained at Leaton', and demands for trained 'Lady-Helps' soon followed from Australia and New Zealand.[50] By 1912 530 women had been trained at the College, which closed down only when the outbreak of war in 1914 caused a sharp drop in emigration generally.[51]

The influence of the BWEA College extended far beyond the relatively modest numbers of its actual trainees. Its 530 graduates formed only a fraction of emigrant women after 1890, but it established an important precedent which others followed quickly. By 1902 there were dozens of similar colonial training colleges operating throughout Britain. Some were run by private individuals for profit, others by members of a philanthropic emigration society; in some cases well-established training schools extended their work to 'colonial training', one of these being the domestic economy school of the University College of South Wales and Monmouthshire.[52] In 1902 the Yorkshire

Ladies' Council of Education framed a special course of domestic instruction 'suited to Colonial life generally, and with special reference to life in South Africa'.[53] Various county councils ran similar courses for 'lady emigrants', among them Lancashire, Hampshire and Sussex, the latter's School of Domestic Science for Women and Girls being established in 1894.[54] The *Imperial Colonist* welcomed with favourable publicity each new training school designed for emigrants. When a Mrs Headlam established a new school in London it remarked that she was

> devoting her house in Chelsea to this purpose for the benefit of girls who cannot afford a long and expensive preparation for earning their own living, or who do not care to mix with those who attend the classes at the Polytechnics or Technical Day Schools.[55]

Mrs Headlam had, in fact, put her finger on a key weakness of all the training schemes: the middle-class women who might stand to benefit from them most were too often those who could not afford them, but this did not prevent the emigrationists from prosecuting their diverse projects with increasing vigour.

Before long the Canadians began to compete with the proliferation of British training colleges. Mary Urie Watson, of the MacDonald Institute in Guelph, Ontario, argued in the *Imperial Colonist* that training in the colony was superior because of the instructors' acquaintance with specifically local conditions.[56] On Vancouver Island a Miss Bainbridge-Smith established the Haliburton College for Gentlewomen, offering household and farm training at £85 a year to students whom she hoped would subsequently buy land in the neighbourhood, and 'carry on their own business, with the friendly advice of the college teachers'.[57] However impractical some of the schemes may have been for impecunious gentlewomen, they all assumed that the typical middle-class Englishwoman was wholly unequipped for colonial life, especially as a home-help, without some prior intensive training. The Colonial Intelligence League was formed in 1910 largely to ensure that only properly trained women were helped to emigrate. It gave a 'practical test in efficiency' to women at several colonial training colleges, and only those successfully obtaining its 'card of credentials' were assisted. In 1913 it opened the Princess Patricia Ranch, a farm settlement for women near Vernon, British Columbia, to provide both occupations and further familiarisation for its emigrants.[58] By this time training had shifted from the interesting sideline of 1890 to the major preoccupation of all the female emigration societies.

The offer of practical domestic training to gentlewomen enhanced the credibility of the emigrationists' rhetoric. After 1890 it became easier to argue that the cultured home-help had a real civilising mission to perform. At first the BWEA stressed that 'only efficient practical women are introduced by the Association',[59] but the emphasis soon shifted from practicality to nobility. In her foreword to the first number of the *Imperial Colonist* Ellen Joyce stressed that the great colonial need was for healthy, cultured women with domestic training 'who will keep up the tone of the men with whom they mix by music, and book-lore when the day is over'.[60] On a later occasion she told a Girls' Friendly Society conference that cultured colonial women preferred cultured and refined home-helps, 'as associates for their growing children as well as for themselves', and added, significantly, that the same well-bred women 'are greatly needed as helpmates for the well-bred men'.[61] The BWEA British Columbia representative welcomed well-trained cultivated home-helps for the morality they brought with them.

There is no greater civilizing power in the world than that which a truly good woman possesses. There are many mothers and sisters in the dear old land across the seas who will never fully know how much they owe to the gentle mannered women who had gone to far-off corners of B.C. to make their home — I write of what I know — the rough jest is hushed and men grow ashamed of a careless life. The sound of the 'soft English voice' brings back to them memories of other days.[62]

BWEA writers stressed that women exercised their greatest moral influence in the domestic sphere, agreeing with the comment of the college matron that the work at Stoke Prior 'is, after all, only woman's natural work'.[63] Miss S.R. Perkins, who had lived in Australia, pleaded for more real gentlewomen to be trained and sent as useful companions to the colonies, where they would more easily resist the temptations and dangers of a rough colony, to which so many lesser women succumbed; as potential wives and mothers they would exert a critical influence on the character of new communities; for the women themselves the simpler life, more frequent recreation, and more sociable neighbours easily compensated for the harder work.

The balance of advantages and prospects is distinctly on the side of those living in the rougher, newer districts. What can be more ennobling, more healthy, or more truly womanly than the doing of

domestic work as our ancestresses did it? . . . Women will be doing
truly good work there in helping some overburdened house mother;
and how new countries benefit by the presence of more women of
culture and high principle none can realise who have not seen for
themselves. They maintain the chivalry of men, raise the tone of
their less favoured sisters, and uphold the standards of morality and
good manners, as only women and women of this type can do.[64]

The enthusiasm for domestic training coincided with a growing
interest in female emigration to the Canadian West, especially British
Columbia, and South Africa. The higher fares to Australia had caused
the new societies to shift their main attention to less distant colonies
during the eighties, and by 1890 the general increase in emigration to
Western Canada and Southern Africa induced them, as usual, to follow
the fasionable trail of most emigrants to relatively new settlements.[65]
The real emigration booms to both these regions occurred after 1900,
but during the nineties the societies laid the foundations of an intensive
system of female emigration. Representatives from both areas reported
insatiable demands for genteel home-helps. The BWEA representative in
Vancouver, Mrs Skinner, who also worked through the local YWCA
employment bureau, reported in 1907 that she had managed to provide
only 200 qualified middle-class women in the face of requests for 900.[66]
Gentlewomen were 'overwhelmingly in demand' in Western Canada, and
'only women of good family' were accepted as 'lady home-helps' in
British Columbia and the North-West.[67] In 1903 Miss Johnson reported
that Natal had no need for the 'ordinary departmental servant', but
rather for young gentlewomen and lower middle-class women.[68] Most
striking was the exodus of women to South Africa immediately after
the Boer War. Empty troop ships returning from England took out
women for a nominal charge, and the pressure on BWEA facilities was
so great that their South African Expansion Committee re-formed into
the separate South African Colonisation Society.[69] Politicians like
Joseph Chamberlain, the Colonial Secretary, and Lord Milner, the
South African High Commissioner, attended the societies' meetings to
encourage female emigration, especially to South Africa, as an imperial
duty, and the societies rapidly became willing instruments of imperial
policy.[70]

The combination of female emigration propaganda with the heady
enthusiasm of *fin-de-siècle* imperialism gave a unique twist to the
rhetoric of the feminine civilising mission, which was stronger at the
end of the century than it had been during mid-Victorian years. Notions

of imperial destiny and class and racial superiority were grafted on to
the traditional views of refined English motherhood to produce a concept of the Englishwoman as an invincible global civilising agent. The
emigrationists' general argument was that cultivated British women had
an 'Imperial mission' to perform by bringing their British ideals to an
abandoned generation of male pioneers who were threatened with alien
assimilation; these ideals, furthermore, could only be implanted by
women who occupied their 'proper sphere' in the colonies as civilised
domestic helps, teachers, wives and mothers. The founders of the CIL
hoped that their work would 'help to keep the British Empire for the
British race'.[71] and the editor of the *Spectator*, addressing a BWEA
annual meeting, argued that emigration was the only way to influence
rising states with 'our Anglo-Saxon ideals'; only women could build
colonial homes, without which the Empire could not exist.[72] Miss
J.R. Chitty feared that it was too easy for colonies to lose their
'Imperial heritage' after the first generation of predominantly male
settlers; it was woman's vital mission to counteract this evil tendency
by making attractive homes for Englishmen abroad 'that they may cease
to think of themselves as exiles, but may realize that they have but
migrated from one part of the family estate to another, and are still
among their own people'. In their 'potential motherhood' women held
the key to the situation.

> Away in the back-blocks, the whole early training of the children
> falls upon the mother alone. Upon her it depends to make a living
> reality of all that lies quite outside their circumscribed lives, above all
> the Church and Empire.[73]

In a later article, Chitty took her argument further, claiming that the
colonies had a great need for British 'women of leisure', who had some
capital but no great economic need to emigrate. Their emigration would
be an imperial duty to give personal service as social workers, educators
and even wives to a generation that had grown up ignorant of Britain; 'it
is the Englishwoman who can best teach them the way, because they
start with all the advantages of that sex privilege which the Briton wraps
around the motherhood of his race'.[74] The doctrine reached the peak
of its expression in Dora Gore Browne's poem 'To England's Daughters'
in 1904. Englishwomen, who traditionally 'Bore aloft the torch of
freedom', were now entrusted with a higher duty 'to keep the flaming
torch of loyalty on fire,/In the land of your adoption, for the honour
of your home', as 'future nursing mothers of the English race to be'.[75]

Here was Edward Gibbon Wakefield's old tenet in revised form, and just as his notion had sprung initially from the threat of alien convictism in Australia, so the new version grew from the fear of alien influences in Canada and South Africa.

The major threat in Canada was that the country would become cosmopolitan rather than British, and the emigrationists voiced alarm when they saw that the Canadian immigration boom early in the twentieth century attracted Europeans other than Britons. Ellen Joyce was shocked that a Winnipeg newspaper should have to be printed in four different languages, Russian, German, French and English, to reach that city's polyglot population. To counteract this others had to be convinced 'that the Empire, and not the Island, is woman's sphere'.[76] England's supremacy depended on keeping Canada British, and if, through indifference, it fell into alien and foreign hands 'then we shall go under and share the fate and decay of older nations'. The cure was a determined application of the 'Science of Empire Building', or sending the right women where they were needed from an imperial point of view. And if any listeners thought Joyce was speaking in platitudes, she could recall specific examples of the kind of women Canada needed:

A cultured woman takes her love of culture within herself, and in the winter evenings has longer hours for study than we have, or generally use. I only wish that my acquaintance with English Literature had been half as good as that of the wife of a Major in the North West Mounted Police, or that I had kept up my music as she had kept up hers . . . We know quite well that the duties of a housewife do not interfere with her being one of the most educated women in the world.

With such educated women, Joyce argued in 1913, it would be decided within the next five years whether Canada was to be 'British or Cosmopolitan'.[77]

The racial argument was, predictably, strongest in South Africa, and could be used to magnify potential threats from either Boers or indigenous Africans. During the Boer War the view that the Dutch population might eventually be swamped by a mass migration of Englishwomen gained increasing currency among emigration promoters. Even when the absurdity of the view was recognised it usually survived in a modified form, as in the hope that Englishwomen might instil English virtues among the Boers by example, or that they should at least be sufficiently numerous to prevent Englishmen from having to marry

Dutch women. Before the war ended the BWEA predicted that the great migration interest of the future would be in South Africa, for 'the possibility of the settler marrying his own countrywomen is of Imperial as well as family importance'.[78] The Countess of Malmesbury urged the task of the 'repopulation' of South Africa on the BWEA 'by sending out the right sort of women, fitted to be the wives of settlers and the mothers of loyal subjects'.[79] By 1903 Lord Onslow, the Colonial Under-secretary, felt it necessary to remind the SACS that the Government's encouragement of female emigration arose from no desire to swamp the Boer element, but after a long and bloody war it would be absurd 'that we should not also look after the interests of our own people'.[80] Most writers and speakers interpreted Onslow's view loosely. Lilian Orpen thought the English governess in a Dutch family had 'a splendid opportunity of serving the Empire by instilling British principles into the minds of the children', and 'helping to counteract the evil and disloyal influence by which they are surrounded'.[81] S.R. Perkins felt that the educated home-help who made herself valued and welcomed in a Dutch family, 'may feel that she is doing a real work for the Empire',[82] and J.C. Wedgewood, Liberal MP, told a SACS annual meeting that such women could conquer the Boer antipathy for things British. 'These people are not only going out to be married, but as missionaries of our Empire.'[83] In 1909, shortly before the Union Act gave South Africans self-government, the Earl of Crewe, then Colonial Secretary, was still reassuring the SACS that racial differences were actually disappearing, and might happily be still further obliterated by intermarriage of Dutchmen with Englishwomen.[84] By this time the temperature of the Dutch-English racial conflict had cooled, but a more apparent bogey was readily available in the insidious presence of the threatening African.

As the Boer question subsided, the argument shifted to an emphasis on the need for the preservation of the white race in South Africa. L.S. Amery maintained in 1908 that the SACS had made it amply clear that it had no intention of swamping the Dutch with a mass of English servants and teachers, but rather of improving the quality of social life and education for both white races; this could only be attained in a white man's country, and so long as Africans continued to perform domestic duties and influenced the children's upbringing the country did not belong wholly to the white man; women, therefore, must first replace the Africans in the household.[85] It was an argument which appealed easily to a generation reared on imperial notions of the white man's burden and the natural inferiority of Africans. In 1904 the

Governor of Natal, Sir Henry McCallum, told the SACS that his colony
needed Englishwomen as servants to ameliorate the lot of colonial
housewives whose children were being raised by Kaffir servants, with
deplorable results, 'for daily contact with a lower race must induce a
familiarity with lower ideals'.[86] Lord Robert Cecil praised the South
African Union Government of 1910, maintaining that the aim of the
SACS should now be 'to furnish South Africa with a white female
population, true colonists and settlers, who would live there and make
homes for white men', and Sydney Goldman, at the same meeting,
thought the object of emigration 'was surely to strengthen the Anglo-
Saxon race in South Africa, to keep pace with the increasing vigour of
the natives'.[87] Emigration workers invariably saw the situation in more
vivid terms. Eleanor Tyrrell highlighted the moral dangers of the shortage of Englishwomen by depicting the lonely settler in a life 'face to
face with primitive Nature. She has a way of making her demands
imperatively felt'. Without moral and social support it was difficult
always to adhere to the 'straight path'.

> Dick knows a man not so far away, a Harrowboy, he was, whose
> little house is clean, his bed comfortable, his dinner well-cooked,
> and ready when he wants it. A coloured woman seems to do ex-
> tremely well for Smith, and nobody says anything about the half-
> caste child that is occasionally seen. Smith is jolly and contented,
> works hard on his farm, and his farm prospers.

The idle women of England had a duty to emigrate in order to prevent
this degradation, for the sake of the men, for themselves and the
Empire.[88]

The arguments for domestic competence and racial dominance were
part of a rhetoric which made marriage and motherhood the end-
product and highest ideal of female emigration. The complementary
disproportion of the sexes in Britain and the colonies was still the most
striking evil for emigrationists, and Greg's old solution of the emigration
of potential wives seemed the natural and practical remedy. From its
beginning the Women's Emigration Society propaganda concentrated on
the fruitful marriage prospects for its emigrants and the imperial benefit of sending properly educated women as mates for educated colonists.[89] At times the rhetoric was sufficiently blatant to prompt criticism.
Colonel Sir Gerard Smith, an ex-Governor of Western Australia, complained that too many speakers, 'in advocating female emigration — not
to Western Australia alone — have dwelt on the advantages which await

emigrants in the shape of marriage, as if marriage were the be-all and end-all of human existence and aspirations'.[90] In 1907 the BWEA reminded its 'country-workers' that the accusation of being a 'matrimonial society' under camouflage was a perpetual hindrance to its operations; quite to the contrary, it maintained, 'Work is inscribed on our banner, the security of immediate employment – and this does not commend itself to the woman whose primary object is to "get settled".'[91] The warning was accurately based to the extent that the society's major practical work was devoted to finding colonial employment rather than spouses for its emigrants. But there was a striking rift between practice and propaganda. The emigration societies were among the most active promoters of marriage, and most of the articles in the *Imperial Colonist* openly stated or implied that colonial motherhood was the greatest need and highest aspiration for an educated woman.[92] Ellen Joyce remarked that in emigration 'Success usually means matrimony',[93] and Miss Clark was not afraid to admit that in the Canadian West women schoolteachers 'invariably have the choice of the matrimonial market'.[94] Other writers thought such noble prospects deserved more eloquent language. Mrs Shepstone saw no shame for a woman in anticipating 'that supreme development of her own being, which should make her part of the most important and powerful influences necessary to our Empire'.[95] In 1909 Dr G.R. Parkin argued that home life, with women's 'light and influence', was the secret of Britain's imperial power and greatness, 'which is transferred to homes abroad by the good wives and mothers sent out to every part of the world'.[96] The selfish younger generation of British women came in for criticism for their reluctance to venture abroad as pioneer help-mates.

> Why, if it is well for the young Englishmen of the upper and middle-classes to face Colonial life, should it be considered impossible for their sisters? . . . Are our women so neurotic, so deteriorated since the early days of America, India and Australia, that they will not help their men to conquer new worlds, give them the one really strong incentive to Colonial settlement, new sons and daughters to carry on the English tradition in wider spaces?[97]

The gulf between reality and rhetoric is suggested by Eve Grahame's admission that many girls reacted contemptuously when matrimonial possibilities were mentioned in connection with emigration; as if to underplay the point, she felt constrained to add the reminder that 'in Canada there is almost a certainty of marriage for any attractive girl who wishes to settle and have a home of her own'.[98]

Most of the writers who made so much of the civilising mission rhetoric were equally frank about their anti-feminist sentiments. Not surprisingly, since, by the 1890s, the contentious 'marriage question' and appearance of the 'New Woman' were at issue, the two attitudes invariably went together. Emigrationists judged the female excess in Britain to be the root cause of both female unemployment and feminist unrest, and assumed that once the sex disproportion had been eradicated by emigration both these symptoms would disappear in a society where most women could find their natural destiny as wives and mothers. Mrs Piers Dutton, who had recently visited Rhodesia, maintained in 1913 that even the successful working women of England, the typists, governesses and schoolmistresses, still felt 'a sense of something missing'; the lonely London typist 'may have a few women friends, but too often a normal human society of both sexes is beyond her reach'. In such circumstances her sense of injustice easily prompted her to look to the vote as a solution, 'but a vote will not touch the causes, social and economic, that make for hardship in the existence of the woman-worker'. On the other hand, in a 'well-organized Community' like Rhodesia women felt they had a good part to play in social life, and there was no sign of 'the violent symptoms of the great feminine unrest' which plagued an overcrowded England.[99] S.R. Perkins deplored the fact that, because of the female surplus, women were forced into occupations 'in which a woman's special aptitude finds no play'. The 1901 census had revealed that many women were engaged as commercial travellers, chemists, bill discounters, auctioneers, dentists and undertakers, all 'to the detriment of those duties, most important of all to the State, of rearing the citizens of the future, which they alone can perform'. Feminists were striving for women to have equal access to just such occupations as Perkins described, but she insisted that all of them were aberrations for women, who would be far better off as much needed housewives in the colonies.[100] J. Weston, describing the life of the 'colonial lady-help' in a woman's magazine, insisted that

> whatever may be said by the advanced suffragists, the natural destiny of the sex is marriage, and so much the worse for the world when the majority think otherwise.[101]

Female emigration appealed most easily to those who rejected feminist views and who recoiled from the apparent turmoil wrought by the feminists; by 1914 the emigrationists could still agree with the 1881 strictures of Viscountess Strangford on the need for women to colonise:

> And after all *what is* the mission of women? Is it not to be the help-
> meets of our Men and mothers of our Boys? I am told that women
> look *higher* now; but I myself know no mission so high as this — nor
> any education that can be given to women high enough to fit them
> for it: for those who would mould the future are surely of the
> highest importance in the Present.[102]

A few years prior to the First World War the emigrationists won
support from a new and unexpected source, the eugenics movement.
From 1909 Caleb Williams Saleeby, a young eugenist, turned his attention to a growing preoccupation of the movement, the disproportion of
the sexes in Britain and its racial implications. Saleeby claimed intellectual kinship with Herbert Spencer, but together with early eugenists like
Francis Galton and Karl Pearson he departed from Spencer's *laissez-
faire* social Darwinism by advocating specific social measures, such as
birth-control and temperance, to secure the survival of the fittest and
racial perfection.[103] Eugenics, he argued, was the business of the patriot;
'National eugenics' was vital for the survival of the British Empire,
which was a beneficent force for good throughout the world. The basic
need was for a fuller exploitation of racial genius, and eugenics should
be able to raise the average level of intelligence while simultaneously
providing the right environment in which genius could prosper. Certain
social problems prevented the attainment of these ideal conditions,
however, one of the most important being the 'woman question', for
which Saleeby blamed the surplus of over a million and a quarter
women in Britain. He admitted that the surplus was largely a natural
phenomenon, in that the root cause was a higher infant mortality among
males than females, but its long-term solution lay in the realisation of
the 'ideal of race culture', or a reduction of the birth-rate to the extent
where all children were 'already loved and desired in anticipation'.[104] In
Parenthood and Race Culture in 1909 Saleeby rested his argument on
this single solution, namely birth-control, but two years later in *Woman
and Womanhood* he extended his interest to short-term solutions, and
recommended emigration as a means to eliminate the female surplus.

In his second book Saleeby deplored the emigration of more males
than females, arguing that Britain must either cease exporting its males
or send an equal number of women to accompany them. Women's co-
operation was essential to the founding of new nations, and the colonies
needed more white women to prevent the growth of a 'half-caste' popu-

lation. In Britain the alternative to female emigration would be poly-
gamy, or at least 'something immeasurably worse', prostitution, a deplorable symptom already of the disproportion between the sexes.
Hence the growing surplus of females threatened the very practice of
monogamy, which was essential to Saleeby's 'race-culture'. But quite
apart from that, the causes of the sex disparity at home — such as infant
mortality, child mortality, war and excessive male emigration — were
evils in themselves, in the case of emigration because it limited Anglo-
Saxon unions and threatened racial improvement throughout the
Empire.[105]

The emigrationists were quick to welcome this espousal of their
cause, agreeing that large scale female emigration to the dominions 'is a
measure of fundamental statemanship and indispensable if, for example,
the White Empire is to be saved for British blood and British ideals'.[106]
But Saleeby's agreement went deeper by incorporating the same kind of
anti-feminism evident in emigration propaganda. The object of all
Saleeby's proposals was to ensure that 'the best women must be the
mothers of the future', and to this end all other matters must be sub-
ordinated. He agreed with Spencer's dictum that all female activities
which were incompatible with motherhood were liabilities to the
nation; a woman was, in effect, an instrument for furthering the progress of 'race-culture':

> Women, being constructed by Nature, as individuals, for her racial
> ends, they best realize themselves, are happy and more beautiful,
> live longer and more useful lives, when they follow as mothers or
> foster-mothers in the wide and scarcely metaphorical sense of the
> word, the career suggested in Wordsworth's lovely lines. [A tribute
> to motherhood] [107]

It was not essential, he insisted, that all women must marry, but
spinsters should, at least, become 'foster-mothers' by working at characteristically feminine duties, extensions of the mothering role, like
teaching and nursing. Female higher education ought to concentrate on
a curriculum directed towards motherhood, specifically household econ-
omics and child psychology. The feminists were misguided to the extent
that most of their aims were incompatible with eugenics; in fact,
according to Saleeby, many varieties of feminism would be 'ruinous to
the race'. Instead he advocated 'Eugenic Feminism', a doctrine which
purportedly allowed women the same right to consideration, recognition and opportunity as men, but at the same time asserted that the

best means for women to fulfil themselves was in motherhood. He supported female suffrage and the prospect of female Members of Parliament — he was taken with the potential wisdom of the 'elder matron' as MP — because he was convinced that women's vote would serve the cause of eugenics, but he was opposed fundamentally to the feminist drive for equal access to the professions and other traditionally male employment preserves.[108] For all its apparent scientific grounding, Saleeby's position, like that of the eugenics movement generally on the woman-question, differed little from that of mid-Victorian moralists intent on confining women to their 'proper sphere'. But his enthusiasm for emigration was consistent with that of the emigration promoters, and it highlights the extent to which female emigration, preoccupied with domestic training, marriage and motherhood, had become, at least in its rhetoric, an anti-feminist movement.

Female emigration propaganda, with support from eminent politicians, journalists and scientists, achieved widespread credibility and respectability, but it is not clear how far the propaganda accurately reflected the colonial lives of the societies' emigrants. Certainly some emigration workers themselves were not unaware of the tendency of their speeches and writings, and one admitted that it was wise first to entice the genteel sheltered woman to a point where she would at least be willing to face a course of domestic training, the first step in preparing for the roughness of colonial life. The BWEA and SACS received many letters from 'young ladies' wanting colonial employment but not wishing 'to emigrate' or do 'anything menial'. Three months of training often brought such women down to earth, but in the meantime a few euphemisms could be helpful:

> Sometimes it is better not to 'call a spade a spade', but by talking of technical training with big T.T. and domestic economy and women's work (also in capitals), or home experience and manual not menial work, with allusions to the development of the young nations and building up of the Empire, to arrive at the same point as if we had written back at once to say 'you must be prepared to undertake the family wash!'[109]

The persistent colonial opinion on the prime need for rough hard work, adaptability and willingness to face hardship and privation was never suppressed by the emigrationists,[110] but it is questionable whether their noble compensations of social equality and being made 'part of the family' always lived up to the idyllic expectations.

A frank corrective to some of the more effusive propaganda was published in 1912. Ella C. Sykes, a wealthy English gentlewoman, undertook a visit to Canada for the Colonial Intelligence League in 1911 to study women's employment conditions; instead of making the customary inquiries, however, she masqueraded as a genuine inexperienced home-help, and published her impressions of six different engagements on her return. Most of her experiences were not encouraging for the prospective educated home-help. Even after overcoming her initial incompetence she found that her education and previous social position counted for nothing. In recently emigrated English families and in Canadian families in towns she was treated as an ordinary servant with no concession towards being considered 'one of the family'. In isolated farm and prairie homes, where the atmosphere was more comradely, the work was so hard as to amount to a perpetual round of drudgery, which left no time for reading or the other pursuits of an educated woman. Only in Victoria, where the older population regularly sought 'lady-helps', and a few other locations in British Columbia did she find that the educated home-help's treatment lived up to that depicted in emigration propaganda. But she still concluded that most educated women would be better off as Canadian home-helps than in England; if they avoided the more sophisticated towns they would not be looked down on socially as in England. Sykes did in fact suffer some humilating experiences in the more class-conscious families, but after all her varied experience she insisted that if she had to earn her living she would 'not hesitate for a moment between the wide, free life of Canada and my probable lot in an overcrowded England'. On balance she thought it would be 'well worth a girl's while to put up with some discomfort and toil in the Dominion, where she is badly needed, and where, if of the right type, she will in all likelihood succeed beyond her anticipations'.[111] A review of her book in the *Imperial Colonist* insisted that Sykes would have avoided her unpleasant experiences if she had obtained positions through BWEA representatives instead of independent advertisements, but by and large it agreed with her general conclusions and reiterated the opinion that the best place for the home-help was in British Columbia.[112]

The colonial home-help was certainly unlikely to have found the utopia promised in the emigrationists' rhetoric, but most of the direct evidence suggests that emigration could offer more of a real solution to the distressed gentlewoman, mainly for socio-psychological reasons, than could most alternatives in Britain. Some writers made much of the claim that the South African lady-help was best off because African servants performed the heaviest work,[113] but the printed letters from emigrants indicate far more satisfaction with circumstances surrounding their home life and social intercourse than actual duties and remuneration. 'LGC' went as a governess to Bloemfontein, South Africa, and was at first shocked that she was expected to assist in household duties like any home-help, but she soon adapted to this novelty and found other compensations in the different customs of the country: 'one learns not to mind these things a bit, I look upon it all as a huge picnic',[114] Repeatedly the women implied that the biggest change for them had been in their basic way of life rather than in income, and the Old World stigma attaching to 'menial work' simply never arose after their initial experience. A Vancouver 'companion-help' thought her new circumstances admirably suited to similar women in England.

> Why don't they come out here some of these white slaves in England? Why, why? I have always taken good salaries myself, but have met many of these poor girls, and only hope that I may in writing to provincial English papers induce some of them to come out here and enjoy with me this simple, natural, though not lazy life.[115]

Such letters abound in the publications of the various emigration societies, and although the societies would be inclined naturally to print the most favourable letters, there is no evidence of any significant number of failures or dissatisfaction, which was quick to communicate itself through disgruntled colonial employers. The consistent impression is that the educated home-help survived and succeeded because she was freed from the more class-bound conventions of British society.[116]

For women who were not satisfied with the life of a home-help the societies' advice to use the position as an initial 'stepping-stone' to more challenging employment seems to have been followed widely. Many went with that exact intention, and the BWEA Training College reported that numbers of its students regularly became teachers, typists and hostel superintendents after a year as home-helps.[117] The societies saw this as a question of adaptability, for after a year of colonial domestic work most women were much more likely to succeed in any other occupation.

> Of the many ladies and middle-class girls 'placed' by the W.E.A. in the Colonies, those who were now doing best were those who took a at once any work they could get, and who, having thus proved their

willingness and their capabilities, had by degrees been enabled to better their position.[118]

The Colonial Intelligence League, formed in 1910, was directed primarily to ensuring that this kind of progress took place. It sought to place women in 'other professions besides those of Teacher and Home-Help' but insisted that they first be prepared to work as home-helps.[119] This approach began during the late nineties and became increasingly common in the years immediately preceding the World War. It was a sign that a new type of educated woman was beginning to emigrate, a woman for whom 'the cruel crush of life' no longer centred round the governess's schoolroom but round 'the soul-destroying typewriter, so largely her only resource, grinding out youth, joy and life, day after day, for small pay, in hot indoor narrowness'.[120] Distressed gentlewomen still existed in thousands at the beginning of the twentieth century, and they remained a major preoccupation of the emigrationists, but the trained typist, clerk or nurse, was relatively new to the colonial scene, and, reflecting recent changes in British society and the position of women, came increasingly within the orbit of the emigration societies.

We have already seen how, after 1880, the new emigration societies, unlike the FMCES, made emigration available to a much wider range of middle-class women. Undoubtedly the home-help idea proved to be a realistic solution for women of varied backgrounds, at least in the short-term, although the lower middle-class girl, who had usually done some housework in her own home, often had the advantage in that she required little or no special training before emigrating. Proud though the BWEA was of its Leaton Colonial Training Home, it acknowledged that there were 'multitudes' of women who they 'dare not encourage to run the risk of emigration without previous training, but who cannot afford it'.[121] By the turn of the century, though, an increasing number of women were training for more specialised careers in secretarial work, nursing and teaching.[122] The fact that the well-educated minority still monopolised the better paid jobs in Britain meant that it became more realistic for partly trained women, especially those from lower middle-class families, to seek to pursue their careers abroad, where the prospects and pay were generally better.[123] Distressed gentlewomen, who, by definition, were untrained for employment when they most needed it, and were unable to afford the necessary training or undergo a schooling period without income, again suffered in relation to the more socially mobile lower middle class. By Edwardian years such

women were being urged to turn to increasingly eccentric but unprom-
ising occupations such as the 'lady-gardener'.[124] Teaching remained a
possibility, whether as a schoolmistress or private governess, but the
emigration societies, acknowledging the colonial demands for adequate
training, insisted that prospective teachers of any kind be properly
educated, with some form of certificate or diploma.[125] By the twentieth
century it was as difficult for the truly distressed gentlewoman to emigrate as it was for her to obtain respectable and remunerative employment in Britain.[126]

During the decade preceding 1914 the societies devoted increasing
time to the new professions and trades dominated by lower middle-class
women, largely at the expense of untrained and ill-qualified distressed
gentlewomen. Essentially this was a function of the rapid growth in the
populations of colonial towns, especially in Canada. In 1909 the
Alberta Deputy Minister of Education, D.S. MacKenzie, visited England
and appealed to the BWEA to send out more qualified teachers; the
demand in elementary schools far outstripped local supply, and women
with an English certificate could be certain of immediate
employment.[127] Secondary and specialist teachers were usually required
first to take some Canadian training, but the opportunities for qualified
primary schoolteachers were unlimited. The new schools effectively
supplanted the governess, and except for in remote rural areas the
Canadian governess became a rarity.[128] The well-trained stenographer
also found colonial employment an easy matter, but, as Ella Sykes
discovered, each city was over-supplied with 'indifferent typists' so that
good training was essential.[129] The CIL during its four years of active
existence before 1914, continued to cater to the home-help, but was
involved increasingly in finding professional and semi-professional work
for qualified women, and this, indeed, was the reason for its original
formation.[130] The BWEA itself, which maintained its traditional
approach of assisting women of all classes, with the emphasis on educated women, signified the shift of focus by a noteworthy change in
terminology. Until 1909 its annual reports classified educated emigrants
into two groups: 'Ladies' and 'Middle-class'; from 1910 it dropped the
term 'Ladies' and instead used 'Educated women', 'Middle-class and
business' and a finer breakdown of other occupations such as 'Teachers,'
'Nurses' and 'Stenographers'.[131] Yet in spite of this clear recognition of
specialisation in women's work the emigrationists' rhetoric continued to
expound the domestic helpmeet's civilising mission. Changes in both
British and colonial social and economic structures forced the emigration societies to become sophisticated placement agencies for trained

and qualified women, but their traditional and anti-feminist inclinations remained enshrined in pious and sentimental propaganda.

The societies' work was at its peak when, in 1914, the outbreak of war brought most active operations to an abrupt end. Numerically their achievements look moderately impressive, especially compared with those of their predecessors, but it is not always easy to establish the precise social origins of their protegées. There are no total figures for the WES, which operated from 1880 to 1884, but between them the BWEA, SACS and CIL helped approximately 20,000 women to emigrate in the thirty years between 1884 and 1914, or on average just over 660 each year.[132] A large proportion of these were working-class women who received assistance and protection but no financial aid, and there are insufficient records to determine the exact numbers and origins of middle-class emigrants. The closest analysis, which must still be heavily qualified, can be made from the BWEA annual reports. After 1906 the BWEA began to list class origins or occupations of some of its Canadian emigrants; unfortunately the same was not done for Australasian and American emigrants, and nearly half of those listed were indistinguishable as to class, being described only as 'escorts to friends, relations, situations' etc., if the society did not provide actual financial assistance. With these reservations it is possible to form a conservative estimate of the proportion of women helped to emigrate to Canada only by the BWEA in these years.

Table 5: Female Emigrants Assisted to Canada by BWEA, 1906-14

Year	Total female emigrants	Total to Canada	'Middle-Class', incl. 'Ladies', 'Educated' etc.	Class unidentified: 'GFS' 'Escorts', 'Widows'. etc.
1906	604	538	110	69
1907	706	639	98	99
1908	417	356	70	142
1909	398	318	85	202
1910	932	803	158	451
1911	1012	905	215	337
1912	1126	956	155	752
1913	1007	857	146	407
1914	504	396	42	170
Totals	6706	5768	1079	2629
Percentage of Total to Canada			18.5%	45.5%

Source: Compiled from BWEA *Annual Reports*, 1906 to 1914. Nurses are not included in the middle-class column.

Table 5 reveals that 18.5 per cent of the Canadian emigrants were variously classified as middle-class while 45.5 per cent were not distinguished by class at all; the proportion, therefore, may have been higher than indicated here. In 1912 Lady Knightley, the BWEA president, and Ellen Joyce told a Dominions Royal Commission that approximately 20 per cent of BWEA and SACS emigrants were educated women.[133] After the Boer War the SACS itself helped an average of 400 women a year, and the widespread use of African servants tended to create a relatively larger demand in South Africa for genteel home-helps. The CIL assisted 269 women, all of them educated, between 1911 and 1914, and its own work probably accounts for the decline in the numbers of middle-class emigrants sent after 1911 by its sister organisation, the BWEA.[134] The figures do seem to indicate, at least, that a varied range of middle-class women were turning to emigration in increasing numbers on the eve of the World War. The national figures are of only slight help in confirming this trend, since even after 1900 approximately 70 per cent of female emigrants were not classified as to occupation, and most middle-class home-helps, for example, would have been entered as domestic servants. Still, even these inadequate figures reveal a marked increase in middle-class occupations after 1903, as shown in Table 6.

Table 6:[135] Adult Female Emigrants from Great Britain, 1899-1911

Year	Total female emigrants	Teachers, clerks, or professional women	Miscellaneous or occupation not stated
1899	57,248	274	36,348
1900	63,909	256	41,555
1901	65,213	666	45,653
1902	73,663	686	56,864
1903	86,687	1,698	66,815
1904	96,224	1,737	70,275
1905	88,279	1,351	65,982
1906	105,139	1,656	77,474
1907	128,920	1,812	96,868
1908	97,174	2,165	71,371
1909	103,138	2,225	73,102
1910	136,699	2,769	97,402
1911	156,606	3,751	110,642

Source: I. Ferenczi (ed.), *International Migrations* vol. I, *Statistics*, p. 635, Table viii.

In the late Victorian and Edwardian periods single women were emigrating more readily without the assistance of voluntary organisations, and the BWEA was convinced that far more women emigrated independently than under its auspices[136] Emigration was no longer the hazardous experience it had once been, and independent women could safely spurn the aid of a protective society. Ella Sykes met some of these women in Canada and was impressed with their self-reliance.[137] At last the facilities and opportunities for emigration had developed to a point where they might nearly do justice to the enterprising spirit of countless single middle-class women. But how far the opportunities reached the most needy women of the middle class remains uncertain.

Much of the evidence in this chapter does indeed point in a familiar direction already clear from the experience of the FMCES and earlier schemes: that emigration, while offering a real solution to many of the distressed gentlewoman's problems, was denied to her in favour of better qualified, more upwardly mobile women, especially from the lower middle class. The gradual decline of the governess and of genteel domestic service abroad, and the rise of more specialised occupations for women in Britain and the colonies certainly suggest an unmistakeable trend, in which impecunious gentlewomen unable to afford training could only be the losers. But the point should not be pushed too far. After 1880 the numbers alone are, for the first time, large enough to confirm the readiness of genteel women without prospects to risk the uncertainties and hazards of emigration. The clientele of the societies' domestic training colleges was overwhelmingly middle-class in origin, mostly, it seems, composed of models of the distressed gentlewoman stereotype. Moreover, to the extent that the home-help idea was a real solution, it was so largely for genteel women who lacked qualifications for other work at home or overseas. In many respects, then, the emigration societies fulfilled the high expectations they created. But their pervasive rhetoric, which obscured the real social origins and occupations of most emigrants, cannot be used as evidence for this conclusion. Widely publicised propaganda told women that the chief qualifications for successful emigration were their sex and their breeding. Only when women looked more closely at the practicalities did they discover that education and basic training were the real qualifications, and the more specialised the better. In the final analysis it was their adaptability and willingness to put their much vaunted gentility at risk which proved to be the most relevant and helpful qualifications.

Notes

1. Blanchard, the wife of the dramatist, Edwart Litt Leman Blanchard, was better known as Mrs E.L. Blanchard and under the pen-name of 'Carina'. She had

travelled to New Zealand in the course of her work as an emigration agent. Pratt, *A Woman's Work for Women*, pp. 64-9; Pratt, *Pioneer Women in Victoria's Reign*, pp. 62-66; WEA, Introductory brochure describing the preliminary meeting of 12 Jan. 1880; *Borough of Marylebone Mercury*, 3 June and 1 July 1882. Cf. Monk, pp. 7-13.

2. Pratt, *A Woman's Work for Women*, pp. 69-71; United British Women's Emigration Association, *Annual Report*, 1891-2, p.7; South African Colonisation Society, Report of First Annual Meeting, 13 May 1903, *Imperial Colonist*, vol. II, June 1903, pp. 65-7; Colonial Intelligence League, *Annual Report*, 1910-11, pp. 4-9. Cf. Monk, pp. 13-17.

3. UBWEA, *Annual Reports*, 1889, pp. 4-5, 1892-3, p. 7; BWEA, Sub-Committee for Diffusing Information, Minutes, 5 June and 12 June 1903, 'Rules for Associates,' *Record Book*, 1903-5 (Fawcett Library); A. Ross, 'Paragraph for Parish Magazines,' *Imperial Colonist*, vol. X, Feb. 1912, p. 31.

4. BWEA, *Annual Report*, 1901, p.41. Lady Knightley of Fawsley, an active worker and speaker for the BWEA, became editor of the new journal. *Imperial Colonist*, vol. I, Jan. 1902, pp. 2-5.

5. E. Joyce, 'Emigration Notices – Canada', *Imperial Colonist*, vol. XI, Dec. 1913, p. 211; 'Notes of the Month', Ibid., vol. VI, Oct. 1907, pp. 1-2.

6. BWEA, *Annual Reports*, 1908, p. 13, 1911, p. 11. Until 1902 the BWEA had leased the 'Working Women's House' in Horseferry Road, Westminster, *Annual Reports*, 1900, p. 29, 1901, p. 37. On the Liverpool hostel see E. Joyce, *Emigrant's Rest for Women and Children* (London, 1887).

7. The British Ladies' Female Emigrant Society had selected matrons from 1848 to 1888, and its example prompted the colonial governments to employ them to supervise its own assisted female emigrants; after the death of the society's secretary, Miss Tipple, in 1888, the Society for the Promotion of Christian Knowledge selected and paid matrons for BWEA women, and the BWEA assumed full responsibility in 1897. UBWEA, *Annual Reports*, 1891-2, p. 8, 1897, p. 12; 'Early History', *Imperial Colonist*, vol. VI, Dec. 1908, pp. 8-11.

8. YWCA, *Important Notice to Young Women About to Emigrate* (n.d., brochure on Loma House, Sydney, in News Cuttings, Book 1, p. 27, Fawcett Library); UBWEA, *Annual Reports*, 1896, p. 14, 1910, pp. 24-8; *Imperial Colonist*, vol. VI, June 1908, p. 5, July 1908, pp. 3-7, vol. VIII, Oct. 1910, pp. 159-61.

9. R. Strachey, *The Cause, A Short History of the Women's Movement in Great Britain*, p. 210. Cf. B. Harrison, 'For Church, Queen and Family: The Girls' Friendly Society, 1874-1920', *Past and Present*, No. 61, Nov. 1973, pp. 107-38.

10. The society reported 'great annoyance' that 'Mrs. Tuckwell, BWEA' had been reported in *The Times* of 29 August 1912 to have joined a deputation from the Women's Social and Political Union to urge Robert Borden, the Canadian Prime Minister, to give the vote to Canadian women. 'The President at once wrote to Mr. Borden to explain to him that Mrs. Tuckwell had absolutely no right to represent the BWEA, which is an entirely non-political body, neither Suffragist nor Anti-Suffragist'. The note of expediency here is obvious, but it was not evident in the activities of the FMCES. 'What are we doing?' *Imperial Colonist*, vol. X, Nov. 1912, pp. 182-3.

11. Pratt, *A Woman's Work for Women*, pp. 72-3.

12. The society claimed to have adopted the new policy 'without at all losing sight of its primary object – the protection and care of women'. UBWEA, *Annual Report*, 1889-90, p. 10.

13. It does not follow that all contemporary female philanthropists were anti-feminist. Women like Florence Nightingale and Mary Carpenter certainly had reservations about the direction of the women's movement, but there is no clear dichotomy, and feminist reformers and philanthropists like Josephine Butler and

temperance workers were probably more generally representative. Cf. B. Harrison, 'State Intervention and Moral Reform in nineteenth-century England', in P. Hollis (ed.), *Pressure from Without in early Victorian England* (London, 1974), p. 291. An exception among emigration workers, notable for her feminist outlook, was Lady Knightley of Fawsley, editor of the *Imperial Colonist*, who supported women's suffrage and worked with the Working Ladies' Guild and Society for Promoting the Employment of Women. J. Cartwright (ed.), *The Journals of Lady Knightley of Fawsley, 1856-1884* (London, 1915), pp. 293-4; Harrison, 'For Church, Queen and Family . . . ', pp. 113, 122-3.

14. UEEA, *Finance Committee Minutes*, 11 March 1885-29 March 1886 (Fawcett Library); BWEA, Sub-Committee for Diffusing Information, 1903-5, Minutes, 8 Oct. 1903 (Fawcett Library); BWEA, *Annual Reports*, 1904, p. 13, 1909, p. 14, 1912, p. 12.

15. See the annual reports of the BWEA, which listed occupational classifications of many of the emigrants; the 1907 report, for example, listed 122 'industrial workers', 166 servants and 22 dressmakers out of 538 women sent to Canada; p. 13.

16. C.E. Collet, 'Prospects of Marriage for Women,' in *Educated Working Women*, pp. 48-49 (reprinted from the *Nineteenth Century*, April 1892). Collet herself was one of the four early MA graduates from London University.

17. Ibid., p. 53.

18. Occupations of Males and Females, England and Wales, Summary Tables, vol. III, 1891 Census, *PP* 1893-94, CVI (7058), p. vii, Table 4; 1881 Census, *PP* 1883, LXXX (3722), p. vi, Table 4. Cf. Holcombe, pp. 18-19 and *passim*.

19. C.E. Collet, 'The Economic Position of Educated Working Women,' (Paper delivered in South Place Chapel, Finsbury, 2 Feb. 1890), *South Place Ethical Society Discourses* no. 25 (pp. 205-16) (London, 1890). pp. 207-10.

20. 'Training for English Girls as Colonists', *The Queen*, 11 April 1891, p. 566.

21. See above ch. 5.

22. Crawshay, *Domestic Service for Gentlewomen: A Record of Experience and Success*, p. 38.

23. LMH (Hubbard), pp. 43-5; see also ch. 5, above. For sceptical but antifeminist reaction see 'Daughters as Lady Helps,' *Saturday Review*, vol. XLII, 5 Aug. 1876, pp. 161-2.

24. A. Ross, *Emigration for Women* (London, 1886), p. 16.

25. BWEA, *Annual Report*, 1909, p. 14. The BWEA Secretary, Miss Grace Lefroy, in press interviews, was at pains to stress the society's opposition to the emigration of domestic servants. *Cassell's Saturday Journal*, 3 July 1895, p. 835; *Morning Leader*, 24 Nov. 1897, p. 3.

26. 'Some Situations offered for Useful Helps', *Imperial Colonist*, vol. III, Oct. 1904, pp. 116-17; see also enclosure with vol. V and vol. VI, May 1907, pp. 3-4.

27. In 1912 the BWEA obtained a grant from the Corporation of the City of London only after a determined defence against the charge that 'we are very short of servants in this country; you are endeavouring to get them out of the country'. Speech of Lord Mayor of London to BWEA annual meeting, 1913; ibid., vol. XII, April 1914, pp. 57-65.

28. E. Joyce, 'Home Helps', Circular sent to Western Canada, 22 Aug. 1906, ibid., vol. V, Oct. 1906, pp. 148-50.

29. Miss G.B. Clark, 'Are Educated Women Wanted in Canada?' Pt. I, ibid., vol. VIII, Feb. 1910, pp. 22-4.

30. Ibid., vol. V, Nov. 1906, pp. 160-1.

31. UBWEA, *Annual Report*, 1894, p. 10.

32. Eleanor Tyrrell, 'Colonial Life for Girls,' *Imperial Colonist*, vol. IX, Feb.

1911, p. 244; Eve Grahame, 'Women Who Can Do Things', vol. XII, May 1914, pp. 75-7.
33. Mrs C.H. Cambell – 'Opportunities in Canada, The West in Particular', ibid., vol. VI, Aug. 1907, pp. 3-5.
34. G.B. Clark, 'Women's Chances in the West', ibid., vol. VIII, March 1909, pp. 39-41.
35. 'Horticulture as a Career for Women', ibid., vol. VI, Feb. 1908, pp. 7-10, reprinted from *The Times*, 26 Dec. 1907, p. 8.
36. CIL, *Annual Report*, 1910-11, pp. 10-11; YWCA, *Important Notice to Young Women About to Emigrate.*
37. UBWEA, *Annual Report*, 1890-1, pp. 11-12; interview with G. Lefroy in *The Echo*, 13 April, 1895, p. 22; E.L. Blanchard, 'The Emigration of Women', in *Work and Leisure*, May 1880, vol. V, pp. 129-34.
38. Letter from E. Joyce in *Our Paper, The Monthly Organ of the Women's Help Society*, Nov. 1894, p. 699. G. Lefroy in *Cassell's Saturday Journal*, 3 July 1895, p. 835; Blanchard, ibid.
39. Ross, pp. 5-8.
40. UBWEA, *Annual Report*, 1897, p. 13.
41. 'Emigration of Educated Women', *The Queen*, 4 Dec. 1886.
42. Mrs W. Browne (Hon. Sec., WES), *Emigration for Women* (n.d.) p. 4.
43. BWEA, *Annual Report*, 1906, p. 11.
44. E. Joyce speech at a 'private conference at HRH Princess Christian's House', 13 July 1904, *Imperial Colonist*, vol. III, Aug. 1904, p. 87.
45. Ibid.
46. 'Training for English Girls as Colonists', *The Queen*, 11 April 1891, p. 566.
47. Miss Vernon, *Leaton Colonial Training Home* (Winchester, 1905, second edition), pp. 4-9; 'The Work of a Woman's Emigration Society', Pt. II, *The Queen*, 25 Oct. 1890, p. 613; BWEA, *Annual Report*, 1909, pp. 22-4.
48. Letter from 'One of the Foundresses of the Leaton Colonial Home', *St. James's Gazette*, 20 April 1897, pp. 4-5. Vernon noted that 'although the greater number of girls trained at Leaton came from the middle classes, a good many ladies have also been among the pupils'. Vernon, pp. 13-14.
49. BWEA, *Annual Report*, 1907, pp. 22-5.
50. 'A Visit to the Colonial Training College for Ladies at Stoke Prior', *Imperial Colonist*, vol. X, June 1912, pp. 102-5; BWEA, *Annual Reports*, 1906, p. 26, 1909, pp. 22-3, 1912, p. 24.
51. BWEA, *Annual Reports*, 1912, pp. 23-4; 1914, pp. 10-11.
52. 'Training Schools', and G. Lefroy, 'Where to Train and How to Train', *Imperial Colonist*, vol. I, Oct. 1902, pp. 91, 92-6, which give a complete list and description of the existing colonial training schools in 1902; see also ibid., Dec. 1902, pp. 115-16.
53. Ibid., vol. I, May 1902, pp. 42-3.
54. Ibid., vol. I, Oct. 1902, pp. 92-6; Dec. 1902, pp. 115-16.
55. Ibid., vol. III, Feb. 1904, pp. 20, 23. Some of the better known colleges were the 'Colonial Training Branch of the Horticultural College', Swanley, Kent, the 'Country and Colonial School for Ladies', Arlesley, Herts., run by Miss Turner, a BWEA worker, and the home at Haslemere, Surrey, run by the Rev. and Mrs E. Tritton-Gurney. Ibid., vol. II, March, 1903, pp. 32-3; vol. VIII, June 1910, p. 82; vol. I, Aug. 1902, p. 76. In 1914 the BWEA college at Stoke Prior became affiliated with the nearby 'Barnt Green Nursery' in order to teach 'mothercraft' and infant care to educated women about to emigrate. BWEA, *Annual Report*, 1914, p. 11.
56. 'MacDonald Institute', *Imperial Colonist*, vol. VII, April 1909, p. 57. In 1914 a graduate of the MacDonald Institute began giving colonial training, 'repro-

ducing Canadian conditions', at Hoebridge Farm, Woking, Surrey, established by Lady Gwendolen Guinness; 'Overseas Training School for Women', ibid., vol. XII, May 1914, pp. 79-80.

57. 'Training for Ladies in British Columbia,' ibid., vol. X, Jan. 1913, pp. 225-6.

58. CIL, *Annual Reports*, 1911-12, pp. 9-10, 1913-14, pp. 10-11.

59. UBWEA, *Annual Report*, 1891-92, p. 12.

60. *Imperial Colonist*, vol. I, Jan. 1902, pp. 3-5.

61. 'Thirty Years of G.F.S. Imperial Work', read at GFS Imperial Conference, York, 17 July 1912, Pt. II, ibid., vol. X, Sept. 1912, p. 154.

62. Mrs Skinner, 'In British Columbia', ibid., vol. II, April 1903, pp. 39-41.

63. 'A Visit to the Colonial Training College for Ladies at Stoke Prior', ibid., vol. X, June 1912, pp. 102-5.

64. S.R. Perkins, 'Emigration', read to the Royal Institute of Public Health, Folkestone Congress, July 1904, ibid., vol. III, Nov. 1904. p. 125-8.

65. The CIL revived interest in the emigration of 'Lady elps' to Australia, and the Victorian Government subsidised its candidates with £9 ach, but it devoted the bulk of its work to British Columbia. CIL, *Annual Reports*, 1911-12, pp. 5-6, 1913-14, pp. 10-13.

66. The plentiful supply of Chinese servants in British Columbia kept down the demand for regular working-class servants, 'Emigration Notices', *Imperial Colonist*, vol. VI, Aug. 1907, p. 11. See also the letter from 'E.E.' to G. Lefroy, Victoria, 4 July 1907, in BWEA, *Annual Report*, 1907, p. 33.

67. E. Lewthwaite, 'Useful Helps for Western Canada', *Imperial Colonist*, vol. I, March 1902, pp. 19-20.

68. E. Johnson, 'Domestic Helps in Natal', *Imperial Colonist*, vol. II, April 1903.

69. BWEA *Annual Reports*, 1902, pp. 40-2, 1903, p. 11.

70. Milner supported the BWEA's work in the first *Imperial Colonist*, vol. I, Jan. 1902, p. 1, and in 1907 spoke at the annual meeting of the SACS, ibid., vol. VI, June 1907, pp. 3-7. Chamberlain's speech at the 1901 BWEA meeting 'crystallized a wave of thought which had been moving in the minds of statesmen and both military and commercial men', to the effect that 'the settling of new countries could not, it was felt, be carried out or maintained unless "women-settlers" followed the men pioneers'. *Annual Reports*, 1901, p. 16, 1900, pp. 51-7. In 1902, through Milner's influence, the South African Government allotted £15,000 annually for female emigration to the Transvaal and Orange River Colonies; copies of telegrams in *Imperial Colonist*, vol. I, Oct. 1902, pp. 89-90.

71. CIL, *Annual Report*, 1910-11, p. 12.

72. John St Loe-Strachey to meeting of 23 March, 1909, BWEA, *Annual Report*, 1908, p. 34. Strachey, a staunch Unionist and Imperialist, owned and edited the *Spectator* from 1898 to 1925. *DNB* (1922-30), pp. 816-18.

73. J.R. Chitty, 'Imperial Patrotism,' *Imperial Colonist*, vol. III, Feb. 1904, pp. 15-16.

74. Chitty, 'The Young Old Maid as Emigrant', ibid., vol. V, Aug. 1906, pp. 116-18.

75. Ibid., vol. III, Dec. 1904, pp. 133. See the complete poem in Appendix II.

76. E. Joyce, 'Thirty Years of G.F.S. Imperial Work', read at GFS Imperial Conference, 17 July 1912, ibid., vol. X, Aug. 1912, pp. 138-41.

77. Joyce, 'The Imperial Aspect of G.F.S. Emigration', read at GFS Imperial Conference at the Imperial Institute, London, June 19,1913, ibid., vol. XI, Aug. 1913, pp. 123-31. For a similar argument from the Standing Committee on Emigration of the Royal Colonial Institute see ibid., vol. IX, Aug. 1911, pp. 346-8.

78. BWEA, *Annual Report*, 1900, p. 12.

79. Susan, Countess of Malmesbury, 'The Future of South Africa,' *Imperial Colonist*, vol. I, Feb. 1902, pp. 10-11.

80. Speech to SACS annual meeting, 13 May 1903, ibid., vol. II, June 1903, pp. 65-7.

81. L. Orpen, 'Governesses in South Africa,' ibid., vol. III, May 1904, pp. 50-3.

82. S.R. Perkins, 'Openings for Women in South Africa,' ibid., vol. IV, Aug. 1905, pp. 87-8.

83. Speech of 23 May 1906, ibid., vol. V, June 1906, pp. 80-2. Wedgewood, a descendant of the Staffordshire potter, had just been elected for Newcastle-under-Lyme, *DNB*, (1941-50), pp. 941-3.

84. Speech, as chairman, to SACS annual meeting, 10 June 1909, ibid., vol. VII, July 1909, pp. 98-100.

85. Speech to SACS annual meeting, 13 May 1908, ibid., vol. VI, June 1908, pp. 6-8.

86. Speech to SACS annual meeting, 1904, ibid., vol. III, June 1904, pp. 64-5.

87. Speeches to SACS annual meeting, 6 May 1910, ibid., vol. VIII, June 1910, pp. 83-5.

88. E. Tyrrell, 'A Few Home Truths', ibid., vol. IX, March 1911, pp. 266-8.

89. An account of the opening meeting of the WES Northern Branch deplored the shortage of good wives for colonial men 'of good birth, of honest life, following the most wholesome of occupations, who would give all that life is worth to have a woman like his sisters come and make his home complete', while in Britain, 'there are hundreds of women, well bred and well educated, who have been practiced in home duties, but who find no room for the exercise of these duties. These are just the women who are wanted as wives in the colonies. They need feel no sense of injury in the plain statement of the fact.' Anon. pamphlet, 'The Northern Branch and "Home" of the W.E.S.', reprinted from the *Borough of Marylebone Mercury*, 3 June 1882.

90. 'Western Australia', *Imperial Colonist*, vol. I, July 1902, pp. 60-2.

91. 'A Word to Our Country Workers', ibid., vol. VI, May 1907, pp. 3-5.

92. The BWEA annual report for 1909 expressed a wish to direct women 'from other occupations to take up domestic duties in Canada, so as to fit them eventually for homes of their own'. p. 14.

93. Joyce, 'On Openings for Educated Women in Canada', read at a conference of the Central Bureau for the Employment of Women, 18 June 1906, *Imperial Colonist*, vol. V, July 1906, pp. 100-4.

94. G.B. Clark, 'Women's Chances in the West', ibid., vol. VII, March 1909, pp. 39-41.

95. 'Some Views of the Emigration of Women to South Africa', ibid., vol. I, Sept. 1902, pp. 79-82.

96. Speech at BWEA annual meeting, 23 March, 1909, *Annual Report*, 1908, p. 34.

97. D.A. Bowen, 'Waste Women', *Imperial Colonist*, vol. XI, Feb. 1913, pp. 27-8.

98. 'Women Who Can Do Things', ibid., vol. XII, May 1914, pp. 75-77.

99. P. Dutton, 'Rhodesia for Women', ibid., vol. XI, Aug. 1913, pp. 131-2.

100. S.R. Perkins, 'Emigration', from a paper read to the Royal Institute of Public Health Folkestone Congress, July 1904, ibid., vol. III, Nov. 1904, pp. 125-8.

101. J. Weston, 'What Women May Do — The Colonial Lady Help', *Woman*, no. 123, 4 May 1892, pp. 3-4.

102. Viscountess Strangford speech at WEA meeting, Grosvenor House, 22 June 1881, in brochure *Women's Emigration Society* (Fawcett Library, News cuttings, Book 1).

103. Pearson and Galton did not share Saleeby's unreserved fervour for the temperance cause. Cf, F. Copleston, 'Herbert Spencer – Progress and Freedom', in H. Grisewood (ed.), *Ideas and Beliefs of the Victorians* (first published 1949, New York, 1966), p. 90; D.W. Forrest, *Francis Galton, The Life and Work of a Victorian Genius* (London, 1974), pp. 282-3.

104. C.W. Saleeby, *Parenthood and Race Culture: An Outline of Eugenics* (London, 1909), pp. x-xi, 291-4. Saleeby graduated MD from Edinburgh in 1904, was the Royal Institute Lecturer in Eugenics in 1907, 1908, 1914, 1917 and 1923, Vice-President of the National Temperance League, and in 1920-1 chairman of the World League against Alcoholism. *Who Was Who* (London, 1941), vol. III, 1929-40, pp. 1189-90.

105. C.W. Saleeby, *Woman and Womanhood: A Search for Principles* (London, 1911, US edition, 1912), pp. 267-86.

106. *Imperial Colonist*, vol. IX, April 1911, p. 282.

107. Saleeby, *Woman and Womanhood*, pp. 6-14.

108. Ibid., pp. 6-24, 128-31.

109. 'How Not to do it', *Imperial Colonist*, vol. VI, Sept. 1908, pp. 8-9.

110. The unmistakeable impression conveyed by published answers to a questionnaire sent to Western Canadian housewives in 1886 was that women must be ready to work hard, stoop to any manual chores and be prepared to face privations and set-backs before being successful. Anon., *What Women Say of the Canadian North-West. A Simple Statement of the Experience of Women Settled in all parts of Manitoba and the North-West Territories* (1886). Emigration propaganda continually repeated that 'fine ladies are not wanted' as emigrants. 'Emigration for English Girls, A Chat with Mrs. Joyce', *The Spinning Wheel, For Wives, Mothers and Daughters*, vol. IV, 8 Sept. 1894.

111. E.C. Sykes, *A Home-Help in Canada* (London, 1912), pp. ix, 302-4 and *passim*. Sykes was already well-travelled, having accompanied her brother, Sir Percy Sykes, to Persia in 1894; she was the first woman to ride from the Caspian Sea to India, which she described in *Through Persia on a Side Saddle* (London, 1898); *Who Was Who*, vol. III, 1929-40, p. 1319.

112. *Imperial Colonist*, vol. X, Jan. 1913, pp. 214-15.

113. See, for example, 'A Talk with Miss Lefroy', *The Echo*, 13 April 1895, p. 22; S.R. Perkins, 'Openings for Women in South Africa', *Imperial Colonist*, vol. IV, Aug. 1905, pp. 87-88; speech of Richard Jebb to SACS annual meeting, 10 June 1909, ibid., vol. VII, July 1909, pp. 100-2.

114. Letter to Miss Wilson, Scottish correspondent, UBWEA, 20 Sept. 1897, UBWEA, *Annual Report*, 1897, p. 34.

115. 'E.R.' a 'young lady' to G. Lefroy (BWEA secretary), Vancouver, (n.d.), UBWEA, *Annual Report*, 1898, p. 29.

116. See, e.g. 'G.H.' to Lefroy, Kelowna, B.C., 17 May 1912, a home-help who, after describing her new talents at milking cows, caring for chickens and ducks, added that she would never want to live in England again. BWEA, *Annual Report*, 1912, pp. 41-2. One woman with a genteel background 'had the courage to go out as a general servant', and prospered eventually as a home-help. *Imperial Colonist*, vol. II, July 1903, p. 80. See also the report of the BWEA annual meeting, 28 Feb. 1905, ibid., vol. IV, April 1905, p. 40.

117. Report of Stoke Prior Training College, 1910, BWEA, *Annual Report*, 1910, p. 27. See also emigrants' letters, e.g. in UBWEA, *Annual Report*, 1892-93, p. 18.

118. 'Women's Emigration Association', 'An account of a paper read by Miss Lefroy on "Emigration" at an "At Home" ' held by Mrs. Younghusband', *The Queen*, 15 Feb. 1896, p. 272. See also M. Montgomery Campbell, 'Ca-na-da, A Contradiction in Terms', *Imperial Colonist*, vol. II, Feb. 1903, pp. 17-18.

119. 'Colonial Intelligence for Educated Women', *Imperial Colonist*, vol. VIII, April 1910, p. 51.

120. Mrs J. Hopkinson, 'On Colonisation of Women in South Africa', read to the British Association on board SS *Durham Castle*, 13 Oct. 1905, ibid., Special 'British Association' issue, Feb. 1905, pp. 37-43.

121. BWEA, *Annual Report*, 1892-3, p. 22.

122. Cf. Holcombe, *passim*.

123. See, for example, the discussion of Canadian secretarial work, reporting that conditions were better and working hours shorter. BWEA, *Annual Report*, 1908, p. 24.

124. There was considerable interest expressed in gardening, or horticulture, as a respectable career for women in Edwardian years, and each time the colonial possibilities of the occupation were canvassed, but for the impoverished gentlewoman it involved similar specialised training to any other career. See especially Viscountess F.G. Wolseley, *Gardening for Women* (London, 1908), pp. xiv, 1-7, 89, 232; *The Times*, 26 Dec. 1907, p. 8; J. Hopkinson, 'On Colonisation of Women in South Africa', Feb. 1906, pp. 38-40.

125. UBWEA, *Annual Report*, 1900, p. 25.

126. Miss G.B. Clark noted in one of her surveys of employment prospects in Canada that 'It should always be remembered that Canada has a horror of the useless gentlewoman', 'Are Educated Women Wanted in Canada?' Pt. III, *Imperial Colonist*, vol. VIII, April 1910, pp. 52-5.

127. 'British Teachers for Canadian Schools', *Imperial Colonist*, vol. VII, April 1909, pp. 55-6.

128. G.B. Clark, 'Are Educated Women Wanted in Canada?' Pt. III, ibid., vol. VIII, April 1910, pp. 52-5; BWEA, *Annual Reports*, 1912, pp. 27-32, 1913, p. 28. Ella Sykes drew attention to the other advantages accruing to the rural colonial teacher besides better pay: one of her acquaintances 'had the best social position in the district, and the pick of all the husbands'. Sykes, pp. 228-31.

129. Sykes, pp. 233-4; see also G.B. Clark, 'Are Educated Women Wanted in Canada?' Pt. II, *Imperial Colonist*, vol. VIII, March, 1910, pp. 39-42.

130. The CIL committee was composed partly of BWEA and SACS members who were interested in the problems of educated women exclusively, but half of the committee was made up of members of the Head Mistresses Association, this concession being a condition of their help. The first report of the CIL recognised that its formation was necessary because 'During the last ten or fifteen years the position of the educated woman in this country has become every day more difficult.' *Annual Report*, 1910-11, pp. 7-9; see also report for 1912-13, pp. 24-5.

131. BWEA, *Annual Reports*, 1909, p. 10, 1910, pp. 16-17, 1911, p. 15.

132. By 1911 the BWEA and SACS had together aided 16,000 women. During the subsequent three years the BWEA helped 2,637 the CIL 269 and the SACS 1,425, giving a conservative total of 20,331. *Imperial Colonist*, vol. IX, Sept. 1911, p. 362; vol. X, Jan. 1912, pp. 1-2; Feb. 1912, pp. 17-18, vol. XII, Jan. 1914, p. 2. July 1914, p. 110: BWEA, *Annual Reports*, 1911-14, CIL, *Annual Reports*, 1911-14. 'Reports on the Emigrants' Information Office for the Year Ended 31 Dec. 1912,' *PP* 1913, vol. XLV (Cd. 6670), p. 21. On the sudden halt of emigration activity see the BWEA and SACS reports for 1914 and 'Our Work in War Time', *Imperial Colonist*, vol. XII, Dec. 1914, p. 205.

133. Evidence of Joyce and Knightley to Dominions Royal Commission on Natural Resources, Trade and Legislation of Certain Portions of H.M. Dominions, Pt. I, Migration, *PP* 1912-13, XVI (Cd. 6516), p. 45.

134. CIL, *Annual Reports*, 1911/12-1914/15.

135. Changes in the methods and categories of recording after 1911 make it impossible to provide comparable figures for 1912/14; see also Carrier and

Jeffery, pp. 58-60.
136. UBWEA, *Annual Report*, 1900, p. 25; see also Dr E.C. Sparrow, 'Canada for Girls', *Imperial Colonist*, vol. XI, Feb. 1913, pp. 29-32. It was not unusual for wealthier colonial residents to hire women on a visit to England and return with them, thus avoiding dependence upon voluntary organisation. UBWEA, *Annual Report*, 1889-90, p. 10.
137. Sykes, pp. 3-4, 76. Some idea of the pressure among women for emigration compared to those actually assisted by the societies is derived from the figures of actual applicants; in 1906, for example, when the BWEA aided 604 women, it had 3,501 applicants and conducted 2,126 interviews. *Annual Report*, 1906, p. 12. In 1901, when the South African Expansion Committee (subsequently SACS) sent 670 women to South Africa, it had 7,311 applications. 'What We Are Doing', *Imperial Colonist*, vol. I, Dec. 1902, pp. 110-11.

CONCLUSION

The emigrant gentlewoman had much to gain from leaving Britain. Emigration offered escape from excessive competition, from a steadily narrowing field of suitable employment, and from the requirements of a rigid code of gentility. The emigrant's colonial destination, being a younger, sparsely settled society, although no egalitarian utopia, at least promised employment opportunity, and it did so in the critically meaningful context of greater freedom of action which created a real possibility for redefinition of her social identity. Emigration could become a genuine solution to the problem of distressed gentlewomen, even thoug though circumstances too often seemed to conspire against the women most in need of it.

Yet the complexity and ambiguity arising from much of the evidence in the previous chapters finally raises more questions than it answers, especially in relation to class and to the wider meaning of women's adaptability in the face of change. These areas of ambivalence and their implications deserve closer examination, but first the areas of greater certainty should be clarified.

Adaptability and determination are not qualities that have been associated traditionally with Victorian distressed gentlewomen, nor with Victorian middle-class women generally. But the most persistent theme throughout this study has been the certainty of women's adaptation to the rigorous experience of emigration. Regardless of the nuances of their class backgrounds most emigrants found scope for expanded enterprise, and, where they can be identified, were unequivocal about their more optimistic life prospects and their personal outlook. The pattern of adaptability so evident in the colonial lives of Mary and Ellen Taylor was also present among the courageous pioneers who braved the conditions of working-class emigrant ships to obtain a cheap passage to Australia in the 1830s, among the accomplished governesses sent out by the FMCES and among the trained colonial lady-helps after 1890. Adaptable people like Annie Davis[1] in 1864 and 'E.R.'[2] in 1898 were quick to recommend their own solution to others in England, up to the point of urging that middle-class women would be better off as servants in Australia and Canada than as exploited governesses in Britain. The huge disproportion between the women who actually emigrated and those who applied to the emigration societies but could not afford the necessary training or associated expense, confirms the willingness of women to risk the kind of personal upheaval implied in Annie Davis' advice from Sydney to 'undergo a little domestic training and come out here to take your chance with others'.[3] It is difficult, from this kind of evidence to present a clear and rounded alternative picture to that embodied in the familiar helpless stereotype of the distressed gentlewoman, but the evidence clearly demands substantial rethinking of that stereotype.

While it is clear that middle-class women were fully capable of adapting to colonial life, it is equally clear, paradoxically, that the most disadvantaged were repeatedly deprived of the opportunity to do so. Until the 1860s only the most adventurous or desperate among distressed gentlewomen were willing to risk the hazards of disreputable emigrant ships. But once emigration became more respectable and special facilities and voluntary societies began to cater to the exclusive needs of middle-class women, new barriers appeared rapidly. The charge of 'matrimonial colonisation' was sufficient to deter middle-class feminists in the sixties and seventies from encouraging any but the most highly qualified governesses from emigrating, so that the real beneficiaries were an elite who had already capitalised on educational reforms in Britain and who had the advantage in the domestic employment market. Only with the new societies and their lady-help schemes after the 1880s did more unprepared and unqualified distressed gentlewomen begin to benefit from some of the opportunities of emigration. But once established the opportunities were short-lived. As colonial employment requirements shifted to more skilled female occupations like nursing, schoolteaching and office work, the advantage returned to those possessing the requisite skills, either through education or apprenticeship — or at least to those who could still afford to acquire the training. The real casualties in this situation were the women whose parents continued to insist that a practical and advanced education for their daughters was a waste of time and money.[4] New employment opportunities in the colonies now left them at a disadvantage, just as educational reform and an expanding economy had caused their position to deteriorate in Britain.

The most persistent rationale used to justify female emigration from Britain was the feminine civilising mission. From Edward Gibbon Wakefield in the thirties to the late-Victorian and Edwardian emigration societies, enthusiasts insisted that a due proportion of respectable and cultivated women were essential to guarantee morality, British culture, social order and hierarchy and the survival of Anglo-Saxon values. By the late nineteenth century, with the increased stress on racial themes, the racial aspects had overshadowed the class aspects of the argument, but by this time the rhetoric urging women to civilise the colonies had become far more intense. Paradoxically, this occurred at a time when female middle-class emigrants were leaving in large numbers as trained or skilled workers, and when the rhetoric persuading them to 'make homes for settlers' was being shown to be irrelevant. The reasons for the widening gap between propaganda and practice are not hard to find. The revival of interest in the value of respectable English motherhood in the colonies was more than just a response to national and racial threats to the Empire. It was also an integral part of the conservative reaction against the apparent threat of the 'New Woman' and associated social changes in Britain evident in the late nineteenth century. Greater female mobility and increased female employment meant that more and more women were visibly exercising their freedom from old constraints, in however small a way. To conservatives like John St-Loe Strachey, editor of the *Spectator*, the new freedoms constituted a sexual revolution not unrelated to the wider crumbling of Victorian moral and political values. To H.G. Wells' justification of extra-marital sex and birth-control in his novel, *Ann Veronica*, Strachey flatly replied that 'one man and one woman is the law of fecundity'.[5] Not surprisingly, Strachey was also among the many enthusiastic Imperialists who lectured to the BWEA on the need to influence rising states with the 'Anglo-Saxon ideals' of English motherhood, arguing that the Empire could not exist without respectable women who would go out to build colonial homes.[6] Strachey's notion of female emigration was a comfortable and convenient reaction to the threatening spectre of female emancipation, easier divorce and birth control. The rhetoric of the feminine civilising mission continued to serve this ideological purpose despite its increasing irrelevance to the actual course of female emigration.

Against these certainties there are areas of uncertainty which are bound to qualify some of the conclusions or raise further questions. In most cases the evidence used has not been detailed or thorough enough to allow precision in identifying and quantifying the class backgrounds of the female emigrants examined. Too often it has been necessary to make inferences about them from the women's British or colonial occupations, in a few cases even from the tone of their letters. There are obvious risks here, and while most of the findings do seem to be consistent, there is sufficient doubt for them to remain tentative.

The class problem is most pronounced in the complex relationship between daughters of the lower middle class and those of the presumably more gently nurtured middle and upper middle class. Women from all these classes have been encountered throughout this study in the position of distressed gentlewomen. How far is this justified? Who, in fact, were the real distressed gentlewomen?

There are obvious dangers in lumping together a group of women drawn from the entire range of the middle class under the category of distressed gentlewomen. The upwardly aspiring daughters of the lower middle class, particularly, seem, on the surface, to belong to an entirely different group. Most of them have been seen correctly to have had the advantage in new employment fields after the mid-nineteenth century.[7] As the chief beneficiaries of the huge expansion in white-collar and technical occupations, the bulk of them hardly qualify as distressed gentlewomen. The disparity is underlined by their relatively less genteel social origins. But as feminists never tired of complaining, the lower middle class aspired not only to the wealth but to the values of a higher class.[8] To that end many of them were capable of giving their daughters the same kind of limited education in genteel 'accomplishments' traditionally associated with the prosperous middle class. Reformers soon realised that the distressed gentlewoman was less the product of a single class than of a process which left women to face the employment market with few qualifications apart from their well-cultivated gentility. The process could produce lower middle-class victims just as it produced victims from the upper and middle middle class. Late-Victorian emigration promoters thought that women from humble backgrounds who had been used, for example, to doing housework in their own homes, would adapt more easily to the process of emigration, but it is far from clear, from the evidence presented here, that there were major differences in adaptability attributable to class background. The differences that mattered were, on the one hand, between the women with economic security or marketable qualifications, and, on the other hand, those with claims to gentility but deprived of security and in need of qualifications, whose adaptability depended on their courage and wits, regardless of their class origins. These findings have emerged as much by implication from indirect sources as from detailed personal material, and should not be regarded as being more than tentative, and an invitation to further investigation and analysis. Certainly the relationship between different levels of middle-class women is a complex and vital one needing more illumination. If their key problems are viewed as being essentially similar, traceable to the same sources in Victorian values, the complexities might be reduced.

The optimistic picture of distressed gentlewomen adapting successfully to colonial environments also needs some qualification. There were, at the opposite end of the spectrum, clear non-adaptors as well. Women like Frances Haydon[9] who was declared insane in Hobart Town and Rosa Phayne[10] who detested her Australian work as much as she detested Australian society were quite unable to benefit from the upheaval of emigration. So too were the 'fine ladies' who, colonial correspondents complained, refused to undertake 'anything menial'.[11] Such casualties seem to have been exceptions among a majority of adaptors, but the stress on adaptability, courage and enterprise among the majority of emigrants should in no way be taken to minimise the severity and scope of the distressed gentlewoman's plight. A central theme of this study has been that successive obstacles prevented most distressed gentlewomen from exploiting a solution of genuine promise, just as the same women became casualties of most improvements in female education and employment in Britain. The transition to urban-industrial society had, in many ways, exerted a more severe and longer lasting effect on single middle-class women than on most other groups, since the certainties of their older domestic role and social place were not replaced by any clearly delineated alternative in the new order. The fact that so many women adapted in the face of such weighty disadvantages is no case for suggesting that the problems were slight, or of their own making; nor is it to suggest that they could all succeed, given the will, in a world of open opportunity. But it does suggest that the women who could and did adapt possessed ordinary human qualities which are quite inconsistent with the traditional view of woman as victim.

The specific process of adaptability experienced by women in colonial societies is bound to raise further questions. The evidence from propagandists on the need for middle-class emigrants to be willing either to assist in domestic work as governesses or even to become full-time home-helps, and the clear message from most emigrants that they found such menial work in no way demeaning, is overwhelming. But it is difficult to reconcile this evidence with the usual — and largely convincing — picture of rough domestic toil in colonial households, most of which possessed a minimum of servants and a minimum of labour-saving devices.[12] Colonial motherhood, for all its praise from late-Victorian propagandists, was dominated by hard, unremitting labour, diverting as a temporary novelty, perhaps, but leaving little time or energy for other interests on a permanent basis.[13] But for single, middle-class women — if they remained that way — the situation was rather different. The letters in chapter 5 illustrate that their tolerant attitude towards harder, presumably more demeaning work, was inseparable from their new found relative liberation from a range of social constraints, a less rigid definition of gentility, easier mobility and more informal social relationships. The atmosphere of colonial egalitarianism which allowed this process need not be exaggerated; the point is that it was sufficient to allow women caught in a narrowing circle of diminishing opportunity in Britain to find a way out.

Further questions might usefully be asked about the conditions making for adaptability among Victorian women. There is no compelling reason why loss of the protection and security associated with the patriarchal home should have left women completely helpless. The constricting power of gentility was inseparable from the net of patriarchal security, and it is not fanciful to suggest that the death of a father or the loss of family fortune which forced daughters to leave home might have increased women's scope for independence and action. Harriet Martineau experienced this process at the age of 27, when her family's remaining capital was wiped out in 1829. Her family had been left in reduced circumstances after her father's partial ruin and death in 1826, but for three years they had managed to maintain a convincing front of gentility. For Martineau and her sisters the second loss had quite opposite effects from what might have been expected. She was 'left destitute . . . with precisely one shilling in my purse'. But she described her reaction as one of relief rather than depression.

The effect upon me of this new 'calamity,' as people called it, was like that of a blister upon a dull, weary pain, or series of pains. I rather enjoyed it, even at the time; for there was scope for action; whereas in the long, dreary series of preceding trials, there was nothing possible but endurance. In a very short time, my two sisters at home and I began to feel the blessing of a wholly new freedom. I, who had been obliged to write before breakfast, or in some private way; had henceforth liberty to do my own work in my own way, for we had lost our gentility. Many and many a time since have we said that, but for that loss of money, we might have lived on in the ordinary provincial method of ladies with small means, sewing and economizing and growing narrower every year: whereas by being thrown, while it was yet time, on my own resources, we have worked hard and usefully, won friends, reputation and independence, seen the world abundantly, abroad and at home, and, in short, have truly lived instead of vegetated.[14]

Obviously it is a hazardous business to generalise from the experience of a prominent writer like Harriet Martineau to the anonymous lives of distressed gentlewomen, although it should be noticed that in 1829 Martineau had not achieved the eminence that came in later years. At the very least her experience can be used to pose wider questions about women's ability to adapt in the nineteenth century. The resourcefulness of middle-class emigrants seems to confirm the wider relevance of Martineau's reaction, and while emigrants may have been unique among distressed gentlewomen in Britain, it does not follow that their lives tell us nothing about the more inarticulate unrecorded women who shared the same problem but failed to obtain the same solution. It cannot be reiterated too strongly that the history of the exceptional in this sense can tell us a great deal about the more typical and less distinguished who can never be identified directly. If social history is to deal with more than a series of abstractions based on statistical certainties the female emigrants and Harriet Martineaus of the world will have to be considered carefully.

Victorian distressed gentlewomen had to confront a series of obstacles which prevented them from exercising independence and obtaining a livelihood. The dicates of respectability narrowed their permissible range of employment in Britain; reforms designed specifically to alleviate their problems repeatedly put them at a greater disadvantage. Piecemeal educational reform, middle-class feminism, philanthropy, an expanding economy, and even emigration, rarely worked in their favour but instead forced them to fall back on their powers of adaptability. That so many adapted to the extent they did is a remarkable tribute to their determination and to a potential which Victorian ideals of womanhood did little to cultivate. Victorian society seemed determined, often unwittingly, to make casualties of its single women; that is not to say that it always succeeded.

Notes

1. A. Davis to FMCES, Sydney, 17 June 1864, *Letter Book No. 1*, pp. 123-7; see above, ch. 5, notes 53 and 70.
2. 'E.R. to G. Lefroy, Vancouver, (n.d.), UBWEA, *Annual Report*, 1898, p. 29; see above, ch. 6, note 115.
3. Davis to FMCES, 17 June 1864.
4. It follows that only the extension in the twentieth century of more universal and secondary education for women, which reduced the arbitrary power of fathers over their daughters' education, brought a real diminution in the existence of distressed gentlewomen as a recognised social problem, though it did not end inequal-

ities in female employment. In 1897 only 20,000 girls were attending recognised (i.e. with a curriculum approximating that of boys' schools) secondary schools; in just over twenty years the number increased to 185,000 and by 1936 it was 500,000. Kamm, *Hope Deferred*, p. 233.

5. S. Hynes, *The Edwardian Turn of Mind* (Princeton, 1968), pp. 198, 293-4.

6. Speech of J. St-Loe Strachey at BWEA annual meeting, 23 March 1909, BWEA, *Annual Report*, 1908, p. 34.

7. McGregor, p. 87.

8. On the aspirant ideology of the lower middle class cf. Crossick, introduction, pp. 21-31.

9. See above, ch. 2, note 53.

10. R. Phayne to FMCES, Melbourne, 13 Aug. 1869, *Letter Book No. 1*, pp. 341-6; see above ch. 5, note 55.

11. See above, ch. 6, note 109.

12. Cf. Raewyn Dalziel, 'The Colonial Helpmeet: Women's Role and the Vote in Nineteenth-Century New Zealand', *The New Zealand Journal of History*, vol. II (2), Oct. 1977, pp. 115-16, 123. Beverley Kingston, *My Wife, My Daughter and Poor Mary Ann: Women and Work in Australia* (Melbourne, 1975), pp. 15-25, 29-55.

13. See Sarah Greenwood's observation on the lack of time for her children's education. Drummond, pp. 73-7, see above ch. 3, note 64.

14. Martineau, *Harriet Martineau's Autobiography*, vol. I, pp. 141-2.

APPENDIX I

Comparison of British and Colonial Occupations of Middle-class Emigrants, 1832-1836

Ship and destination	STATED ORIGINAL OCCUPATIONS		SUBSEQUENT OCCUPATIONS IN COLONY									Total female emigrants on ship
	G'ness or middle-class	Nursery G'ness, teacher	G'ness, teacher	Nursery G'ness	Dom. service (gen. servant, nursery maid)	Dress-making or needle-work	Actress	Married on arrival	Joined family or friends	Insane	Unknown or not yet employed	
Sarah Hobart Town	6 —	— 4	— —	— 1	2 2	— —	— —	3 1	— —	— —	1 —	115
Strath-fieldsay Hobart Town	17 —	— —	8 —	— —	— —	1 —	1 —	— —	6 —	1 —	— —	256
Canton Sydney	6 —	— 1	1 —	— —	1 —	1 —	— —	— —	2 —	1 1	— —	171
Charles Kerr Launceston	11 —	— 4	10 1	— 2	— —	— —	— —	— —	— —	— 1	— —	156
James Pattison Sydney	17 —	— 11	4 1	3 1	1 3	1 5	— —	— —	2 —	— —	6 5	288
Boadicea Hobart Town	5 —	— 12	1 1	— 2	1 3	— —	— —	— —	— —	— —	3 6	194
William Metcalfe Hobart Town	3 —	— 2	3 1	— 1	— —	— —	— —	— —	— —	— —	— —	110

Ship and destination	G'ness or middle-class	Nursery G'ness, teacher	G'ness, teacher	Nursery G'ness	Dom. service (gen. servant, nursery maid)	Dress-making or needle-work	Actress	Married on arrival	Joined family or friends	Insane	Unknown or not yet employed	Total female emigrants on ship
Duchess of Northumberland Sydney	NO LIST	NO LIST	–	2	–	–	–	–	–	–	–	227
Layton Sydney	8 –	– 10	NO LIST									234
David Scott Sydney	13 –	– 5	NO LIST									247
Amelia Thompson Launceston	NO LIST		6	–	–	–	–	–	–	–	–	172
Bussorah Merchant Sydney	NO LIST	NO LIST										217
Duchess of Northumberland (II) Sydney	NO LIST	NO LIST										236
Lady McNaughton Sydney	NO LIST	NO LIST										80
Total	86	49	37	12	13	9	1	4	10	4	21	2,703

Source: Ch. 2, note 41.

APPENDIX II

'To England's Daughters' Dora Gore Browne

Do you feel the heart of England beating high with love and yearning
As her daughters gather round her, ere they sever from her knee?
'Oh, my children!' hear her speaking, 'when your steps from home are
    turning,
See you keep my fame unsullied, be you true to God and me.

'For I bid you to remember how from days of ancient story
Every loyal English daughter, who was worthy of the name,
In whose heart the glow was kindled for her country's highest glory,
Bore aloft the torch of freedom, adding lustre to the flame.

'And to you 'tis now entrusted with a meaning larger, higher,
You, my daughters, as you go to join your kinsfolk o'er the foam,
'Tis for you to keep the flaming torch of loyalty on fire,
In the land of your adoption, for the honour of your home.

'Yes! for God and for your country now 'tis yours to make the story,
You, the future nursing mothers of the English race to be.
In your arms his love will lay them, and he looks for England's glory
To her loyal sons and daughters in her homes beyond the sea.

'God be with you, then, and speed you, as you cross the heaving waters,
God be with you, as you land upon our kinsmen's distant shore,
Let them feel that Mother England sends the noblest of her daughters,
Forges living links of Empire, links to bind us more and more.

'Keep your anchor firmly grounded on the steadfast Rock of Ages;
Keep your eyes upon His cross who died to save us in his love;
Seek the Holy Spirit's guiding, as life's ocean round you rages,
He will lead you to the haven, to the Father's home above'.

From the *Imperial Colonist*, vol. III, December 1904, p. 133.

BIBLIOGRAPHY

(A) Manuscript Sources

(1) *Private Collections*

Dixon Letters, Leeds City Museum
Herbert Papers, Wilton House, Salisbury

(2) *Fawcett Collection, City of London Polytechnic*

(a) *Female Middle-Class Emigration Society*
Letter Book Number One, 1862-76
Letter Book Number Two, 1877-82.
(b) *British Women's Emigration Association* (formerly *United Englishwomen's Emigration Association and United British Women's Emigration Association*)
Minute Book (UBWEA), 1896-1901
Finance Commitee records (UEEA), 1885-6
South African Committee Correspondence, 1899-1900
Sub-Committee for Diffusing Information (BWEA), 1903-5
Hostel Minute Book (BWEA), 1909-12
(c) *South African Colonization Society*
Minutes of Committee Meetings, 1902-19
(d) *Colonial Intelligence League*
Records of Committees and Council Minutes, 1911-19
(e) *Fawcett Library Autograph Collection of Correspondence*, vol. II

(3) *Colonial Office Records, Public Record Office, London*

CO 384 Emigration, Original Correspondence
CO 385 Emigration, Out-letters
CO 386 Colonial Land and Emigration Commission, Original
     Correspondence and Out-letters
CO 201 New South Wales, Original Correspondence
CO 202 New South Wales, Out-letters
CO 280 Van Diemen's Land, Original Correspondence
CO 408 Van Diemen's Land, Out-letters
CO 309 Victoria, Original Correspondence

(B)   Printed Sources

(1)   *Parliamentary Papers*

(a) *Reports* (in chronological order)

Report of Assistant Commissioners appointed to inquire into the state of Popular Education in England, 1861. *PP* 1861, XXI (2794-II) Pt. II

Report from Schools Inquiry Commissioners. *PP* 1867-8, XXVIII (3966) General Report, vol. I; (3966-I) Miscellaneous Papers, vol. II; (3966-IV) Minutes of Evidence, vol. V

General Report, Royal Commission on Secondary Education, 1895. *PP* 1895, XLIII (c.7862)

Report from Dominions Royal Commission on Natural Resources, Trade and Legisliation of Certain Portions of HM Dominions. Part I, Migration, *PP* 1912-13, XVI (c.6516); Final Report, *PP* 1917-18 1917-18, X (c.8462)

(b) *Census Reports* (in chronological order)

Great Britain, General Report, 1851. *PP* 1852-3, LXXXVIII (1691-I), Pt. I

England and Wales, General Report, 1861, *PP* 1863, LIII (3221), Pt. I

England and Wales, Preliminary Report, 1871. *PP* 1871, LIX (381) (381)

England and Wales, General Report, 1871, *PP* 1873, LXXI (872-I) Pt. II

England and Wales, General Report, 1881, *PP* 1883, LXXX (3797)

England and Wales, General Report, 1891, *PP* 1893-4, CVI (7222)

England and Wales, General Report, 1901, *PP* 1904, CVIII (2174)

England and Wales, General Report, 1911, *PP* 1917-18, XXXV (8491)

(c) *Accounts and Papers*

Annual Reports of the Colonial Land and Emigration Commissioners, 1842-73

Papers Relating to Emigration

PP 1831, XIX (328), p. 113

PP 1834, XLIV (616), p. 291

PP 1835, XXXIX (87), p. 705

PP 1836, XL (76), p. 461

PP 1837, XLIII (358), p. 101

PP 1840, XXXIII (113), p. 19

PP 1842, XXXI (301), p. 49

PP 1843, XXXIV (109), p. 9, (323), p. 367
PP 1847-8, XLVII (986), p. 481
PP 1849, XXXVIII (593), p. 97
PP 1850, XL (1163), p. 29
PP 1851, XL (347), p. 1, (347-II), p. 135
PP 1852-3, LXVIII (1627), p. 25
PP 1854, XLVI (436), p. 111
Answers to the Circular of Questions to the Commissioners of
Popular Education, 1861, *PP* 1861, XXI (2794-V), Pt. V
Report on the Emigrants Information Office for the Year Ended
31 December, 1912. *PP* 1913, XLV (c.6670)
(d) *Miscellaneous Parliamentary Papers*
Hansard, *Parliamentary Debates*
Victoria, *Votes and Proceedings of Legislative Council*, 1852-4
Victorian Year Book, Melbourne, 1874

(2)   *Reports of Societies*

(a) *Reports of Emigration Societies*
British Women's Emigration Association, *Annual Reports* 3 vols.
(1888-1918), Fawcett Library
Colonial Intelligence League. *Annual Reports* (1911-15), Fawcett
Library
Female Middle-Class Emigration Society. *Reports* (1861, 1862-72,
1880-82, 1883-5), Fawcett Library
Herbert, Sidney. *First Report of the Committee of the Fund for
Promoting Female Emigration* (London, March, 1851)
(b) *Miscellaneous Reports and Transactions*
Governesses' Benevolent Institution. *Annual Reports* (1843-54)
National Association for the Promotion of Social Science.
Transactions (1857-84)
Society for Promoting the Employment of Women. *Annual
Report* (1879)

(3)   *Newspapers*

(a) *Newspapers published in London*
Australia and New Zealand Gazette
Borough of Marylebone Mercury
The Echo
Illustrated London News
Morning Chronicle
Morning Leader

New Zealand Journal
Our Paper
South Australia News
Spectator
St James's Gazette
The Times
(b) *Newspapers published outside London*
Argus, Melbourne
Bradford Daily Telegraph
Cleckheaton Guardian, Yorkshire
Liverpool Mercury

(4) *Periodicals*
Blackwood's Magazine
British and Foreign Review
Cassell's Saturday Journal
Chambers's Edinburgh Journal
The Christian Lady's Friend and Family Repository
Colonial Magazine and East India Review
Dublin University Magazine
Edinburgh Review
Emigrant's Penny Magazine
English Woman's Journal
Foreign Quarterly Review
Fraser's Magazine
Household Words
Imperial Colonist
Madame Aubert's Governess List
Monthly Review
National Review
Punch
Quarterly Review
The Queen
Saturday Review
The Spinning Wheel for Wives, Mothers and Daughters
Tait's Edinburgh Review
Victoria Magazine
Westminster Review
Woman
Woman's Gazette
Women and Work

Work and Leisure

(5)   *Contemporary Books, Pamphlets and Articles*

Ansell, Jr. C., *On the Rate of Morality at Early Periods of Life, the Age of Marriage. . . and other Statistics of Families in the Upper and Professional Classes* (London, 1874)

Barker, Lady M.A., *Station Amusements in New Zealand* (Christchurch, 1953, orig. pub. 1873)

—— *Station Life in New Zealand* (Christchurch, 1950, first pub. 1870)

Barnes, Howarth, *Training Colleges for Schoolmistresses* (London, 1891)

Blessington, Lady Marguerite Gardiner, *The Governess* (London, 1839)

Boucherett, Jessie, *Hints on Self-Help: A Book for Young Women* (London, 1863)

Brontë, Ann, *Agnes Grey* (London, 1847)

Brontë, Charlotte, *Jane Eyre* (London, 1847)

Brontë, Charlotte, *Shirley* (London, 1849)

Browne, Phillis, *What Girls Can Do* (London, 1880)

Browne, Mrs. Walter, *Emigration for Women* (n.p., n.d. c.1880-4)

Buley, E.C., *Australian Life in Town and Country* (London, 1905)

Butler, Josephine E., *Woman's Work and Woman's Culture* (London, 1869)

Cadman, H. Ashwell, *Gomersal Past and Present* (Leeds, 1930)

Carmichael, Rev. Henry, *Hints Relating to Emigrants and Emigration* (London, 1834)

Cartwright, Julia (ed.), *The Journals of Lady Knightley of Fawsley, 1856-1884* (London, 1915)

Chapman, H.S. 'Emigration: Comparative Prospects of Our New Colonies', in *Westminster Review* XXXV, (Jan. 1841), 131-87

Chisholm, Caroline, *The A.B.C. of Colonization* (London, 1850)

Chisholm, Caroline, *Emigration and Transportation Relatively Considered* (London, 1847)

Clacy, Mrs. Charles, *A Lady's Visit to the Gold Diggings of Australia in 1852-53* (London, 1963, first pub. 1853)

—— *Lights and Shadows of Australian Life* 2 vols. (London, 1854)

Clayden, Arthur, *The England of the Pacific, or New Zealand as an English Middle-Class Emigration Field* (London, 1879)

Clayden, Arthur, *A Popular Handbook to New Zealand* (London, 1885)

Cobbe, Frances Power, *Essays on the Pursuits of Women* (London, 1863)

Collet, Clara E. *The Economic Position of Educated Working Women* (London, 1890)

—— *Educated Working Women: Essays on the Economic Position of Women Workers in the Middle-Classes* (London, 1902)

—— *Women in Industry* (London, 1911)

Collins, Wilkie, *Armadale* (London, 1866)

—— *No Name* (London, 1862)

Crawshay, Rose Mary, *Domestic Service for Gentlewomen: A Record of Experience and Success* (London, 1874)

—— *Domestic Service for Gentlewomen: A Record of Experience and Success, with additional matter* (London, 1876)

Cunningham, Peter M., *Two Years in New South Wales* 2 vols. second edition (London, 1827)

Davidson, Mrs H.C., *What our Daughters Can Do for Themselves* (London, 1894)

Davidson, L.C. *Hints to Lady Travellers at Home and Abroad* (London, 1889)

Davies, Emily, *On Secondary Instruction as Relating to Girls* (London, 1864)

Dickens, Charles, *David Copperfield* (London, 1849-50)

Eastlake, Lady Elizabeth, 'Lady Travellers', in *Quarterly Review* LXXVI (June, 1845), 98-135

—— '*Vanity Fair* and *Jane Eyre*', in *Quarterly Review* LXXXIV (Dec. 1848), 153-185

Ellis, Mrs Sarah, *The Daughters of England* (London, 1842)

—— *The Women of England* (London, 1839)

Farr, William, *Remarks on a Proposed Scheme for the Conversion of Assessments Levied on Public Salaries . . . into a 'Provident Fund' for the Support of Widows and Orphans of Civil Servants of the Crown* (London, 1849)

Fitzgerald, P.H., *Memories of Charles Dickens, with an Account of Household Words* (Bristol, 1913)

Fraser, Donald, *Mary Jane Kinnaird* (London, 1890)

Gaskell, Elizabeth C., *The Life of Charlotte Brontë* (London, 1958, first pub. 1857)

—— *Wives and Daughters* (London, 1866)

Gissing, George, *The Odd Women* (London, 1893)

Godley, Charlotte, *Letters from Early New Zealand by Charlotte Godley* ed. J.R. Godley (Christchurch, 1951)

Greg, William R., *Enigmas of Life* (London, 1891)

—— *Literary and Social Judgements* second edition, (London, 1869)

—— 'Why are Women Redundant?' in *National Review* XXVIII (April 1862), 434-460

Grogan, Mercy, *How Women May Earn a Living* (London, 1880)

Hadland, Selina, *Occupations for Women other than Teaching* (London, 1886)

Hall, Mrs S.C., *Stories of the Governess* (London, 1852)

Herbert, Sidney, *First Report of the Committee of the Fund for Promoting Female Emigration* (London, 1851)

—— *The Needlewomen and Slopworkers* (London, 1849)

Historical Records of Australia ed. J.F. Watson, (Sydney, 1914 etc.)

Hogan, James F., *The Irish in Australia* (London, 1887)

Houston, Arthur, *On the Emancipation of Women from Existing Industrial Disabilities Considered in its Economic Aspect* (London, 1862)

Hubbard, Louisa M., *The Handbook of Women's Work* (London, 1876)

—— *Work for Ladies in Elementary Schools* (London, 1872)

Jameson, Anna, *Memoirs and Essays* (London, 1846)

Joyce, Ellen, *Emigrant's Rest for Women and Children* (London, 1887)

—— *Emigration, A Paper Read at the Girls' Friendly Society Winchester Diocesan Conference, Southampton, October 25, 1883* (London, 1884)

—— *Letters on Emigration* (London, 1884)

—— *Thirty Years of Imperial Work with the Girls' Friendly Society* (Winchester, 1912)

Kingsbury, Elizabeth, *Work for Women* (London, 1884)

Kingston, W.H.G., *How to Emigrate: or The British Colonists. A Tale for all Classes* (London, 1850)

Krafft-Ebing, Dr. R. von., *Text-Book of Insanity, Based on Clinical Observations* English transl. (Philadelphia, 1904)

Ladies at Work, (London, 1893)

Lewis, Sarah, *Woman's Mission* (London, 1839)

Low, Jr. S., *The Charities of London* (London, 1850)

M.A., *The Economic Foundations of the Women's Movement*

Fabian Society Women's Group (London, 1914)

MacKenzie, Eneas, *The Emigrant's Guide to Australia* (London, 1855)

——— *MacKenzie's Australian Emigrant's Guide* (London, 1852)

——— *Memoirs of Mrs. Caroline Chisholm* (London, 1852)

Marshall, John, *A Reply to the Misrepresentations which have been put forth respecting Female Emigration to Australia* (London, 1834)

Martineau, Harriet, *Deerbrook* (London, 1839)

——— 'Female Industry', in *Edinburgh Review* CIX Apri (April 1859), 293-336

——— *Harriet Martineau's Autobiography* (London, 1877)

——— *History of England During the Thirty Years' Peace*, 2 vols. (London, 1849-50)

——— *Society in America* 3 vols. (London, 1837)

Maurice, Mary Atkinson, *Governess Life: Its Trials, Duties and Encouragements* (London, 1849)

——— *Mothers and Governesses* (London, 1847)

Meredith, Louisa Anne, *My Home in Tasmania, During a Residence of Nine Years* 2 vols. (London, 1852)

——— *Notes and Sketches of New South Wales* (London, 1844)

Merivale, Herman, *Lectures on Colonization and the Colonies* third edition. (London, 1861)

Milne, John Duguid, *Industrial and Social Position of Women in the Middle and Lower Ranks* (London, 1857)

Montgomery, Robert, *Woman, The Angel of Life* (London, 1833)

Moodie, Susanna, *Roughing it in the Bush* (Toronto, 1962, first pub. 1852)

More, Hannah, *Coelebs in Search of a Wife* 2 vols. 3rd edition (London, 1809)

——— *Strictures on the Modern System of Female Education* 2 vols. (London, 1799)

Muzzey, Artemas Powers, *The English Maiden: Her Moral and Domestic Duties* (London, 1841)

Nightingale, Florence, 'Cassandra', (1852) from *Suggestions for Thoughts to Searchers after Religious Truth* in R. Strachey *The Cause* . . . 395-418

Osborn, Christabel, and F.B. Low, *Manuals of Employment for Educated Women* 3 vols. (London, 1890)

Parkes, Bessie Rayner, *Essays on Women's Work* (London, 1865)

——— *A Passing World* (London, 1897)

The Perils of Girls and Young Women Away from Home (London, 1884)

Phillips, L. *A Dictionary of Employments Open to Women* (London, 1898)

Pratt, Edwin A. *Pioneer Women in Victoria's Reign* (London, 1897)

——*A Woman's Work for Women* (London, 1898)

Ross, Adelaide, *Emigration for Women* (London, 1886)

Ruskin, John, *Sesame and Lilies* (London, 1865)

Rye, Maria S., *Emigration of Educated Women* (London, 1861)

Saleeby, Caleb Williams, *Parenthood and Race Culture: An Outline of Eugenics* (London, 1909)

——*Woman and Womanhood: A Search for Principles* (London, 1912)

Sewell, Elizabeth Missing, *Autobiography* (London, 1907)

——*Principles of Education* 2 vols (London, 1865)

Shaw, William, *An Affectionate Pleading for England's Oppressed Female Workers* (London, 1850)

Shirreff, Emily A.E., *Intellectual Education and its Influence on the Character and Happiness of Women* (London, 1858)

——*The Work of the National Union* (London, 1872)

Sidney, Samuel, *Female Emigration – as it is – as it may be: A Letter to the Rt. Hon. Sidney Herbert, M.P.* (London, 1850)

Smith (afterwards Bodichon) Barbara Leigh. *Women and Work* (London, 1857)

Stanmore, Lord, *Memoir of Sidney Herbert* (London, 1906)

Stewart, Mrs J., *The Missing Law: or Woman's Birthright* (London, 1869)

Strickland, Catherine Parr, *The Backwoods of Canada* (London, 1846, first pub. 1836)

——*The Canadian Settlers' Guide* 10th edition (London, 1860)

Stuart, J.A. Erskine, *The Bronte Country* (London, 1888)

Sykes, Ella C., *A Home-Help in Canada* (London, 1912)

——*Through Persia on a Side-Saddle* (London, 1898)

Taylor, Mary, *The First Duty of Women* (London, 1870)

——*Miss Miles, or, A Tale of Yorkshire Life Sixty Years Ago* (London, 1890)

Thackeray, William M., *Vanity Fair* (London, 1848)

Therry, Roger, *Reminiscences of Thirty Years Residence in New South Wales and Victoria* (London, 1863)

Thompson, Flora, *Lark Rise to Candleford* (London, 1954)

Trollope, Anthony, *Australia and New Zealand* 2 vols. (London, 1873)

—— *Phineas Finn* 2 vols. (London, 1869)

Vanderbilt, A.T., *What to do with Our Girls* (London, 1884)

Vernon, Miss, *Leaton Colonial Training Home* 2nd edition (Winchester, 1905)

Wakefield, Edward Gibbon, *England and America* 2 vols. (London, 1833)

—— *A Letter from Sydney* (London, 1929, first pub. 1829)

—— *A View of the Art of Colonization* (London, 1849)

Welton, Thomas A., *On the Inaccuracies which Probably Exist in the Census Returns of Ages* (Liverpool, 1876)

What has Mrs. Chisholm Done for New South Wales? (Sydney, 1862)

What is a Lady? (London, 1885)

What Women Say of the Canadian North-West (n.p. 1886)

White, Arnold (ed.), *The Letters of S.G.O.* 2 vols. (London, 1890)

Wolseley, Frances Garnet, *Gardening for Women* (London, 1908)

Woman's Rights and Duties Considered with Relation to their Influence on Society and on their own Condition, by a Woman 2 vols. (London, 1840)

Yonge, Charlotte, *Womankind* (London, 1876)

(6)   *Modern Articles*

Alexander, Sally, 'Women's Work in Nineteenth-Century London: A Study of the Years 1820-1850,' in J. Mitchell and A. Oakley *The Rights and Wrongs of Women* (Harmondsworth, 1976), 59-111

Beales, H.L., 'The Victorian Family' in Grisewood, H., *Ideas and Beliefs of the Victorians* (New York, 1966), 343-50

Branca, Patricia, 'A New Perspective on Women's Work: A Comparative Typology,' in *Journal of Social History* VII, 4 (1974), 407-28

Copleston, Frederick, 'Herbert Spencer — Progress and Freedom' in Grisewood, H., *Ideas and Beliefs of the Victorians* (New York, 1966), 86-93

Crowther, M.A., 'British Social History' in *Historical Journal* XX, 4 (1977), 991-9

Dalziel, Raewyn, 'The Colonial Helpmeet: Women's Role and the Vote in Nineteenth-Century New Zealand' in *The New Zealand Journal of History* III, 2 (Oct. 1977), 112-23

Davidoff, Leonore, 'Mastered for Life: Servant and Wife in Victorian and Edwardian England' in *Journal of Social History* VIII, 4 (1974), 407-28

—— Jean L'Esperance, and Howard Newby. 'Landscape with Figures: Home and Community in English Society' in J. Mitchell and A. Oakley, *The Rights and Wrongs of Women* (Harmondsworth, 1976), 139-75

Edgerley, C. Mabel, 'Mary Taylor, The Friend of Charlotte Brontë' in *Transactions, The Bronte Society* X (1944), 214-21

Glass, D.V., 'Marriage Frequency and Economic Fluctuations in England and Wales, 1851 to 1934' in L.T. Hogben, *Political Arithmetic: A Symposium of Population Studies* (London, 1938), ch. 6.

Hammerton, A.J., ' "Without Natural Protectors": Female Immigration to Australia, 1832-36' in *Historical Studies* XVI, 65 (1975), 539-66

Harrison, Brian, 'For Church, Queen and Family: The Girls' Friendly Society, 1874-1974' in *Past and Present* 61 (Nov. 1973), 107-38

—— 'State Intervention and Moral Reform in Nineteenth-Century England' in P. Hollis, *Pressure from Without in Early Victorian England* (London, 1974), 289-322

Leser, C.E.V., 'The Supply of Women for Gainful Work in Britain, 1881-1951' in *Population Studies* IX, 2 (1955), 142-58

McGregor, O.R., 'The Social Position of Women in England, 1850-1914: A Bibliography' *The British Journal of Sociology* VI (1955), 48-60

Musgrove, Frank, 'Middle-Class Education and Employment in the Nineteenth Century' in *Economic History Review* XII, 1 (1959), 99-111

Peterson, M. Jeanne, 'The Victorian Governess: Status Incongruence in Family and Society' in M. Vicinus, *Suffer and Be Still* (Bloomington, 1972), pp. 3-19

Sonstroem, David, 'Millet Versus Ruskin: A Defense of Ruskin's "Of Queen's Gardens" ' in *Victorian Studies* XX, 3 (Spring, 1977), 283-97

(7) *Modern Books*

Banks, J.A., *Prosperity and Parenthood* (London, 1954)

Banks, J.A. and Olive, *Feminism and Family Planning in Victorian England* (Liverpool, 1964)

Best, Geoffrey, *Mid-Victorian Britain, 1851-75* (London, 1971)

Bloomfield, Paul, *Edward Gibbon Wakefield: Builder of the British Commonwealth* (London, 1961)

Branca, Patricia, *Silent Sisterhood: Middle-Class Women in the Victorian Home* (London, 1975)

Carrier, Norman H. and James R. Jeffrey, *External Migration: A Study of the Available Statistics (Studies on Medical and Population Subjects*, No. 6) (London, 1953)

Carrington, C.E., *John Robert Godley of Canterbury* (London, 1950)

Carrothers, W.A., *Emigration from the British Isles* (London, 1929)

Chadwick, Mrs. Ellis H., *In the Footsteps of the Brontës* (n.p., 1914)

Chamberlain, Mary, *Fenwomen: A Portrait of Women in an English Village* (London, 1975)

Clark, Alice, *Working Life of Women in the Seventeenth-Century* (London, 1919)

Crossick, Geoffrey (ed.), *The Lower Middle-Class in Britain, 1870-1914* (London, 1977)

Crow, Duncan, *The Victorian Woman* (London, 1971)

Davidoff, Leonore, *The Best Circles: Society, Etiquette and the Season* (London, 1973)

Drummond, Alison (ed.) *Married and Gone to New Zealand* (London, 1960)

Dunbar, Janet, *The Early Victorian Woman 1837-1857* (London, 1953)

Ferenczi, I. (ed.), *International Migrations* 2 vols. (New York, 1929)

Fleming, G.H., *Rossetti and the Pre-Raphaelite Brotherhood* (London, 1967)

Forrest, D.W., *Francis Galton: The Life and Work of a Victorian Genius* (London, 1974)

Gerin, Winifred, *Charlotte Brontë: The Evolution of Genius* (Oxford, 1967)

Grisewood, H., *Ideas and Beliefs of the Victorians* (New York, 1966)

Harrison, J.F.C., *The Early-Victorians, 1832-51* (London, 1971)

Hartman, Mary S., *Victorian Murderesses: A True History of Thirteen Respectable French and English Women Accused of Unspeakable Crimes* (London, 1977)

Heasman, Kathleen J., *Evangelicals in Action* (London, 1962)

Hitchins, F.H., *The Colonial Land and Emigration Commission* (Philadelphia, 1931)

Hogben, Lancelot (ed.), *Political Arithmetic: A Symposium of Population Studies* (London, 1938)

Holcombe, Lee, *Victorian Ladies at Work: Middle-Class Working Women in England and Wales, 1850-1914* (Newton Abbot, 1973)

Hollis, Patricia (ed.), *Pressure from Without in Early-Victorian England* (London, 1974)

Houghton, Walter E., *The Victorian Frame of Mind* (New Haven, 1957)

Howe, Bea, *A Galaxy of Governesses* (London, 1954)

Hudson, Derek, *Munby, Man of Two Worlds: The Life and Diaries of Arthur J. Munby, 1828-1910* (London, 1972)

Hynes, Samuel, *The Edwardian Turn of Mind* (Princeton, 1968)

Johnson, S.C., *A History of Emigration from the United Kingdom to North America* (London, 1913)

Kamm, Josephine, *Hope Deferred: Girls Education in English History* (London, 1965)

—— *Rapiers and Battleaxes: The Women's Movement and its Aftermath* (London, 1966)

Kiddle, Margaret L., *Caroline Chisholm* (Melbourne, 1950)

Kingston, Beverley, *My Wife, My Daughter and Poor Mary Ann: Women at Work in Australia* (Melbourne, 1975)

Korg, Jacob, *George Gissing: A Critical Biography* (Seattle, 1963)

Lansbury, Coral, *Arcady in Australia: The Evocation of Australia in Nineteenth-Century English Literature* (Melbourne, 1970)

McBride, Theresa, *The Domestic Revolution: The Modernization of Household Service in England and France, 1820-1920* (London, 1976)

McGregor, O.R., *Divorce in England: A Centenary Study* (London, 1957)

Mackenzie, Norman I., *Women in Australia*, London, 1963

Madgwick, R.B., *Immigration into Eastern Australia, 1788-1851* (London, 1937)

Middleton, Dorothy, *Victorian Lady Travellers* (London, 1965)

Miller, John, *Early-Victorian New Zealand* (London, 1958)

Mills, R.C., *The Colonization of Australia, 1839-1842* (London, 1915)

Mitchell, B.R., *Abstract of British Historical Statistics* (Cambridge,

1962)

Mitchell, Juliet and Ann Oakley, *The Rights and Wrongs of Women* (Harmondsworth, 1976)

Monk, Una, *New Horizons: A Hundred Years of Women's Migration* (London, 1963)

Morrell, W.P., *The Gold Rushes* (New York, 1941)

Musgrove, Frank, *The Migratory Elite* (London, 1963)

Nadel, George, *Australia's Colonial Culture* (Melbourne, 1957)

Neff, Wanda F., *Victorian Working Women, 1832-50* (New York, 1929)

Osborne, Charles C., *Letters of Charles Dickens to the Baroness Burdett-Coutts* (London, 1931)

Pinchbeck, Ivy, *Women Workers and the Industrial Revolution, 1750-1850* (London, 1930)

Samuel, Raphael (ed.), *Village Life and Labour* (London, 1975)

Shepperson, Wilbur S., *British Emigration to North America* (Minneapolis, 1957)

Sherrard, O.R., *Two Victorian Girls* (London, 1966)

Shorter, Clement K., *Charlotte Brontë and Her Circle* (London, 1896)

—— *The Brontës: Life and Letters* 2 vols. (London, 1908)

Stevens, Joan (ed.), *Mary Taylor, Friend of Charlotte Brontë: Letters from New Zealand and Elsewhere* (Auckland, 1972)

Strachey, Ray, *The Cause: A Short History of the Women's Movement in Great Britain* (London, 1928)

Summers, Ann, *Damned Whores and God's Police: The Colonization of Women in Australia* (Ringwood, 1975)

Thompson, E.P. and Eileen Yeo (eds.), *The Unknown Mayhew* (Harmondsworth, 1973)

Thompson, Paul, *The Edwardians* (London, 1975)

Thomson, Patricia, *The Victorian Heroine: A Changing Ideal, 1837-1873* (London, 1956)

Vicinus, Martha (ed.), *Suffer and Be Still: Women in the Victorian Age* (Bloomington, 1972)

—— *A Widening Sphere: Changing Roles of Victorian Women* (Bloomington, 1977)

Ward, Louis E., *Early Wellington* (London, 1928)

West, Katherine, *Chapter of Governesses: A Study of the Governess in English Fiction, 1800-1949* (London, 1949)

Williams, Raymond, *Culture and Society* (London, 1963)

Wise, Thomas J. and J. Alexander Symington, *The Brontës: Their*

Lives, Friendships and Correspondence 4 vols. (Oxford, 1932)
Woodham-Smith, Cecil, *Florence Nightingale* (London, 1951)
Young, G.M., *Victorian England: Portrait of an Age* (London, 1936)

INDEX

DATE DUE
